BUILDING
MORE
EFFECTIVE
UNIONS

BUILDING MORE EFFECTIVE UNIONS

Paul F. Clark

ILR Press AN IMPRINT OF
Cornell University Press
ITHACA AND LONDON

First Published 2000 by Cornell University Press
First printing, Cornell Paperbacks, 2000

Printed in the United States of America

Library of Congress Cataloging-in-Publication Data
Clark, Paul F., 1954–
    Building more effective unions / Paul F. Clark
        p. cm.
Includes bibliographical references and index.
    ISBN 0-8014-8705-6 (pbk.: acid-free)
    1. Labor unions—United States.   2. Labor union members—United States—Attitudes.   3. Labor unions—Organizing—United States.   I. Title.
    HD6508 .C563 2000
    331.88   dc21
                                                                00-009656

Cornell University Press strives to use environmentally responsible suppliers and materials to the fullest extent possible in the publishing of its books. Such materials include vegetable-based, low-VOC inks and acid-free papers that are recycled, totally chlorine-free, or partly composed of nonwood fibers. Books that bear the logo of the FSC (Forest Stewardship Council) use paper taken from forests that have been inspected and certified as meeting the highest standards for environmental and social responsibility. For further information, visit our website at www.cornellpress.cornell.edu.

Paperback printing   10 9 8 7 6 5 4 3 2

®

Contents

Acknowledgments

Over the last twenty-five years I have had many opportunities to work with a wide variety of unions and their members, both on labor education programs and on research projects. While I hope that my efforts on behalf of these unions have been of some value, I know that I have learned a great deal in the course of this work. What follows draws heavily on those experiences, and I acknowledge the contributions of participants in those programs and projects toward bringing this book to fruition. I especially want to thank John DiTollo and John Miller of the National Association of Letter Carriers, Rick Bloomingdale and Bill George of the Pennsylvania AFL-CIO, and Dick Davis of the United Steelworkers in this regard.

I have also learned a great deal from colleagues on the academic side, both past and present. I have been particularly fortunate to work with many fine labor scholars and labor educators at Penn State over the years. Their support and insights are acknowledged and appreciated.

This book benefited greatly from early collaboration with four colleagues—Julian Barling of Queen's University, Clive Fullagar of Kansas State University, Kevin Kelloway of St. Mary's University, and Daniel Gallagher of James Madison University—all of whom contributed conceptually and substantively until other responsibilities pulled them away from the project. Dan Gallagher's contributions were particularly substantial.

I would also like to thank Jeff Grabelsky of the Cornell School of Industrial and Labor Relations, Mark Erlich of the New England Regional Council of Carpenters, Jesse Bostelle of the Service Employees, Michael Eisenscher of the Project for Labor Renewal, and Bob Bruno of the University of Illinois for their help with the case studies.

Parts of the manuscript were read by Bob Bussel, Greg Giebel, Gil Gall, Jack Fiorito, and participants in the Pennsylvania AFL-CIO COPE and CWA Summer

Schools held at Penn State. The constructive criticism and encouragement they provided helped me to move forward with the project.

At various times I received funding to conduct research that is incorporated in this book. I extend my thanks to the Department of Labor Studies and Industrial Relations at Penn State, the Pennsylvania AFL-CIO, and the George Meany Center for Labor Studies for this financial support.

As in previous projects with Cornell ILR Press, I have benefited from Fran Benson's enduring patience and insightful editorial skill. I heartily recommend her and ILR Press to authors looking for a home for their work. Thanks also to Jackie Dowdell, Trudie Calvert, and Ange Romeo-Hall for their help in getting the book out.

I also want to thank Darlene, Molly, and Bryan Clark for allowing me to monopolize the computer and the second floor and for providing a foundation for life and work.

If we are lucky, each of us encounters a few individuals who have an enormous influence on the people we become professionally. I have been fortunate to have two such mentors, both named Lois. I wish to acknowledge Lois S. Gray and the late Lois Nowicki for their guidance and their friendship. This book is dedicated to them.

While these colleagues and friends have all contributed in various ways to shaping this book, any shortcomings are mine alone.

Introduction

Strong and viable unions play a necessary and important role in American society and in its industrial relations system. Building strong unions in today's economic, political, and social environment, however, is a very difficult task.

Much has been written about the "big" issues facing labor—the globalization of the economy; labor laws that do little to protect workers' rights; a political system in which money, rather than ideas and principles, is the bottom line. Much has also been written about strategies to deal with these issues—the adoption of a new "organizing" model of unionism; the restructuring of individual unions and of the American Federation of Labor–Congress of Industrial Organizations (AFL-CIO); a new, more effective, political action program; and the establishment of a truly international labor movement that can cross borders with the same ease as multinational corporations. Somewhat less attention has been given to the one thing each of these strategies is dependent on—an increasingly active, involved, informed, and engaged union membership at the local level.

While committees, commissions, centers, and task forces at the national union and federation levels wrestle with the best ways to adapt to a global economy, the best strategies to confront global corporations, and the best tactics to fight labor's political and legislative battles, local unions can, and should, be building a more effective labor movement from the bottom up.

This book was written to assist unions and union leaders in building a stronger labor movement by more effectively mobilizing their membership.[1] To accomplish this task, American unions need to draw on every resource at their disposal. One

---

1. Most of the discussion in this book refers to union members, but many of the principles and tools examined are also applicable to nonmembers in a bargaining unit or to potential members involved in the organizing process. Also, while the discussion focuses on local, district, and national unions, many of the issues and strategies discussed are equally applicable to local labor councils, state federations, and the national AFL-CIO.

potentially useful, but largely overlooked, resource available to the labor movement is behavioral science.

Behavioral science is the study of people, their behavior, and the organizations they form. Over time, behavioral science research has learned a great deal about these subjects. In recent years, behavioral science researchers have increasingly turned their attention to unions and union members. Much of this research, however, has not been readily or easily accessible to union leaders and activists, remaining largely in the province of behavioral scientists themselves.

This book is intended to make selected behavioral science research and its practical implications for unions available to those interested in building a stronger labor movement. Toward this end, the book was written with a broad audience in mind. One of the audiences for which it was written is that part of the labor movement that has the greatest opportunity to put the ideas to work—officers and activists at the local union level.

I hope that more experienced union officials and staff at the district/region and national levels will also find the book useful. If so, it may not be because the ideas presented are entirely new to them but because the book pulls together important issues and strategies, ties them together in the context of an overall model, and uses behavioral science to give the conclusions additional credence.

In addition, I hope that the book will be useful to labor educators, industrial relations academics, and academics from related disciplines as a starting point for examining important behavioral science research about unions. I also hope that they will find the model of union commitment and participation, which draws on the work of numerous scholars but is original in its configuration, to be a contribution. Ultimately, the book will have played a constructive role if it generates thoughtful discussion and debate about labor's future.

Union leaders and behavioral researchers have not had a close relationship in the past. In recent years, however, both have been interested in the issue of organizing. Organizing is essential to the labor movement's future, yet in the past the movement has struggled to achieve significant results in this area. At least some union leaders have begun to pay attention to a growing body of research that has direct strategic implications for how unions conduct organizing campaigns.

Union leaders have paid less attention to other areas and issues that have been the subject of behavioral research. If unions do succeed in bringing large numbers of new members into the fold, they will immediately be confronted with the challenge of retaining those members, as well as building commitment and generating participation among them toward the work of the organization. If unions are less than successful in the organizing arena, retaining existing members and winning their support and involvement become even more important. Behavioral science can provide some insight on these issues.

This book will look at how behavioral science can help build stronger unions. It will examine the research to date on organizing and discuss what unions can learn from that work. It will, however, go beyond this one issue to discuss what behavioral research has learned about commitment in organizations and what unions can do to increase the commitment of their members to the union. It will also discuss what this research has discovered about the relationship between organizational commitment and participation and what unions can do to generate greater involvement on the part of their members. And it will look at how these and other behavioral principles apply to the fundamental work of unions in such critical areas as political action, handling grievances, communication with members, image-building, organizational culture, and leadership.

Because this book is aimed at a broad audience, its focus is on clearly communicating the relevant findings of behavioral research and identifying strategies for putting those findings to work on behalf of labor organizations. For this reason, the book will forego detailed discussions of methodologies. It will also strive to avoid the use of scientific jargon. This is not to suggest that what follows is a "cookbook" or a "how-to" manual. Building effective organizations is far too complex an endeavor for such an approach. Rather, the book will introduce theories and research that provide insight into the behavior of individuals and organizations and suggest approaches and strategies based on this work. Citations are provided to enable the reader to investigate more fully the research introduced.

Where possible, specific examples of behavioral principles in practice will be used to illustrate how unions might employ these findings to build stronger organizations. In addition, Chapters 3 through 10 each close with a case study that discusses how the principles in that chapter are being put to use by the labor movement.

This book will not directly address relevant skills such as the negotiation of contracts, the presentation of arbitration cases, or the recognition and filing of unfair labor practices. Certainly these skills are necessary for building stronger unions, and the book does address the impact these processes have on members' attitudes and behaviors. Sufficient material is already available to individuals who wish to develop or improve their skills in these areas. The same cannot be said for the issues covered in this book.

Finally, this book is not a comprehensive treatment of all the behavioral research relevant to unions. Although it does contain a lengthy bibliography pulling together much of the behavioral science literature relating to unions, there is more research on behavior in organizations generally, and even on unions specifically, than can be dealt with here. For that reason, it has been necessary to make hard choices about which research to include. Others may have chosen differently, but this is my own best judgment as to the behavioral science research that is of most direct and immediate importance to the work of building stronger labor organizations. In this sense, this book represents a step forward, rather than the final word, on this subject.

An Outline of the Book

This book is intended to introduce the reader to behavioral science research and principles that can play a role in building more effective unions. Chapter 1 examines the concepts of behavioral science and union effectiveness that are of central importance to all that follows. Chapter 2 introduces another concept that is at the heart of this book—member participation. This chapter makes the case that the primary mechanism available to unions for building more effective organizations is member participation (Likert, 1961; Lawler, 1986). It also presents a model of member participation and union effectiveness that is referred to throughout the book. This model suggests that an individual's behavior is a result of two key factors— the personal characteristics of that individual and the environment in which the behavior takes place. One of the most important individual characteristics shaping behavior is a person's attitudes. In a union context this suggests that union participation can be encouraged by positively influencing a member's attitudes toward the union.

Chapters 3 through 10 examine different strategies that behavioral science suggests are effective in influencing individual members' participation in the union. Chapter 3 examines how behavioral research can help unions organize new members and retain their current memberships. Chapter 4 looks at the importance of orienting and socializing new members into the union. How unions can gain greater support for, and participation in, the political efforts of the union is the focus of Chapter 5, while Chapter 6 looks at what behavioral science has to say about the handling of contractual grievances. Chapter 7 looks at how information and communication strategies can be effectively used to increase participation and build stronger unions.

Chapter 8 looks at the impact that labor's public image has on union effectiveness and discusses strategies for building a more positive union image. Chapter 9 focuses on how to build a "union culture" that will encourage and sustain positive and supportive attitudes and increased participation among members. Chapter 10 examines leadership skills and how these skills can assist unions in implementing the numerous programs and activities discussed in the earlier chapters. Finally, Chapter 11 briefly reviews the themes touched on throughout the book.

Union Acronyms

ACTWU	Amalgamated Clothing and Textile Workers Union
AFA	Association of Flight Attendants
AFGE	American Federation of Government Employees
AFL-CIO	American Federation of Labor-Congress of Industrial Organizations
AFSCME	American Federation of State, County, and Municipal Employees
AFT	American Federation of Teachers
ALPA	Air Line Pilots Association
APWU	American Postal Workers Union
CWA	Communications Workers of America
FOP	Fraternal Order of Police
IAFF	International Association of Fire Fighters
IAM	International Association of Machinists and Aerospace Workers
IBEW	International Brotherhood of Electrical Workers
IBT	International Brotherhood of Teamsters
NALC	National Association of Letter Carriers
NEA	National Education Association
NFLPA	National Football League Players Association
OCAW	Oil, Chemical, and Atomic Workers
SEIU	Service Employees International Union
UAW	United Automobile, Aerospace, and Agricultural Implement Workers of America
UFCW	United Food and Commercial Workers
UFW	United Farm Workers
UMW	United Mine Workers of America
USW	United Steel Workers of America

BUILDING MORE EFFECTIVE UNIONS

1

Behavioral Science
and Union Effectiveness

After two unsuccessful efforts to organize workers at ABC Industries, the Allied Workers Union (AWU) won a representation election by 597 votes to 565. In the years that followed, the AWU negotiated a couple of impressive contracts. Although the employer resisted at every turn, favorable economic conditions allowed the union to overcome this resistance. Because few bargaining unit members had any experience with unions, AWU staff took on much of the responsibility for bargaining and administering the contract. Thus there was little opportunity for leaders to develop in the bargaining unit or for the staff to educate, inform, and involve the membership itself. Following a dramatic downturn in the economy, the union entered its third round of negotiations with the employer. This time the union became entangled in a bargaining dispute that led to a strike. After a couple of weeks on the picket line, members began returning to work. Upon their return, some of the dissatisfied workers filed a decertification petition. The union quickly settled the contract, but the damage had been done. When the decertification election was held, the AWU was voted out.

Most informed observers of the labor movement agree that to meet the many challenges they face, unions need to become more effective at all levels. Doing so is a huge and formidable undertaking for national, regional, and local labor groups. Clearly, one of labor's greatest challenges is to mobilize the talents, ideas, and energy of its members. If the goal is to build more effective unions, the membership is the place to start.

This book is based on the belief that behavioral science can help unions and union leaders build a stronger labor movement by increasing the level of members' commitment to, and participation in, their union. In the vignette at the beginning of this chapter, the hypothetical union clearly suffered from a lack of commitment and participation on the part of its members. In fact, a basic understanding of some of the principles of behavioral science could have helped the AWU avoid the problems it experienced. For example, if the AWU had understood the importance of the socialization process in building members' commitment to the union, it might have developed an orientation program to introduce the newly organized members at ABC Industries to unionism. If it understood that keeping members informed about the union was a tried and tested way to get members involved, it might have developed a more effective communications system. And if it under-stood more about leadership, it would have realized the importance of developing a group of leaders from among its membership at ABC.

This is not to suggest that behavioral science is *the* answer to labor's problems. Lo-cal leaders and union activists, particularly those with long experience, have tried and tested tools, techniques, and strategies they regularly employ, with varying degrees of success, to build and rebuild their unions. The premise of this book is that unions can be made even more effective if they carefully evaluate the tools they currently use, are exposed to different variations of these tools, and are given access to new tools.

Much of what union activists and leaders know about building effective organi-zations they have learned from experience. While experience *is* a very good teacher, one of the purposes of this book is to introduce unions to another teacher. That teacher is behavioral science. Behavioral scientists have a long history of studying people, their behavior, and their organizations. While much of the knowl-edge they have acquired can be gained through experience, doing so takes a very long time and requires many painful lessons. To the degree that behavioral science can accelerate the learning process and reduce the amount of learning that must occur through trial and error, it can be a useful companion to experience.

At the very least, behavioral science and its findings may help union activists and leaders better understand the human behaviors they observe on a firsthand basis. An understanding of the principles of behavioral science can also help to place the lessons of experience in a broader perspective. This broader perspective can be helpful to union leaders interested in initiating changes or in analyzing the success or failure of a particular initiative (e.g., an organizing drive, a boycott, or a get-out-the-vote effort).

Employers have long looked to behavioral science for insights that could make their organizations more effective. They have consistently turned to behavioral sci-entists to help them increase the productivity and efficiency of their employees. In-dustrial psychology and organizational behavior have been instrumental in the de-velopment of such management practices as time and motion studies, job design, employment testing, incentive pay plans, and assessment programs (Lowenberg and Conrad, 1998). Behavioral scientists have been the moving force in the docu-mentation and promotion of effective leadership styles. In the past, some employ-ers have also used behavioral scientists to usurp or undermine unions through company unions, phony involvement schemes, and employee selection programs or to defeat them in representation elections (Gordon and Burt, 1981).

For these reasons, unions and union leaders have, historically, been suspicious of behavioral scientists and, in particular, industrial psychologists (Gordon and Burt, 1981; Gordon and Nurick, 1981). Over the last twenty-five years, however, an in-creasing number of behavioral scientists have worked with unions, rather than against them, on research that might benefit the labor movement. Gradually, many unions and union leaders have begun to see behavioral science as a powerful tool that can be used to build more effective labor organizations. This collaboration has produced a growing body of research about unions, union members, and union leaders. Much of this work has occurred because unions have been willing to grant researchers access to their members and leaders. In most cases this partnership has benefited the labor movement.

The research in question has focused on such fundamental issues as union members' commitment and participation (Barling, Fullagar, and Kelloway, 1992); members' satisfaction with union representation (Fiorito, Gallagher, and Fukami, 1988); and members' attitudes toward politics (Clark and Masters, 1996; Clark, 1999), grievance procedures (Gordon and Bowlby, 1988; Clark, Gallagher, and Pavlak, 1991), strikes (Martin, 1986), and workforce reductions (Mellor, 1990). It has also looked at the voting intentions of members and potential members in certification and decertification elections (Barling, Fullagar, and Kelloway, 1992). In an effort to help unions find the most effective approaches, this research has been used to assess union strategies in the areas of organizing, collective bargaining, contract administration, and political action.

Before examining how behavioral science can contribute to union effectiveness, each of these terms will be defined in some detail.

What Is Behavioral Science?

Behavioral science can be viewed as the systematic study of the behaviors or actions of individuals. Alternatively, behavioral scientists attempt to understand, through scientifically based research, why people act or behave in a particular way. In reality, behavioral science looks at more than just people's actions or behaviors. It also seeks to understand the personal factors and environmental forces that cause people to undertake certain courses of action.

Behavioral science research directly or indirectly affects all our lives. In the realm of politics and government, for example, politicians seek to identify and understand the issues or factors that cause voters to support or oppose a particular candidate or referendum.

Political campaigns devote considerable resources to trying to understand voters' attitudes and to influence voting behavior. Interest in human behavior, however, extends well beyond the political arena. For example, the entire commercial advertising industry exists to encourage people to behave (i.e., spend their money) in certain ways. Automobile advertisers, to take just one group, regularly seek to better understand human behavior by gathering information on the importance or value that various target audiences place on certain concerns (e.g., prestige, success, safety, style). Armed with this information and the behavioral science principle that people seek to maximize satisfaction, they can develop an effective advertising strategy to influence the public's buying behavior.

In addition to the political and business arenas, we see the theories of behavioral science put to work each day in our schools and in our families. Educators study the most up-to-date research about how people learn and what teaching strategies are most effective. Parents read about the latest behavioral research on child development to learn how to help their children grow intellectually and emotionally.

Behavioral scientists are not interested only in the study of individual attitudes and behavior. They are also concerned with the interaction of individuals with organizations. In addition, behavioral science is interested in how the leadership and culture of organizations influence their members' behavior, as well as with how organizational effectiveness can best be measured (Moorehead and Griffin, 1998). The study of individual and organizational behavior extends even further to examine the influence of the broader economic, political, and social environment on the functioning of organizations and on the attitudes and behaviors of people within organizations.

Behavioral scientists use theories, methods, and principles from a variety of disciplines or areas of study. Among the fields they draw upon are psychology (the study of mental processes and behavior), sociology (the understanding of human society, its development and institutions), political science (the study of government and the individuals, organizations, and institutions involved in the political process), and economics (the analysis of economic institutions and systems).

Finally, to fully understand the usefulness of behavioral science research it is also necessary to understand a little about science and the scientific method. Science, ultimately, is a "way of knowing" about the world around us. We acquire knowledge in many ways. Sometimes what we accept as knowledge comes from authority figures such as government officials, trusted newscasters, or religious leaders. We accept something as truth because it comes from a trusted source.

Sometimes we accept things as fact because they are, in our minds, self-evident or simply because we have always known them to be true. The notion that the world was flat was accepted for centuries because it appeared to be flat and because this description had long been common knowledge.

Science is a much more objective way of knowing. It is not based on previous knowledge, the pronouncements of authorities, common sense, perceptions, biases, or emotions but rather on the scientific method. This method involves the development and testing of explanations or hypotheses. Scientists test their explanations by gathering evidence or data through experiments, surveys, interviews, and observation. The end result of this testing process is general laws or theories that, together, begin to explain the world around us (Kerlinger, 1973).

The knowledge that results from behavioral science research is applicable to all types of organizations, whether they are private or public, profit or nonprofit, or based on voluntary membership or an employment relationship. Labor organizations, or unions, are no exception. With careful attention to the unique nature of unions, the insights, theories, and tools of behavioral science can assist members and leaders in building a more effective labor movement.

What Is Union Effectiveness?

The term "union effectiveness" is significantly more difficult to define than behavioral science. It could be argued that social and economic justice is the overarching goal of unions. Yet this goal is too broad to be very useful. It is possible to readily identify a series of narrower measures of effectiveness ranging from the achievement of stated goals related to collective bargaining to the simple survival of the organization. Yet such multiple measures will vary across unions.

Even individuals, inside and outside an organization, will hold their own unique standards for measuring union effectiveness based on their needs and priorities. A retired member may judge the union primarily by the pension benefits the union is able to negotiate while a member expecting her first baby may feel the real measure of an effective union is the quality of the maternity plan. A union organizer might judge effectiveness based on the resources the union devotes to organizing while a union treasurer may think a union's bank account is the real yardstick of a union's success or health.

Those outside the union will have their own criteria for judging union effectiveness. Politicians will judge a union's effectiveness by its ability to mobilize its members to vote for the union's endorsed candidates. Managers may base their assessment on the degree to which a union's leaders can keep its members "under control."

The definition of union effectiveness can also change over time and across industries. In the early part of the twentieth century, survival may have been the chief goal of most American unions, while today's unions probably do not consider it the sole measure of success. Similarly, newly organized unions in predominantly nonunion industries may see modest wage increases as signs of success while unions in more heavily organized industries such as auto manufacturing set the bar much higher.

In short, the answer to the question, "What is an effective union?" depends on many factors, including who and when you ask. Union effectiveness is a highly complex, highly dynamic concept. Perhaps the best that can be done is to look at the common elements we find in the definitions of effectiveness spelled out by union members and union leaders themselves. At least four studies have identified such criteria (Fiorito, Gramm, and Hendricks, 1991; Barling, Fullagar, and Kelloway, 1992; Hammer and Wazeter, 1993; Fiorito, Jarley, and Delaney, 1995). The results of these studies can be combined to yield three general measures by which to judge the effectiveness of labor organizations. These three yardsticks are the union's ability to organize new members, the outcomes of its collective bargaining efforts, and the union's effect on society as a whole.

Unions' Ability to Organize New Members

Because the total nonagricultural labor force organized in the United States fell steadily from a high of 34.5 percent in 1946 to just 13.9 in 1999, recruiting new members has become an almost life-or-death issue for American unions, particularly those that predominantly draw their members from the private sector (Bureau of Labor Statistics, 1999). The recruitment of union members occurs in two different contexts.

First, in the vast majority of cases unions exist only in workplaces where a majority of employees have demonstrated a desire to be represented by a union. Hence organizing drives are a central means of bringing new groups of workers into the union. The second type of recruitment takes place where a union has been voted in but does not have a union security agreement. American labor law dictates that most employees must receive the benefits of union representation whether they choose to belong to the union or not. This means that unions must try to convince "free riders" to join even though they receive many of the benefits of a union without doing so. Three measures of a union's effectiveness, therefore, could be the percentage of organizing drives that a union wins, the number of members it brings in through such drives, and the percentage of members it represents who belong to the union.

Organizing is important to unions as both a primary goal (unions are membership organizations; without members they die) and as a means to other ends. Two of the additional measures of union effectiveness discussed here, collective bargaining outcomes (Freeman and Medoff, 1984) and political influence (Delaney, Fiorito, and Masters, 1988), are directly tied to membership levels (see Figure 1.1).

Collective Bargaining Outcomes

Collective bargaining has traditionally been, and remains today, the most important mechanism for the pursuit of social and economic justice for most unions. Bargaining, in the American context, typically has focused on the "bread and butter" issues of wages, benefits, job security, and working conditions (Filippelli, 1984). One way of measuring the effectiveness of union bargaining efforts is to compare union wage and benefit levels with nonunion levels. Department of Labor statistics indicate that in 1996 the weekly earnings of unionized workers were 33 percent higher than those of nonunion workers (AFL-CIO, 1999b). But if the real cost of living is the yardstick by which union bargaining efforts are measured, these efforts have come up short. Over a nearly thirty-year period, average union wage gains have not kept up with inflation.

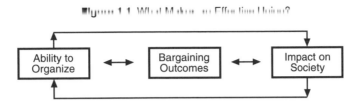

Figure 1.1 What Makes an Effective Union?

In evaluating a union's effectiveness in collective bargaining, it is also important to consider the union's ability to enforce an agreement once it has been negotiated. Grievance procedures, including arbitration, are the chief means for enforcing labor agreements. Union training manuals commonly emphasize that a negotiated contract is only as good as the enforcement behind it. Several studies have concluded that members' attitudes toward the grievance procedure are strongly related to their commitment to the union and their sense of job security (Johnson, Bobko, and Hartenian, 1992; Clark, Gallagher, and Pavlak, 1990).

One researcher has argued that the assessment of union effectiveness in collective bargaining must go beyond the simple consideration of whether unions improve wages, benefits, and working conditions (Kochan, 1980). This researcher argues that any assessment of effectiveness must consider the relationship between the needs and expectations of the members and the gains achieved by the union, thus explicitly linking the criterion of union democracy with collective bargaining outcomes.

The extent to which members' needs and expectations are represented in collective bargaining reflects both the degree to which democracy is valued in the union and the effectiveness of the union in that process. The ability of unions to assess the needs and expectations of their members is of particular importance in today's environment where the makeup of the membership and members' needs and expectations are changing rapidly from what they were in years past.

Union's Impact on Society

A third yardstick for evaluating the effectiveness of a union is its ability to influence society in a way that helps it to achieve the goals previously discussed. Unions have long recognized that union-management relationships do not occur in a vacuum. They also have long been aware that their members have lives beyond the workplace and the union hall. Society, broadly defined, can help a union in the collective bargaining process by supporting the union members during a strike or a boycott or hinder it by withholding support.

Organizing drives are more likely to be successful when they take place in an environment supportive of unions than when they occur in one hostile to them. And, of course, the stance of the government toward unions and their internal governance, toward their attempts to recruit new members, and toward their collective bargaining efforts has historically been a critical factor in the success of unions.

While unions vary on the emphasis they place on impacting society, virtually all unions recognize that they can become more effective by increasing their influence in the community and in the political arena.

Unions are also involved in service, charitable, and political activities because these are yet additional means of moving toward their goal of improving the quality of life for all workers. Unions work with the Red Cross, the United Way, youth groups such as Scouting and junior sports programs, and many other service and charitable organizations. Union political activities include raising money, through political action committees (PACs), to help elect political allies to office. Unions also use "soft money," brought in through dues collections, to participate in get-out-the-vote efforts, rallies, and campaigns and to lobby elected officials on labor-related legislation. A union's overall effectiveness can, in part, be measured by the degree to which it can mobilize members to support and participate in its work in these areas.

Extent of Union Democracy

An additional consideration that some believe is a measure of a union's effectiveness is the extent of democracy in a union. Union democracy has been defined as "control of the governed, whether in a participatory or representative form" (Hochner, Koziara, and Schmidt, 1980). A union that operates democratically would be one in which members are involved in, or at least have the opportunity to be involved in, decision making, the implementation of decisions, and the election of representatives.

The case can be made that union democracy is both an end in itself and directly related to union effectiveness. It is often argued that one of the important benefits of a union is that it gives members a voice in the workplace. Democracy helps to ensure that when this voice is exercised, it truly represents members' wishes. It is also argued that democratic practices help to mobilize members, "unearth" and train potential leaders, and check corruption and incompetence (Strauss, 1999; Summers, 1999).

A case is sometimes made, however, that too much democracy can impede a union's effectiveness. Buttressing this point is the fact that democratic processes can be cumbersome, preventing unions from acting quickly and decisively. It might also be argued that democracy sometimes takes decisions out of the hands of those best equipped to make them (leaders) and places them in the hands of less well-equipped members. Perhaps there is some optimal level of democracy for labor organizations. If this is, indeed, the case, there is no consensus among union leaders or behavioral scientists as to what that level is.

Although there are many possible ways to evaluate union effectiveness, these three criteria—the union's ability to organize and recruit new members, win gains at the bargaining table, and influence society through community activities and political action—and possibly internal democracy, seem to capture many of the goals of unions as suggested by both labor organizations themselves and the research literature.

The discussion of these dimensions suggests a high degree of interrelatedness. For example, the ability of the union to maintain a strong membership base is closely related to its ability to win gains at the bargaining table, influence elections, and effectively lobby legislators. Conversely, the union's ability to win gains at the bargaining table and be effective politically will play an important role in its efforts to attract new members (Kochan, 1979; Fiorito, 1987).

Different unions place different emphases on these activities and the same union might place different emphases on these activities at different times. For example, there has long been a debate in the labor movement over "business" versus "social" unionism, with advocates of the former showing less interest in community and political involvement than advocates of the latter (Fiorito, 1992). In recent years unions have begun to rethink their priorities, and many labor organizations have placed a renewed emphasis on organizing after several decades during which their primary focus was collective bargaining and political action (Shostak, 1991; Sweeney, 1996). Ultimately, however, the interrelatedness of these dimensions suggests that to remain viable, unions need to pay close attention to all four areas.

Member Participation and Union Effectiveness

Unions are, by definition, the coming together of many individuals with some common interests. These individuals form the union's foundation. The strength or effectiveness of the organization depends, to a significant degree, on the extent to which the union-related behaviors of these individual members contribute to the union's organizing and recruiting efforts, collective bargaining outcomes, political and community influence, and democratic processes. Each of these functions can be enhanced by an increase in the quantity (or level) and the quality of member participation.

Member participation in local union activities has been the focus of empirical inquiry for over forty years (Barling, Fullagar, and Kelloway, 1992). Unions may value democracy in decision making as an end itself (Fullagar and Barling, 1987), and participation has widely been viewed as a central determinant, or index, of union democracy. Members can participate in many ways, including attending union meetings, assuming leadership positions, and voting in union elections (McLean Parks, Gallagher, and Fullagar, 1995). These activities substantially increase members' involvement in the union decision-making process (Anderson, 1979). Participation provides members with a "voice" (Hirschman, 1970) in the union and the workplace and serves as a check on the tendencies of individuals or small groups to dominate the organization. While participation may not be a sufficient condition for union democracy, it is a necessary one (Barling, Fullagar, and Kelloway, 1992).

Member participation is also related to a union's ability to organize and recruit new members. Although in the past, union organizing drives were initiated and conducted mostly, and sometimes exclusively, by paid organizers, many unions today recognize the need and value of involving rank-and-file members in organizing campaigns (Sweeney, 1996; Bronfenbrenner, 1997). Members can hand out literature and serve as a presence at a targeted workplace; they can conduct or assist with home visits. In their contacts with potential members they can provide first-hand knowledge of the benefits the union can provide. Given the time-intensive nature of such campaigns, this requires significant levels of voluntary participation on the part of a union's membership.

Membership involvement is also critical to a union's success in the collective bargaining and contract administration process. The negotiation of labor agreements requires that members participate on planning and bargaining committees. Also, if a union becomes engaged in a dispute with an employer, its bargaining position will be strengthened by the visible support and active participation of the membership. This may take the form of attendance at rallies, participation in meetings and on picket lines, and other demonstrations of support (Gallagher and Strauss, 1991; Strauss, 1991).

Finally, unions need the active participation of their members to enforce an agreement effectively. The union leaders who negotiate a contract cannot be in every workplace, in every department, on every shift. Instead, unions depend on rank-and-file representatives, usually stewards or grievance committee members, to make sure that what the union gained in negotiations is not lost in the workplace by management's intentional, or unintentional, breaching of the contract. Ideally, individual members also play a role in enforcing the agreement by knowing their rights under the contract and by bringing possible violations to the union's attention. When violations of the contract are found to have occurred, stewards and local leaders address them through the grievance procedure. Again, this system works effectively only if members and local leaders are committed to participating actively in the union.

The only real resource unions have with which to influence society outside of the collective bargaining arena is their members. Politically, unions want their members to cast their votes for union-endorsed candidates. Union effectiveness in politics is also influenced by the level of participation of the organization's members in get-out-the vote efforts, campaign fund-raising, lobbying efforts, and other political activities. The same dynamic occurs in the area of community service. Unlike business groups, whose contributions are largely monetary, unions donate time and expertise to charities and community service projects. Without membership participation, unions can have limited impact beyond the workplace.

There are certainly many factors beyond member participation that contribute to union effectiveness. This is particularly the case in the collective bargaining arena. A union's bargaining power, for example, is influenced by the supply of, and de-

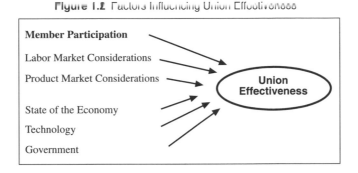

Figure 1.2 Factors Influencing Union Effectiveness

mand for, an employer's product and the supply of, and demand for, the workers needed to produce that product. Bargaining power may also be affected by the general state of the economy, the level and nature of the technology required to produce a product, and the government's involvement in the collective bargaining process. To a large extent, however, these factors lie beyond the influence of a given union. Unions are in a much better position to influence and shape the union-related behavior of their members. Ultimately, of all the factors that determine whether a union is effective, participation is the one over which unions have the most influence (see Figure 1.2).

Behavioral Science and the Special Case of Unions

This book is based on the notion that behavioral science has generated substantial insights into the interaction of individuals and organizations and that unions can use these insights to increase workers' commitment and participation and, ultimately, to build more effective unions. While some of the behavioral science research drawn on here focuses on unions, much of it focuses on other organizations, ranging from business groups to political parties to military organizations. This raises the issue of whether the insights gained through research on other organizations can be applied to the special case of unions.

The answer to this question is a qualified "yes." The answer is qualified because, while unions have much in common with other types of organizations, they are, in many ways, unique. As is true of businesses, some of the driving forces behind unions are economic self-interest, survival, and growth. Like military organizations, unions are organized in a hierarchical fashion and usually have well-defined chains of command. And like voluntary associations, unions depend on their members to give their time freely to help the organization achieve its goals.

The differences between these groups and unions, however, are at least as significant as the similarities. For example, unions differ from business groups in that their interests extend beyond economic self-interest into issues that affect society at large. They differ from military organizations, as well as businesses, in that unions are governed democratically. And unlike private clubs, for example, unions are required by law to provide access and representation to individuals who choose not to become members.

This suggests that if behavioral science research based on other organizations is to be applied to unions, the unique characteristics of unions must always be borne in mind. A longtime observer has described labor organizations as "half army, half town meeting" (Muste, 1928). This suggests that unions are complex organizations with multiple faces. In the area of services, for example, many members see dues as "payment" for a union to provide representation services in the workplace. Unions are, however, in the peculiar situation of having to turn around and ask those same members to volunteer to help them deliver those services.

Traditionally, unions have had an adversarial relationship with employers. This can result in conflict that requires the union to muster its economic strength and engage in economic battle, of a sometimes prolonged nature, with the employer. Unlike their employer-adversary, however, they must engage in these activities and services while operating within a democratic framework, with all the political baggage that comes with democratic government.

Applying behavioral principles in the context of the labor movement is complicated by the fact that unions differ among themselves and that, even within a given labor organization, different parts of a union may operate in different environments and under different rules.

An example is the issue of union membership. In many workplaces, membership is voluntary. Individuals represented by the union can choose to join or not join the union. In other workplaces, where some form of union security clause exists, membership may be mandatory. A person who does not agree to join the union, or at least pay a dues equivalent fee, can be discharged. The different avenues by which individuals become union members suggest that different behavioral strategies may be needed to build commitment and participation among these two categories of members.

Unions are, indeed, unique organizations that face difficult and distinctive challenges. At a fundamental level, however, they do have many things in common with other organizations. Also, the members of unions share many human qualities with members of different types of organizations. If careful attention is paid to tailoring its principles to unions, behavioral science can make a contribution to the building of more effective labor organizations.

A Note: Behavioral Science and Ethics

Some union leaders and activists are uncomfortable with the notion of using behavioral science or psychology in their work. Some believe strategies, tactics, and approaches based on such science are manipulative and associate them with brainwashing or mind control; others see them as inconsistent with democratic practices. Certainly this concern is understandable given the manner in which some employers have used behavioral science to exploit workers and keep unions out of the workplace. But knowingly or unknowingly, each of us uses behavioral science every day as we interact with people. We try to understand why people behave the way they do, and we try to encourage people to act in ways we think are appropriate. Leaders do this when they try to motivate others, salespeople do it when they try to close a deal, and educators do it when they try to devise an effective way to facilitate learning.

Still, it is important always to consider the moral and ethical implications of any given course of action. This should be true for any action, not just those that are consciously based on the findings of behavioral science. Behavioral science is a tool. Like any other tool, if used properly, it can add to the range of resources and strategies the labor movement brings to bear in its work.

2

Union Participation: A Model

Rosa Hernandez works in a nursing home in a large suburb of a major city. She has been active in her union, which recently asked her to recruit other members at her nursing home to staff a get-out-the vote phone bank for the upcoming election. Rosa agrees with her union that one of the candidates running in the election is clearly more supportive of union members' interests than the other candidate. Yet when Rosa asks her co-workers to give up a few evenings to work at the phone bank, only a handful are willing. Some of the newer members tell Rosa that "from what they hear, the union just wants our help in promoting their liberal causes." A few others mention that they don't think the union should be telling its members how to vote and that the union doesn't have any influence on these campaigns anyway. Rosa wonders how she can effectively confront these negative attitudes and opinions about the union's political action program and get the newer members to help out with the phone bank.

As suggested in Chapter 1, the effectiveness of any union is directly tied to the level and quality of the participation of its members. Based on this premise, the critical concern for unions and union leaders becomes how to encourage maximum membership participation.

Types of Union Participation

When most people think of union participation, they probably think of union members engaged in some formal activity such as holding a union office, serving on a committee, or working on a political or organizing campaign. Formal participation can also occur on a more intermittent or occasional basis when members attend a union meeting, vote to elect union officers, or walk a picket line. These activities do not always require a great deal of members' time or effort, but nonetheless they are important ways in which members may choose to participate in their union (McShane, 1986; Gallagher, McLean Parks, and Wetzel, 1987; Fullagar et al., 1995; Sverke, 1997).

The definition of participation can also be extended to include what might be characterized as unstructured, supportive, or informal activities. These might include speaking up in defense of the union, discussing the contract with a new hire, or suggesting to other members how the union could help with a problem. There has been quite a bit of research on informal participation in the field of organizational behavior, although much of it has focused on the behavior of employees in their workplace.

Such informal activities have been labeled "organizational citizenship behaviors," or OCBs, by that field. The research on OCBs has attempted to gain a better understanding of the ways employees go beyond their job roles and engage in extra, informal behaviors that benefit the organization of which they are a part. Researchers of OCBs have identified a range of beneficial informal behaviors, including courtesy (e.g., helping to keep other employees informed), civic virtue (e.g., keeping themselves informed about issues of interest to the organization), and altruism (e.g., helping a fellow employee with a problem) (Organ, 1988; Organ and Konovsky, 1989).

As noted in a 1995 study, the notion of OCBs has relevance for union participation (Fullagar et al.). Most notable is the idea that union members, like the employees in the OCB research, can engage in supportive behaviors that are not formal or structured. While these "union citizenship behaviors" (UCBs) are less noticeable, the sum of individual members' informal participation can have a significant impact on union effectiveness. Unions may also have greater success in encouraging members to engage in these less formal types of participation because there are fewer barriers or qualifications associated with them.

Finally, while the term "union participation" normally refers to activities that union members engage in, it can also be extended to refer to actions nonmembers take in relationship to the union. In an unorganized workplace such actions by nonmembers might include participating in an organizing drive, signing a union authorization card, or voting for the union in a representation election. Where a union is certified but does not have a union security arrangement, joining the union is a significant act of union participation.

To help provide insight into the issue of union participation, this chapter will present a model that is based on well-established principles from behavioral science.

Increasing Union Participation: A Model

In science, a model is something that uses words and symbols to explain how things work. One of the fundamental models in behavioral science suggests that behavior is determined by the interaction of two factors—the characteristics of the individual and the environment in which the individual operates (Reitz, 1987) (see Figure 2.1).

The model depicted in Figure 2.1 is very dynamic. Individual characteristics and the environment, though distinct entities, can interact to influence one another, and

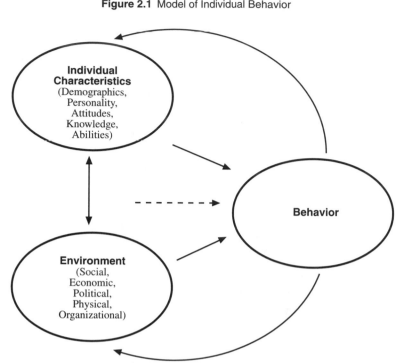

Figure 2.1 Model of Individual Behavior

together they shape a person's behavior. In addition, the behavior that results can, in turn, influence the individual and the environment.[1]

Member participation in the union is a form of behavior. To understand a union member's decision to behave in a certain way (i.e., to participate or not to participate in a union) it is necessary to be familiar with the individual and environmental characteristics that shape this behavior.

Individual Characteristics

In the model presented in Figure 2.1, "individual characteristics" include demographic characteristics; knowledge, skills, and abilities; attitudes and beliefs; and personality traits. Demographic factors can include a person's gender, age, race, education, or work experience, among others. They are important because individual differences can influence a person's behavior. For instance a sixty-year-old union member, nearing the end of his work career, will most likely have signifi-

1. This is a model commonly used by organizational behaviorists. The relationships between the variables are often stated in the equation $B = f(P \times E)$. This equation suggests that "behavior is a function of the interaction between a person and the environment" (Reitz, 1987, p. 22). The term "individual characteristics" is substituted for "personal characteristics" in the model.

cantly different goals, experiences, and, perhaps, beliefs and values, than a twenty-five-year old member.

Differences are also commonly found in the knowledge, abilities, and skills that individuals possess. These factors may have a direct bearing on people's actions or behaviors. It is easy, for example, to envision how a person's abilities to speak in public, to work with others, or to remember names could influence that person's decision to assume or not to assume a leadership role in an organization (Bandura, 1977, 1986).

Researchers have found that female members' participation in union activities is related to both their feelings of self-confidence and their ability to overcome perceived barriers placed in front of them. In fact, the research found that overcoming obstacles to union participation was a problem primarily for women who lacked confidence in their ability to participate in the union (Bulger and Mellor, 1997).

Attitudes and beliefs also may influence people's behavior. Behavioral scientists define attitudes and beliefs as a person's favorable or unfavorable evaluation concerning objects, people, or events (Fishbein and Ajzen, 1975; Cascio, 1991). When people say, "I really like my job" or "all politicians are corrupt," they are expressing an attitude or a belief.

Personality is a fourth individual characteristic that can influence behavior. Personality is the relatively stable set of psychological traits that distinguish one person from another. The link between personality and behavior is readily apparent. People with outgoing personalities, for example, tend to behave differently than people who are shy. The behavior of combative people will differ from noncombative people.

The Environment

Individual characteristics such as attitudes are only one of the two major influences the model suggests are central to shaping an individual's behavior. The environment in which the behavior takes place will also influence a person's behavior. There are many dimensions to the environment in which a person lives. Among them are the social, the political, the economic, the organizational, and the broader physical environments.

The social environment involves the people with whom an individual interacts on a social basis. This environment will include friends and acquaintances, as well as larger groups of people, like peer groups and social organizations with which one is involved. Family constitutes a very important part of an individual's social environment. Each of these groups will have formal or informal rules and guidelines that define acceptable and unacceptable behavior.

The political dimensions of a person's environment also can help shape behavior. A society's laws and legal system are specifically designed to encourage certain types of behavior and discourage (and punish) other types. Prevailing political attitudes in one's immediate environment can also have an impact. Within a small group or in society at large, political attitudes can influence both speech and action.

The economic environment also plays a role in shaping people's behavior. Labor markets and unemployment levels influence whether a person has a secure, well-paying job. Inflation and the prices one pays for goods and services will directly affect a person's buying and spending habits. These economic pressures can, in turn, have an influence on one's actions in other aspects of life.

In any discussion of the environment's impact on behavior, it is important to include the physical environment. Certainly, the behavior of people in New York City and rural Iowa differ in many ways. At least some of these dissimilar behavior patterns can be attributed to the differences in their physical environment. Aspects of the physical environment that can influence behavior include geography, population density, climate, and architecture.

These different environments are not separate and distinct entities; in fact, there is a great deal of overlap among them. Often individuals experience these environments in the context of social, political, or economic organizations. The "organizational environment" may be the environment that has the most immediate influence over a person's behavior. It is also the part of the environment over which organizations have the most control.

Organizations are a central part of every person's life. Whether it be in a social, political, or workplace context, organizations help to shape people's behavior. Organizations have their own environments, which are shaped by the group's resources, its leadership, the rewards it offers to members, its structure, and its culture, among other factors.

What Can Unions Do?

To this point, this chapter has outlined a general model for explaining behavior that could be applied to most any situation and to most any organization. The model suggests that individual characteristics and the environment are the two main phenomena that shape behavior. The model is made much more complicated because each of these has distinct but related dimensions that can influence behavior.

The purpose of presenting this model, however, is to help union leaders and activists better understand how they can influence members' behavior in ways that will help build stronger unions. While it might be interesting, and even helpful, to be able to identify and explain all the individual characteristics and environmental factors that shape behavior, most of these fall beyond the control of unions. Unions and union leaders have very little influence over the gender, age, race, personality, or other individual characteristics of their members.[2] And while union leaders can

2. Although it is true that unions can influence the kind of people who are in their union through the choices they make in organizing, there is little evidence that these decisions are made to influence the de-

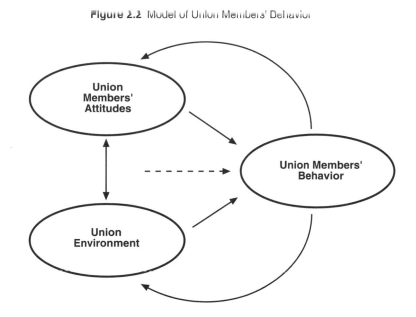

Figure 2.2 Model of Union Members' Behavior

gain insight into members' behavior by understanding the larger social, political, economic, and physical aspects of members' environments, unions' control over these is limited.

There are, however, individual characteristics of a union member's environment over which unions *do* have some control. The model suggests that if unions wish to influence members' behavior, this is where they need to concentrate their efforts (see Figure 2.2).

The most promising individual characteristics for unions to focus their efforts on are members' attitudes and beliefs. Unions have the most control over their own organizational environment. If union leaders can create an environment within their union that encourages and rewards participation in, and support of, the organization, they can encourage the kind of behavior that will most benefit the group.

Shaping Union Members' Attitudes

An important finding of behavioral science is that individuals are not born with their attitudes and beliefs in place. Rather they are, in large part, the product of experiences to which people are exposed and information they receive from a variety of sources, including one's own experience; peers and family; and other societal groups, including religious organizations, schools, the community, the media, and

---

mographic composition of the union. Finding prospective new members is difficult enough for most unions without limiting themselves to certain ethnic or racial groups or to one gender.

unions (Fishbein and Ajzen, 1975).[3] For example, a person's attitude toward his or her job is most likely related to individual experience with that job, while a person's attitude toward organ donation is more likely shaped by information a person receives about the process from family or peers, the media, or religious groups.

New experiences or new information can cause a person to reevaluate, and possibly alter, an attitude. For example, a dramatic restructuring of one's job or the assignment of a new supervisor may change a worker's attitude about his or her job from positive to negative. In the same way, a person who held a negative attitude toward organ donation may adopt a more positive view after reading a news story about the positive impact of such donations.

When applied to a union context, these findings suggest that if participation and involvement in the union are behaviors that unions want to encourage, they need to focus their efforts on fostering those attitudes that will lead to the desired behavior of participation.[4]

An example is the case of Rosa Hernandez described at the beginning of this chapter. Rosa has been trying to get some relatively new members to help staff a phone bank for a union get-out-the-vote drive (behavior) but has been unsuccessful because of the attitudes of the newer members toward the union. What can she do to get her co-workers to help out?

Clearly, Rosa needs to change their attitudes concerning the union and its political action program. Since the newer members who have had less contact with the union show a particular lack of interest, Rosa makes a mental note to try to get these members to a local meeting or other union function in the months ahead. But since that will not help in the short term, she turns to other means, namely peers, to influence their attitudes about unions

Rosa can provide some positive peer influence by identifying individuals in the workplace who are viewed as leaders or who are held in high regard by their co-workers. Rosa could focus her recruitment efforts on these individuals and, if successful, she could encourage them to be vocal about their support for the union's political action program. And Rosa herself, as a peer, certainly can begin to disseminate information that paints a positive picture of the union's political action efforts and that addresses the misinformation the newer members have about the union.

The relationship between attitudes and behavior is complicated by the fact that a given behavior is rarely the result of a single attitude or a single source of informa-

3. Some organizational and industrial psychologists make a distinction between attitudes and beliefs, but others do not. Because I do not believe that the distinctions sometimes made are relevant to the issues addressed in this book, and for simplicity's sake, I use the terms interchangeably.

4. One of the important accomplishments of behavioral research has been to document the relationship between attitudes and behaviors. In the union context, a considerable body of membership-based research has consistently found that union commitment (attitude) is a predictor of union participation (behavior). In other words, individuals who are more committed to the union and union ideals are more likely to participate in various ways in the work of the union. Ultimately, this suggests that if unions wish to encourage member participation, they can do so by increasing the commitment of individual members to the union.

tion. Rather, the thought processes that lead to a particular action or behavior usually involve multiple attitudes and information from multiple, sometimes conflicting, sources. When this occurs, the mind acts like a computer and sorts the different attitudes and information according to their importance to us. Those attitudes and sources designated as more important will have a greater impact on the final decision about how to behave.

Consider the example of job satisfaction. Behavioral scientists have established that job satisfaction (an attitude) is strongly related to people's decisions whether or not to remain employed in a workplace (a behavior). Thus when people quit their jobs, we often find that their behavior is prompted, at least in part, by dissatisfaction about their job (an attitude) (Mobley, 1982). It would not be surprising, however, to encounter individuals who are highly dissatisfied with their jobs but who make the decision to remain in their positions. This is most likely because those individuals hold another job-related attitude that is more important to them than job dissatisfaction. This attitude may involve compensation ("I hate this job, but I will put up with it for the money") or the chances of finding another job ("I hate this job, but any other job I could get would probably be just as bad") or the fact that they have a lot invested in their present job ("I have the highest seniority in my department; I can't give that up!"). Hence understanding how people are likely to behave requires not only an understanding of the attitudes behind their decisions but also the relative importance among attitudes.

Attitudes are often shaped by the opinions of other people. The degree to which an individual's behavior is influenced by the opinions of others depends on the "weight" or "value" an individual gives to those people and their opinions. Teenagers are more likely to give greater weight to the opinions of their peers when it comes to choosing clothes than to the opinions of parents. In a union organizing drive, workers may place greater weight on the opinions of co-workers, family, and friends than on the opinion of a union organizer from outside the community.

A union's ability to influence the attitudes, and the resulting behaviors, of a member or a potential member, will, to a large extent, depend on its ability to identify the most significant people in an individual's life. If one of these significant people has a positive view of the union, the union needs to emphasize and promote that person's views. If a significant person's views are not positive, the union may be faced with the delicate task of deemphasizing the importance or legitimacy of those views.

The Role of Member Commitment

A significant amount of behavioral research over the last twenty years has focused on the attitudes of members and potential members toward unions. This research has looked at a wide range of union-related member attitudes, including attitudes toward unions in general (i.e., whether unions play a positive role in society); perceptions of union "instrumentality" (the degree to which members believe that their union can deliver on issues of importance to them); satisfaction with union performance and union-member relations; feelings about their early experiences in the union (member socialization); views of the operation and effectiveness of the grievance procedure; and opinions about the leadership skills of union stewards and officers.

Union-focused behavioral research has found that a wide variety of attitudes and opinions about unions are ultimately manifested in a broader attitude known as *union member commitment*. Not surprisingly, this research has shown that individuals who are more satisfied with their union's performance, their treatment by union officials, the operation of their grievance procedures, and their first year's experiences with the union are more committed to or supportive of the union than members who have negative attitudes about their union experiences. In many respects, union commitment represents an important or central attitude that captures other attitudes and opinions about union representation (Gordon et al., 1980; Gallagher and Clark, 1989; Clark, Gallagher, and Pavlak, 1991).

The research on union commitment has its roots in work on organizational commitment. Organizational commitment has been defined as the "binding of an individual to an organization" (Gordon et al., 1980, p. 480) and as "a strong desire to remain a member of the particular organization, a willingness to exert high levels of effort on behalf of the organization, and a definite belief in, and acceptance of, the values and goals of the organization" (Porter and Smith, 1970, 2). The research on commitment has looked at many different types of organizations in society, with management organizations garnering the most attention. A great deal has been written, for example, on the commitment of managers and nonmanagerial employees to their employer organizations (Mowday, Steers, and Porter, 1979; Meyer and Allen, 1997). It is, therefore, not surprising that some researchers eventually began examining the commitment of employees to the other major organization present in many workplaces—unions.

The considerable work that has been done on unions in this area over the last two decades was launched by a 1980 study (Gordon et al.). This study found union commitment to be composed of four different parts or facets and developed a scale to measure this attitude.

The first facet of union commitment is *union loyalty*. This facet reflects the fact that members who have a high degree of loyalty will take pride in their association with the union and have a clear awareness of the benefits that stem from membership. The second facet of union commitment is sense of *responsibility to the union*. Committed members will recognize and be willing to fulfill the day-to-day obligations and duties that protect the interests of the union. This would include such activities as keeping the union informed of developments in the workplace and filing grievances when necessary. Members also demonstrate their commitment through their *willingness to work on behalf of the union*, including their willingness to serve as union officers. Although sometimes mistaken as a measure of behavior, this third dimension of union commitment represents intent to behave and is, therefore, attitudinal. The fourth facet of commitment is a member's *general belief in unionism*. This is a broader, catchall, measure of a member's deeply seated attitudes toward unions in general (Gordon et al., 1980).

By determining where a member stands on these four dimensions, we can get a pretty good idea of a member's level of commitment to the union. For instance, if a member were to score high in all four dimensions, we would say that member has a high level of commitment. In contrast, a member who expresses loyalty to his or her union and a belief in unions in general but does not feel a sense of responsibility to the union and is not willing to work on its behalf would, we would conclude, have less commitment.

Establishing an accurate way to measure union commitment has made it possible to examine the relationship of union commitment to a wide range of factors. The relationship between commitment (an attitude) and member participation in union activities (a behavior) has received particular attention (Gordon et al., 1980; Gallagher and Clark, 1989). This research has found that commitment is closely tied to participation in union activities (Fullagar and Barling, 1989; Kelloway and Barling, 1993; Sverke, 1997).

In other words, members who have high levels of commitment are more likely to participate in union activities such as meetings, rallies, and elections. Highly committed members have also been found to be more willing to go on strike in support of bargaining demands (Barling, Fullagar, Kelloway, and McElvie, 1992), more likely to support political action by the union (Fields, Masters, and Thacker, 1987), and more likely to support political candidates endorsed by the union (Thacker, Fields, and Barclay, 1990) than members with low levels of commitment.

In sum, the relationship between commitment and participation in union activities is clear. And high levels of participation in union activities can lead to more effective unions. Strategically, this suggests that if a union wishes to become more effective through increased member participation it can do so by raising the level of member commitment to the union.

General and Specific Attitudes toward Unions

Some of the factors that influence union commitment are outside of the control of unions, although other factors can be influenced, either directly or indirectly, by a union or by individual union activists. Factors that have been found to be closely related to union commitment and that can be influenced by a union and its representatives include a person's overall attitudes about unions and a person's beliefs about a specific union that might be attempting to, or currently does, represent them.

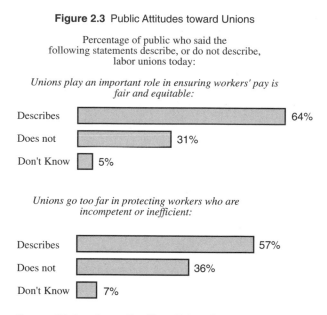

Figure 2.3 Public Attitudes toward Unions

Percentage of public who said the
following statements describe, or do not describe,
labor unions today:

*Unions play an important role in ensuring workers' pay is
fair and equitable:*

Describes   64%
Does not   31%
Don't Know   5%

*Unions go too far in protecting workers who are
incompetent or inefficient:*

Describes   57%
Does not   36%
Don't Know   7%

Source: "Workers Assess Conditions, Unions, Pay," 1997.

General attitudes toward unions include how individuals view the institution of organized labor, its goals, achievements, and leadership, in the abstract (Young-blood et al., 1984; Kochan, Katz, and McKersie, 1986). A 1989 study found that these general attitudes about unions tend to center around two issues—the "big labor" image and "union instrumentality" (Deshpande and Fiorito). The image of unions as "big labor" involves the extent to which people view unions and union leaders as self-interested, opposed to change, autocratic, overly focused on politics, and "blue collar" in orientation. In contrast, general "union instrumentality" reflects people's evaluations of the labor movement's ability to "deliver" or to give members their money's worth for the dues they pay. This might involve the degree to which unions are able to win higher wages, better working conditions, or favorable legislation.

Both dimensions of general attitudes toward unions were reflected in a 1997 *USA Today* Labor Day survey depicted in Figure 2.3.

These results are consistent with those of past surveys commissioned by the AFL-CIO which have indicated that approximately 69 percent of the overall workforce thinks employees are more successful in getting problems resolved with their employer when they bring these problems up as a group rather than as individuals. Yet less than 43 percent say they would definitely or probably vote for a union if given the chance (AFL-CIO, 1999a).

Comments from a 1992 survey of union members represent the range of general attitudes toward unions. For example, one member stated, "I have a bias against unions. My father worked for a company that was put out of business by a union strike. Since then I have been down on unions." Another member stated, "I've never liked unions; all they do is start trouble." A third member had a more positive view: "Unions are the only one fighting for the little man; where would we be without them?" (Clark and Gallagher, 1992).

Behavioral research suggests that such general beliefs often have deep roots and that once in place, they are not easily changed. Research also suggests that these beliefs are very important and play a key role in shaping related attitudes throughout a person's life (Zimbardo and Ebbesen, 1970; Youngblood et al., 1984).

Although sometimes related, attitudes about *specific* unions are different from *general* attitudes. These attitudes focus on how an individual views the specific union that represents, or is attempting to represent, them. Does the union provide services the member believes to be important? Is the union effective in standing up for its members' rights?

In particular, research on unionism has suggested that specific union beliefs can be grouped into three important dimensions—"instrumentality," "union satisfaction," and "perceived union support." Specific union instrumentality refers to the extent to which individuals feel that a given union is able to win tangible gains on behalf of its members (Deshpande and Fiorito, 1989).

Although specific union satisfaction shares some similarities with instrumentality, it also indicates represents a member's feelings concerning the representation that a member receives from the union in his or her workplace. The research suggests that member satisfaction is not simply a matter of unions delivering tangible gains at the bargaining table but also involves the extent to which the union's leadership keeps members informed, gives them a say in running the union, and is responsive to their concerns (Fiorito, Gallagher, and Fukami, 1988; Jarley, Kuruvilla, and Casteel, 1990).

More recently, research in this area has also suggested that members' specific attitudes toward the union reflect the degree to which they believe that their union leadership values members' contributions and cares about their well-being (Shore et al., 1994). Like other research on unions, this work has evolved from the organizational behavior area. The original work on organizational support was based on social exchange frameworks, which suggested that individuals who perceived that the organization was committed to them feel an obligation to be committed to the organization. Using data from a survey of a large Steelworker local union, two researchers found evidence that a strong positive relationship exists between members' perceptions of union support and their levels of commitment to the union (Fuller and Hester, 1998; see Figure 2.4).

Examples of members' attitudes about a specific union include such statements as, "I make quite a bit more per hour than the people over in Ashland. The only reason is that we have a good union and they don't." "I am willing to vote for that union in an organizing election because they have a very good track record in our industry." "I think paying dues to this union is a waste of money. They don't care

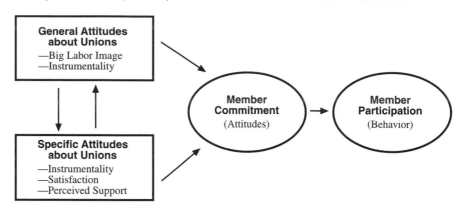

Figure 2.4 The Impact of Specific and General Attitudes on Union Commitment

about us." As these quotes suggest, union members usually have an opinion about how well their particular union is performing.

In some cases, the general and specific views of members may be different. For instance, members may hold a less than positive opinion of the union in their workplace but still view unions in general in a positive light. Conversely, they may view their union positively but hold negative attitudes toward unions in general. It is more likely, however, that members' attitude about unions in general and about their specific union will be consistent.

Since most members have little contact with unions beyond the one in their workplace, a positive or negative experience with that union is likely to shape their beliefs about unions in general. Members probably have a tendency, without a larger frame of reference, to conclude that if their union is doing a good job, other unions must be equally effective.

Attitudes are the product of information people acquire from different sources. Most information shaping people's attitudes comes from three sources: peers and family; other societal groups such as religious organizations, schools, the community, the media, and unions; and their own experience.

People who have had very little exposure to a subject will often rely on the attitudes and information conveyed to them by their family as a basis for forming their own attitudes on that subject. Parents can be influential in this regard, particularly if the information is passed on when a person is most impressionable—during childhood. This is reflected in a comment made by a forty-year-old union member in a survey of union members' attitudes:

> One time in fifth grade, I came home and told everyone in my family how Sister Theresa said the union down at my father's warehouse was no good. My Dad's face got red; he lifted me up until we were eye to eye and said in a very stern voice, "That union puts food on the table and a roof over our heads. Don't ever talk about the

union like that." I remember him telling me that like it was yesterday. I have been a union supporter ever since. (Clark and Gallagher, 1992)

Behavioral research suggests that members' commitment levels can also be shaped by the beliefs of other individuals whose opinions they value such as friends and acquaintances. More significantly, it may include fellow union members and others in the workplace. In an effort to fit in, a new employee entering the workplace for the first time will often try to figure out what the acceptable and even prevailing beliefs are.

Some in that workplace—those who are especially friendly to the new person and those who stand out as leaders, for example—will make more of an impression than will others. These individuals can have a significant influence on the new member's beliefs. If it is clear to the new member that the union is respected and valued in that workplace, the new member may feel more comfortable adopting that view of the union. If the union is continually criticized and ridiculed, the new member's attitude toward the union will likely be negative and the member will probably avoid active involvement in the union.

In addition to family members and peers, people today get information from a multitude of sources, including schools, news publications, radio talk shows, television news programs, World Wide Web sites, and e-mail. All of these sources convey information that is absorbed and processed, to one degree or another. And all of them have the potential to influence attitudes and beliefs.

The prevalent values of a community or a region can greatly influence the way people view the world. This extends to people's attitudes about unions. Unions have traditionally found it difficult to organize in rural, agricultural areas, particularly in the South and the mountains/plains states, because of the conservative, independent values and traditions that predominate in those areas (Kochan, 1979; Fiorito, Gallagher, and Greer, 1986). Some religious denominations have even discouraged their members from organizing unions through religious teachings (Fones-Wolf, 1989).

While there are many secondhand sources that can influence a person's general and specific attitudes toward unions, the adage "experience is a good teacher" suggests that firsthand exposure is likely to be a very significant influence on one's attitudes. This suggests that if a union wants to build commitment among its membership, one of the first things it needs to consider is its own performance.

The Reinforcement of Attitudes

General and specific attitudes toward unions contribute to the more comprehensive attitude toward unions called union commitment. In turn, the level of a member's commitment to the union will largely influence that member's decision whether to take the next step and act on those beliefs. The degree to which mem-

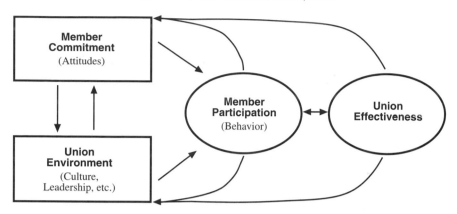

Figure 2.5 Model of Member Participation

bers are willing to participate energetically and enthusiastically in the work the union needs to do in the organizing, bargaining, grievance handling, political, and community action areas, as well as to engage in the more mundane union citizenship behaviors, will have a significant effect on the overall effectiveness of the union.

If this model is to be an accurate reflection of what goes on in a union, however, it cannot stop here. Each time there is movement forward within this model, from commitment to participation, from participation to effectiveness, a whole chain of events is set in motion. For example, members who develop sufficient levels of commitment to cause them to participate in union activities may very well see, close up, how effective the union can be. This experience may reinforce or heighten their commitment, which may cause them to work even harder on behalf of the union, especially if they value the outcome achieved by the union.

Given the idea that behavior can reinforce attitudes, our model can be restated as shown in Figure 2.5. To fully understand behavior, however, it is necessary to look more closely at the other major factor that shapes it, the environment.

The Union Environment

The organizational environment a member experiences also influences behavior. Unions and union leaders probably have more control over the environment they create within their union than over any other single factor that shapes behavior. Unions should carefully consider several aspects of the organizational environment in their efforts to encourage participation and build more effective unions. This book will focus on two of these areas in particular—the overall culture of the union and its leadership.

Culture

One element of the environment that plays an important role in shaping behavior is organizational culture. Within every formal organization there exists an informal organization of unofficial rules, procedures, and interconnections. These mechanisms make up the organization's culture.

Culture exists to communicate and reinforce the norms, values, and priorities of the organization among the members and prospective members. In doing so, an organization's culture gives its members a sense of organizational identity, togetherness, and purpose that promotes commitment to the group. In a sense, culture is the glue that binds members to the organization.

Culture also communicates to members which behaviors are appropriate, approved, or accepted in the organization. Members of an organization with an effective culture will use the values and expectations of that group to decide whether to engage or not to engage in a certain behavior (Wagner and Hollenbeck, 1998).

Unions, like all organizations, have a prevailing culture that underscores their basic values and norms. Among the prevailing values of unions are solidarity, unity, fairness, justice, and equity. If a union creates an environment in which these values are held in high regard, members will be reluctant to engage in actions that are inconsistent with these principles (like crossing a picket line).

An organization's culture is communicated in a variety of ways, including ceremonies, rites, and rituals; heroes, stories, and myths; and symbols and language (Deal and Kennedy, 1982). These phenomena clearly play a role in shaping members' behavior. Unions and union leaders can consciously shape the culture of their organization in a way that encourages member participation. This issue will be discussed in more detail in Chapter 9.

Leadership

Few people would disagree with the notion that leadership is critical to the success of any organization. Labor organizations are no exception to this rule. Part of the reason why union leadership is so important to effectiveness is the role leadership plays in encouraging and facilitating member participation. At the local union level, leaders encourage members to run for elected office or accept appointed positions in the union. Leaders persuade and cajole members to attend union meetings, vote in elections, and walk picket lines.

At the regional and national levels, leaders develop and carry out strategies to increase member participation in organizing drives, lobbying efforts, and political elections. The effectiveness of a union is, in no small measure, tied to the ability of these individuals to get members working on behalf of the union.

Recent research has suggested that there are two general styles of leadership in organizations. Transactional leadership is the traditional approach of most leaders. This form of leadership motivates people by exchanging rewards for services rendered. A transactional leader identifies roles organizational members must play to achieve the organization's objectives. At the same time, these leaders discern what the members need from the organization and communicate to them how the organization will fulfill those needs in exchange for the members performing the necessary roles (Bass, 1990).

A second style of leadership that has received a significant amount of attention is transformational or charismatic leadership. Transformational leaders focus their efforts on communicating group goals to the organization's members and endeavor to convince members to put those goals above their own (Wagner and Hollenbeck, 1998). These leaders work to transform the organizational culture, challenging members to do more than has been asked of them. Evidence suggests that this approach can generate more membership involvement than transactional leadership (Bass, 1998). These leadership styles will be discussed in Chapter 10.

Clearly, the environment a union is able to create will influence union members' behavior. The attitudes of members toward the union are also important in this regard. These are the major premises underlying the model of union member behavior represented in Figure 2.5.

Influences beyond the Union's Control

The model or framework suggested in this book cannot completely explain why a particular union is effective or ineffective. There are many factors beyond a member's attitudes and the organizational environment a union creates that will help determine a union's effectiveness. For instance, members' beliefs about a specific union that represents them can, in part, be influenced by the actions and attitudes of the employer in that workplace. A union faced with an obstinate, aggressive, and unreasonable employer may do all it can to win a decent contract for its members but may ultimately be forced to settle for a less favorable agreement. Despite its best efforts, at least some members will view the union in a negative light for failing to deliver a better contract. The same could be said for the outcomes of members' grievances.

While a union might create a positive union culture and be blessed with impressive leadership, unions do not operate in a vacuum. There are other aspects of individual environment that can influence individual behavior and, ultimately, a union's effectiveness. The state of the economy in general, and the labor market in particular, can have a significant impact on members' attitudes, their behaviors, and ultimately the success of the union. Similarly, the broader social, political, and physical environment may also influence members and labor organizations in important ways. In many cases, these environmental factors will be beyond the influence of unions and union leaders.

Unions, with their limited resources, cannot afford to focus their efforts on things they cannot change. The most effective strategy for unions is consciously to decide what, in a given situation, they have the power to influence and what is beyond their control. The model presented here identifies two areas over which unions can have a significant influence—union members' attitudes and the union's own organizational environment. The remainder of this book will focus on what behavioral science suggests that unions *can* do in these two areas to increase union commitment, increase union participation, and, ultimately, build more effective organizations.

3

Organizing and Retaining Members

Key Points

- Attitudes toward unions in general, and toward the specific union that is organizing the workers, play a critical role in the unionization decision.
- The employee's perception of the union's effectiveness may be the pivotal individual factor or the "fulcrum" of the unionization process.
- Union tactics and strategies play a very significant role in determining the outcome of organizing elections.
- Unions should consider why many employees choose not to vote in union elections.
- Voters in decertification elections are influenced by many of the same factors that influence an individual's vote in a certification election.

"Organizing is the lifeblood of the labor movement." This phrase is often heard in labor circles. Indeed, as organizations whose strength comes primarily from their membership, unions constantly need to recruit new members to maintain their current membership levels, let alone grow, because unions lose members through death, retirement, job loss, and decertification. In 1998, one AFL-CIO official stated that the American labor movement needed to recruit four-hundred thousand new members just to maintain the share of the workforce it had in 1997 (Velasquez, 1999). The main way unions bring new members into the organization is by convincing them to vote for a union during an organizing drive.

This chapter will focus on how behavioral science can help union leaders and activists better understand the decision-making processes employed by prospective members when they cast votes in a representation or decertification election. The insights gained will be used to analyze organizing tactics and strategies. The first part of the chapter will present research on the union representation election process. These studies identify factors that are critical to workers' voting decisions. The second part of the chapter will address an often overlooked, but important, issue related to representation elections—why some people choose *not* to vote in union elections. This section will discuss the implications this phenomenon has for election outcomes and how unions should deal with nonvoters. The third section will look at current research about voter behavior in decertification elections. The final section of the chapter will discuss the influence that family members have on the way people vote in elections.

Voting Behavior in Representation Elections

The general model of behavior outlined in Chapter 2 suggests that individual characteristics and the environment interact to shape behavior. In this chapter the behavior of concern is the casting of votes in union representation and decertification elections. Research in this area has identified some important factors involving the characteristics of individual workers and the environments in which union elections take place. The characteristic over which labor organizations have the most potential influence is individuals' attitudes.

The Role of Attitudes in Organizing

A fair amount of research has been conducted on the critical issue of why people vote for unions (Premack and Hunter, 1988; Barling, Fullagar, and Kelloway, 1992). Study after study has confirmed the important role that attitudes toward unions and toward employers play in this voting decision (Fiorito, Gallagher, and Greer, 1986; Deshpande and Fiorito, 1989). Two studies are particularly instructive in this regard.

Job Dissatisfaction

A 1980 study looked at why workers become interested in union representation. To shed light on that issue, the study used the data from an earlier study in which employees who had been involved in a union election were interviewed at two points in time. The first interview was conducted immediately after the election was announced; the second interview took place following the election. The 1,239 randomly selected employees interviewed in this study were drawn from a wide variety of sectors and geographic locations and represented different unions and different bargaining unit sizes. All had been involved in representation elections that were hard fought. The National Labor Relations Board (NLRB) subsequently determined that unfair labor practices had been committed in twenty-two of the thirty-one elections. Like previous research, this study found that initial interest in voting for a union was stimulated by job dissatisfaction. Specifically, the study found that it was dissatisfaction with working conditions, rather than the nature of the work itself, that led to an interest in unionization. Just how important is job dissatisfaction in stimulating interest in unionization? In this study the researcher's knowledge of employee job dissatisfaction in groups being organized enabled her to predict the actual vote with 75 percent accuracy (Brett, 1980).

A further analysis of the data in this study showed that a second factor, perceived job insecurity, also causes workers to vote in favor of union representation (Brett, 1980). This finding suggests that workplaces in which workers' jobs are threatened represent a potential opportunity for the labor movement. Unions need to consider how they can respond to employees' concerns about job insecurity.

Union Effectiveness

It would be a mistake, however, to suggest that job dissatisfaction or job insecurity alone will lead to a pro-union vote. Research shows that people respond on a rational basis to dissatisfaction in most any situation (Mobley, 1977; Barling 1990). Employees with high levels of dissatisfaction and faced with the option of voting for a union will first consider their general and specific attitudes toward unions. Particularly important is the extent to which employees believe the union can be instrumental or effective in resolving their specific dissatisfactions (see Figure 3.1).

The study described above argues that employees who do not view the union as an effective means to deal with workplace problems are unlikely to vote for the union, regardless of how dissatisfied they are (Brett, 1980). Nevertheless, even employees who are satisfied with their working conditions may vote for union representation if their general and specific beliefs about unions are positive. While this research suggests that employees' attitudes toward unions, and especially their perception of the union's effectiveness, are key factors in representation voting decisions, dissatisfaction remains an important factor in initiating interest in unionization.

The study also found that the decision to vote for a union is largely rational or instrumental rather than emotional. This is an important point that counters the perception, held by some, that union organizers can whip up the emotions of otherwise satisfied workers for their own ends (Brett, 1980).

Attitudes toward Unions in General

While critical in the organization process, employees' job dissatisfaction and perception of the effectiveness of a union may not be sufficient to stimulate a pro-union vote. This research showed that attitudes toward unions in general (in contrast to perceived effectiveness of a specific union) are also important. When employees hold negative views toward unions in general (e.g., unions are too powerful, union dues are too high, unions strike too often), they are less likely to vote for union representation. Employees may be highly dissatisfied and believe that a specific union might help them resolve their dissatisfaction yet choose not to

Figure 3.1 Attitudinal Model of Union Voting

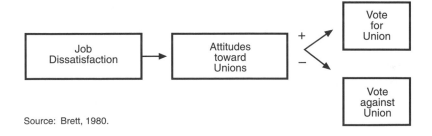

Source: Brett, 1980.

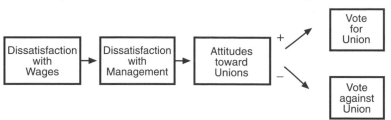

Figure 3.2 Alternative Attitudinal Model of Union Voting

vote for the union because their attitudes toward unions in general are negative. In this way, these general attitudes serve a "gatekeeper" function (Brett, 1980).

In another study, researchers took a very different approach to answering the question of why individuals choose to vote for union representation. Their research involved a meta-analysis of fourteen different studies on the union representation question. A meta-analysis combines, compares, and contrasts the findings of previous studies on a similar issue and, ideally, results in more definitive and reliable conclusions (Premack and Hunter, 1988).

Using this approach, this study was able to go further than the previous one in examining the issue of employee behavior in organizing drives. First, the researchers suggested that to understand why people choose to vote for unions, two aspects of dissatisfaction should be considered—extrinsic job dissatisfaction (dissatisfaction with wages, benefits, and the like) and dissatisfaction with management.

Second, while the previous study accords a triggering role to job dissatisfaction, this study gives this role specifically to dissatisfaction with wage levels, suggesting that poor wages would lead to extrinsic dissatisfaction, which, in turn, would result in dissatisfaction with management (who would be blamed for the low wage levels).

These researchers also suggested that dissatisfaction would lead employees to question whether the union could be effective in resolving their dissatisfaction. As Figure 3.2 suggests, their decision to vote for or against the union would depend on their general and specific attitudes toward unions, especially their perception of the effectiveness of the union (Premack and Hunter, 1988).

Altruistic Considerations

The research discussed above stresses the importance of employee self-interest (individual dissatisfaction and job insecurity and a union's ability to address those concerns) in the employee's voting decision concerning union representation. Given these findings, researchers have generally discounted the importance of unions' appeals to altruism or to a higher purpose, that is, advancing the interests of all workers and improving the well-being of society as a whole.

Union advocates, however, should be aware of one study that analyzed the results of two substantial employee surveys and concluded that altruistic appeals *can* play a "significant and substantial role" in organizing campaigns. At a minimum, this study concluded that narrow self-interest motivations in union voting should not preclude appeals to "nobler" sentiments. In short, the findings suggest that such appeals cannot hurt, and potentially can help, unions in persuading workers to vote yes in organizing elections (Fiorito, 1992).

Stake in the Job

An additional factor that can play a role in a person's decision to support a union is "stake in the job." Many service sector jobs are virtually impossible to organize because those filling those jobs have no long-term stake in them. Individuals who do not plan to hold their jobs for very long usually care little about trying to establish a union that, down the road, might make those jobs better. The fast-food industry is an example of one in which turnover is high and stake in the job is very low. This is also the case for the growing number of contingent, or temporary, workers in American workplaces (Fierman, 1994; Carre, duRivage, and Tilly, 1998; Rogers, 2000).

Commitment to the Union and the Employer

Behavioral science research has examined another aspect of attitudes about which unions involved in organizing campaigns should be aware. Organizing campaigns involve two major organizations—the employer and the union. As is the case for unions, the attitudes an employee holds about the employer can shape that employee's level of commitment to the employer organization.

As the labor ballad "Which Side Are You On" implies, the traditional adversarial model of union-management relations views commitment as an "either or," zero sum, proposition (Gallagher and Clark, 1989). Certainly employers and unions in the midst of organizing drives often behave as if commitment to the employer and union are mutually exclusive. This view of commitment suggests that painting a negative picture of the employer can reduce commitment to the employer and boost

---

"WHICH SIDE ARE YOU ON"

They say in Harlan County,
There are no neutrals there,
You'll either be a union man,
Or a thug for J. H. Blair.

Which side are you on,
Which side are you on.

Written by Florence Reese, 1932

commitment to the union. Employers' efforts to cast the union in the most negative light in the course of an organizing drive are also based on the same reasoning.

Many studies on the relationship between commitment to the employer *and* to the union suggest, however, that there is not always an inverse relationship between the two. These studies have found that employees can be simultaneously committed to both. This phenomenon is called dual commitment or dual loyalty (Purcell, 1953; Fukami and Larson, 1984; Gallagher and Clark, 1989; Gordon and Ladd, 1990).

Sometimes unions need to convince the employees in an organizing campaign that commitment to the union is not incompatible with commitment to the employer. The American Federation of State, County, and Municipal Employees (AFSCME) ran into such a situation in its efforts to organize the clerical workers at Harvard University in 1987 and 1988. At least some of the resistance to the campaign was rooted in the strong attachment the Harvard employees had to the university and the perception that a vote for the union was a vote against Harvard. The union worked hard to convince these employees that giving them some voice in improving employment conditions would ultimately strengthen the university. Their campaign centered around the slogan "It's Not Anti-Harvard to be Pro-Union" (Shostak, 1991, p. 97).

The results of a recent, high-profile study of workers' attitudes further support the notion that many employees hold their employer in reasonably high regard. This nationwide survey of approximately twenty-four hundred workers found that the vast majority of respondents held either a lot (54 percent) or some (32 percent) loyalty to their employer. Furthermore, while most workers surveyed expressed a desire for greater participation in workplace decisions, most thought this could best be achieved through a cooperative, participative group that included management (e.g., a labor-management committee), rather than through traditional employee representation (i.e., a union) (Freeman and Rogers, 1999). These findings suggest that unions need to consider carefully how they portray the employer in an organizing campaign.

Employees may also see a potential conflict between commitment to a union and commitment to a profession, as opposed to an individual employer (Shostak,

1991). Unions involved in the education field have long encountered beliefs that it is "unprofessional" to be involved with a union and that unionism will have a negative effect on the educational process. Education unions have organized successfully because they have addressed these beliefs in their organizing campaigns. The concern of the American Federation of Teachers (AFT) and the National Education Association (NEA) about the teaching profession is prominent in both unions' national constitutions. Section 1 of the NEA's constitution, for example, includes among its objectives "the consistent development and improvement of the profession and its practitioners" and "to work among the American people for broad support of education and improved attitudes toward the profession."

Health care workers also share with teachers and others a deep concern for their profession. Unions attempting to organize these workers need to be sensitive to these concerns. Recent developments in health care present unions with an opportunity to make inroads in an important industry. Managed care initiatives and other cost-reduction strategies have placed increasing pressure on health care workers. These changes have raised concerns among nurses, physicians, and other health care providers that range from inadequate staffing to decreased quality of care to increased liability.[1]

A recent study concluded that nurses who are dissatisfied with the climate for patient care in their hospitals are more likely to vote for a union in a representation election than are nurses who perceive their climate positively. Given these findings, unions' success in this sector may depend on the degree to which they can convince health care workers that organizing can give them greater control over patient care in the face of health care reform (Clark et al., 1999).

Other studies support the idea that an aggressive, conflict-based, antiemployer organizing strategy may not be the most effective means to organize professional, technical, and white-collar workers. This research suggests that, in addition to concerns about professionalism, these workers may also have the most to lose from a contentious campaign. It also suggests that more needs to be learned about differences in attitudes toward conflict across gender, age, and race and about how employer participation programs affect workers' attitudes toward employers in an organizing context (Cohen and Hurd, 1998).

The findings discussed thus far suggest that people's attitudes toward unions play an important role in their decision to vote for or against a union in an organizing campaign. Specifically,

1. Job dissatisfaction plays an important role in stimulating the initial interest in unionization.
2. Job dissatisfaction primarily has an indirect effect on the decision to vote for a union.

---

1. Although a very small percentage of physicians have organized in the past, the American Medical Association (AMA) took a very dramatic step in June 1999 by deciding to form its own union.

3. Attitudes toward unions in general, and toward the specific union that is organiz
ing the workers, play a critical role in the unionization decision.
4. The employee's perception of the union's effectiveness is the pivotal factor or the
fulcrum of the unionization process.
5. Sometimes unions need to convince potential members that being committed to
the union is not incompatible with their commitment to the employer.

The Role of Environment

In addition to individual attitudes, the research on organizing has identified environmental factors that can influence how an employee might vote in a representation election. Environmental factors differ from individual characteristics in that
they largely emanate from outside single individuals and simultaneously affect
more than one person. Such influences might include the employer, the union, the
government, peers, family, and possibly even the physical setting in which workers operate.

One environmental consideration that probably springs to the minds of most
union leaders is the degree to which an employer opposes a union's organizing effort. Considerable research confirms that where an employer creates a hostile environment through such overt actions as intimidation, harassment, surveillance, and
discharge, union support is often reduced (Weiler, 1983; Freeman, 1985; Bronfenbrenner, 1994; Cohen and Hurd, 1998).

Employers can also use "positive" or "preventive" human resource policies to
create an environment that makes union organizing difficult. This "union substitution" strategy is aimed at convincing workers that a union is unnecessary. A 1986
study examined the impact of such "progressive" human resource policies on
unionization and found that they constituted a very effective union avoidance
strategy (Kochan, McKersie, and Chalykoff). Another study in 1987 found that
companies that engaged in union substitution efforts, including employee participation and communications programs and nonunion grievance procedures, are
more successful in remaining nonunion than companies that do not employ these
strategies (Fiorito, Lowman, and Nelson).

In a more recent study, researchers looked at a large number of individual and
organizational (environmental) factors in an effort to determine their influence on
the voting decisions of individual workers. Among the aspects of a worker's environment included in this study were the employer's human resource policies, as
well as certain organizational characteristics of the employer (e.g., the level of cen-
tralization of decision making, size, and the competitiveness of its market) (Fiorito
and Young, 1998).

The results suggest that several aspects of the workers' environment can influence their level of interest in a union. For example, the researchers found, not surprisingly, that cuts in pay tend to increase workers' interest in organizing. Alterna-

tively, they found that incentive pay systems reduce workers' interest. One explanation of the latter finding is that such systems "harmonize workers' and employers' interests by aligning incentives" (Fiorito and Young, 1998, p. 242). Such harmony may translate into lower support for the union.

These researchers also found that the more bureaucratic an employer (multiple layers of management, formal and rigid communications systems, and so on), the greater support there tends to be for a union (Fiorito and Young, 1998).

Another study looked at an additional means by which employers can create an environment that discourages employees from supporting an organizing drive. This research concludes that employee involvement programs can reduce interest in union representation (Rundle, 1998). This finding is reinforced by other studies (Fiorito, Lowman, and Nelson, 1987; Grenier, 1987; Bronfenbrenner, 1993).

Clearly, there are many ways in which employers can manipulate the workplace environment and influence a worker's vote in an organizing campaign. There are also numerous strategies for opposing these tactics. If employers violate existing labor law, unions can file unfair labor practices with the National Labor Relations Board (although some unions are choosing not to go this route because they see the NLRB as increasingly ineffective in enforcing the law [Schlossberg, 1994; Greenhouse, 1998]). Another common strategy of experienced union organizers is "inoculating" workers against these strategies by identifying them and forewarning workers of their use.

In many instances, there is little unions can do to stop employers from manipulating the workplace environment in an effort to influence employees' voting behavior. Unions usually cannot prevent nonunion employers from opposing union efforts to organize or limit the resources they devote to these efforts. Except for when an election campaign is in progress, unions cannot stop employers from implementing preventive human resource policies.

One strategy that a growing number of unions are successfully using to address this issue is the negotiation of neutrality and card check agreements. A neutrality agreement requires an employer to remain neutral if the union attempts to organize its work sites. A card check agreement compels the employer to recognize a union without an election if a majority of bargaining unit members sign cards indicating they want that union to represent them.

These agreements are sometimes negotiated when a union is dealing with an employer with multiple work sites, one or more of which are already organized by the union, or when a union has some other form of leverage with an unorganized employer.[2] Neutrality and card check agreements allow the union to bypass organizing elections in which employers blatantly violate labor law and otherwise place obstacles in the way of workers' desires to obtain union representation.

---

2. One example of the labor movement creatively using its leverage to win neutrality and card check agreements is the Union Labor Life Insurance Company's (ULLICO) efforts to force companies building and operating facilities with money borrowed from its funds to sign such agreements.

NEUTRALITY AGREEMENT—Kaiser Permanente and SEIU, Local 96

Kaiser Permanente agrees to remain neutral during any organizing activity and agrees to recognize SEIU upon a showing of majority interest through a card check conducted by a mutually agreed upon neutral third party.

Unions and union leaders are, understandably, discouraged because of the many aspects of the organizing environment over which they have little control. Rather than dwell on these factors, unions, again, should consider focusing their energies on the things they *can* control.

In recent years, a significant amount of research on the organizing process has been conducted. This research suggests that, despite the hostile environment in which they must organize today, unions can control the outcome of organizing elections to a much greater degree than previously thought (Bronfenbrenner and Juravich, 1998).

One of the most critical findings of this research has been that union tactics and strategies play a greater role in determining the outcome of organizing elections than do any other variables, including employers' characteristics and tactics, the makeup of bargaining units, and the election environment. In short, this research suggests that how unions conduct their organizing campaigns matters a great deal (Bronfenbrenner, 1993,1997).

Work on this issue has tried to determine which tactics are most successful in organizing elections and in campaigns to win a unit's first contract. One such study has suggested that the most effective approach is an "aggressive grassroots rank-and-file strategy focused on building a union and acting like a union from the very beginning of the campaign" (Bronfenbrenner and Juravich, 1998, p. 20). Such an approach emphasizes person-to-person contact, house calls, and small group meetings. It also encourages "active rank-and-file participation in, and responsibility for, the organizing campaign, including developing a large rank-and-file organizing committee representative of the different interest groups in the bargaining unit" (Bronfenbrenner and Juravich, 1998, p. 24). Additional research has supported these conclusions (Jarley, Fiorito, and Delaney, 1998).

This latter point is reinforced by behavioral science research suggesting that people are far more responsive to the opinions of people close to them (family, friends, peers) than to those who are more distant (union organizers from outside the community, for example). Researchers use the terms "proximal," to describe close influences, and "distal," to describe more distant influences. This proximal-distal principle has important implications for organizing, as well as for many other aspects of a union's work (Lewin, 1943; Becker et al., 1996).

These findings also demonstrate the need for a union embarking on an organizing drive to "develop a long range campaign strategy that incorporates building for the first contract into the original organizing process" (Bronfenbrenner and Juravich, 1998, p. 24). This work suggests that unions need to develop a "culture of organizing" that permeates the organization and includes the commitment of significant human and financial resources from all levels to the goal of organizing new members.

Consistent with our model, these recommendations are aimed at transforming both the attitudes of individuals involved in an organizing campaign and the environment in which such a campaign would take place.

Choosing Not to Vote in Union Elections

The research discussed to this point provides insights into why individuals vote for or against union representation in organizing elections. It does not, however, touch on a significant aspect of voting behavior that has, until recently, largely escaped the attention of researchers. This is the issue of why some people choose not to vote in union representation elections.

Under U.S. labor law, a union must receive a majority of votes cast (as opposed to a majority of the votes of all eligible voters) in order to win an organizing election. These elections are often closely contested. One study found that union representation elections are typically decided by about eight votes and that in situations in which the employer wins, the margin of victory is even smaller (Roomkin and Block, 1981). This is a critical issue from the union perspective because, first, the number of people who do not vote are often sufficient to change the outcome of the election. And second, it may be easier to persuade people to vote than it is to get them to change the way they vote, once the decision for whom to vote has been made.

In a 1997 study, researchers surveyed employees shortly after their bargaining unit had voted for union representation. The outcome of the election was very close, with 184 members voting for the union and 180 voting against. Incredibly, 410 members of the bargaining unit did not vote, (Hepburn, Loughlin, and Barling, 1997).

Based on previous research on why people choose to vote in certification elections, the study focused on five predictors of the decision not to vote. The first four factors were level of interest in the election, satisfaction with the employer, general attitudes toward unions, and peer pressure. The fifth factor involved perceived effectiveness (or voting instrumentality). In contrast to studies discussed previously that focused on the effectiveness of the union in addressing workplace problems, this study assessed the degree to which individuals believed their vote would be important in addressing those problems. This factor was included because employees who see their vote as insignificant are unlikely to vote (Hepburn, Loughlin, and Barling, 1997).

The results suggest that these five factors are related to the decision not to vote in two very different ways. First, nonvoters fall between employees who vote for

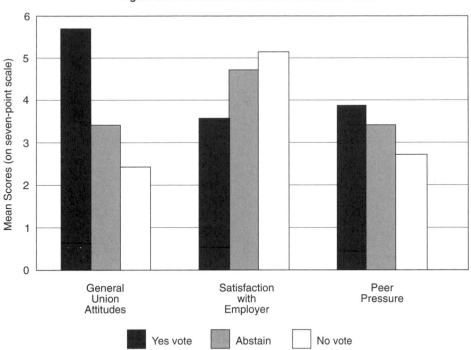

Figure 3.3 Abstainers Fall between Yes and No Voters

Source: Hepburn, Loughlin, and Barling, 1997.

or against the union with respect to attitudes toward unions in general, dissatisfaction with the employer, and peer pressure. In this sense, nonvoters seem to follow a rational process—when their opinions lie in the middle of people who voted for or against the union, they choose not to vote (see Figure 3.3) (Hepburn, Loughlin, and Barling, 1997). Whether intentional or not, an employee's decision not to vote is, in fact, a decision to let those who really care about the issue decide the election's outcome.

Second, and perhaps more important, nonvoters can be differentiated from both groups of voters with respect to how important they believed their individual vote might be (see Figure 3.4). Regardless of how they voted, people who chose to vote were more likely to see their participation as making a difference in the election (Hepburn, Loughlin, and Barling, 1997). This finding is consistent with a significant body of research that has found that individuals are more likely to vote in close elections than in one-sided ones (Aldrich, 1993).

A different study found similar results. Perhaps more important, this subsequent research identified two additional factors that contrast nonvoters with employees who choose to vote. In this study, nonvoters were found to feel less personal responsibility to vote in, and were less knowledgeable about the issues central to, the election (Hepburn and Barling, 1997).

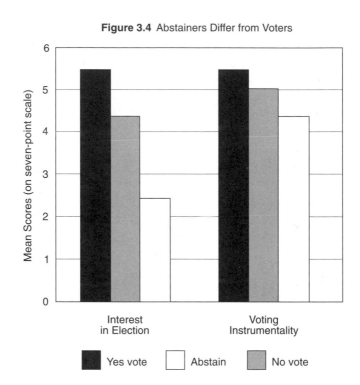

Figure 3.4 Abstainers Differ from Voters

Source: Hepburn, Loughlin, and Barling, 1997.

The findings that employees who chose not to vote in representation elections can be differentiated from voters on the basis of the perceived importance of their individual votes, interest in the election, knowledge of the issues, and feelings of personal responsibility are consistent with a well-established theory of voting behavior from political science called "rational choice" (Aldrich, 1993). The studies described here, as well as rational choice theory, have practical implications for unions. This information could be potentially useful to organizers in deciding what information needs to be communicated to potential nonvoters in the course of an organizing campaign.

These findings present an interesting dilemma for labor organizations regarding the extent to which they should encourage nonvoters to participate in representation elections. While in principle, increasing voter turnout might make the process more democratic, the research suggests that it does not necessarily increase the likelihood that the union will win the election. In fact, several studies have found that as voter turnout increases, chances of a union victory decrease (Becker and Miller, 1981; Hindman, 1988).

If increasing voter turnout reduces the chances of a union win, unions must decide whether to try to keep turnout low or to encourage maximum participation. Insight into which strategy to employ can be found in the long-standing practices of political parties. With few exceptions, political parties devote considerable energy and resources (e.g., phone banks, mailings) to persuading only potential nonvoters who are likely to vote *for* that party to participate in the election. This suggests that unions should encourage only those employees whom the union can reasonably predict will vote for representation to participate in the election. The factors described above can help unions in assessing who these voters are likely to be.

Voting in Decertification Elections

In addition to bringing new members into the labor movement, unions need to retain their current members. One of the ways unions lose members is through decertification, although this accounts for far, far fewer members lost than plant closings and layoffs. Unlike employer-initiated actions, however, unions have some control over the outcome of decertification elections. Unfortunately, unions lose more than two decertification elections for every one they win (National Labor Relations Board, 1997). A better understanding of members' voting behavior in these elections could improve labor's performance.

Two of the three factors discussed as being central to an employee's decision to vote for union representation—perceived effectiveness of the union and general attitudes toward unions—also appear to be central to a member's decision to vote against decertification. The research in this area consistently emphasizes the critical role of perceived union effectiveness. When perceived effectiveness is low, members are significantly more likely to vote for decertification (Chafetz and Fraser, 1979; Bigoness and Tosi, 1984; Summers, Betton, and DeCotiis, 1986).

It should be emphasized, however, that the nature of perceived union effectiveness is somewhat different during certification and decertification elections. During certification elections, employees base their perceptions of how successful the union might be on information received from others (e.g., union organizers, friends or family who may be members of that union). Their own direct experience with the union in question is likely to be minimal.

In decertification elections, however, employees base their perceptions of effectiveness on the past performance of their union. Thus perceptions that the union has not been effective in resolving workplace problems reflects, to a greater degree, the members' personal experience with, and evaluation of, the success or failure of the union.

The research on the role of general attitudes toward unions suggests that prounion attitudes can be important in a member's decision to support or oppose decertification. This conclusion is supported, circumstantially, by the fact that unions that have experienced problems of corruption and violence in the past are involved in relatively more decertification elections than unions that have had few such problems. Unions with positive reputations also are more likely to win decertifications than unions with serious image problems. It seems reasonable to conclude that unions' general public image plays a role in these outcomes (Anderson, O'Reilly, and Busman, 1980; Kilgour, 1987).

In sum, research to date on decertifications suggests that some of the same factors that influence an individual's vote in a certification election, namely perceived effectiveness of the union and general attitudes toward unions, also influence that person's vote in a decertification election. Of these two factors, perceived effectiveness of the union is, again, the strongest predictor of how a union member will vote.

There are many ways in which employers can control the workplace environment and influence a worker's vote in an organizing campaign. In theory, employers should have far less influence in this regard during a decertification campaign because labor law views the decertification process as a decision involving only the bargaining unit members and the union. While it would be naive to think that employers do not get involved in such campaigns (and in some instances actively promote them), unions should have much greater control over the outcome of such elections than they have over representation elections.

Because the process, and sometimes the issues, in decertification elections are similar to those in organizing elections, it makes sense for unions to employ the strategies that are most successful in the organizing process. This means that unions should consider an aggressive, grassroots, rank-and-file strategy when facing a decertification. Of course, a much more positive scenario is for unions and union leaders to pursue such a strategy on a daily basis, beginning with the organizing campaign and continuing through the first contract and beyond. Unions that are seen as effective, as defined in Chapter 1, rarely face decertification votes.

Voting for Unions: Assessing Employees' Priorities

The research discussed above provides evidence that the single most important factor in individuals' decisions about unionization is perceived effectiveness. Individuals are particularly concerned about the union's ability to address their immediate workplace concerns through collective bargaining. One of the first things unions need to do when involved in an election is to identify those concerns.

Occasionally, unions will present a compelling case that they can effectively address certain problems, only to lose the election because the particular issues they focused on were not the priorities of the individuals voting. The research discussed in this chapter has found that organizing strategies that employ systematic means of assessing employees' priorities, such as surveys and house calls, have a greater chance of winning an election than those that do not (Bronfenbrenner, 1993,1997).

Once a union has assessed the issues at the heart of a work group's dissatisfaction, it must then convince the employees that it can effectively address those issues (i.e., be instrumental). Chapter 7 will discuss research findings concerning effective information and communications strategies that unions can use in representation or decertification elections. In the context of an organizing drive, these findings suggest that an effective communications effort must, first, gain the attention of the employees being organized. Second, it must present its message in a way that the employees will comprehend. And finally, it must convince the employees to accept the message.

The Role of Family in Union Elections

Behavioral researchers have known for some time that children are influenced by their parents' jobs. For example, children (especially sons) tend to follow in the occupational footsteps of their parents (particularly their fathers) (Barling, 1990). Children are also aware of the extent to which their parents are satisfied with their work (Abramowitch and Johnson, 1992). Research has found that parents' attitudes toward work indirectly affect the childrens' attitudes (MacEwen and Barling, 1991; Stewart and Barling, 1996).

An individual's general attitude toward unions has been identified as an important factor influencing that person's decision to vote for or against a union in an organizing election. The notion that such attitudes, and ultimately an employee's willingness to join a union, might be influenced by a parent's union experience has been of particular interest to researchers. Surprisingly, the research has found that children of union members do not necessarily have a more positive attitude toward unions than do children of nonmembers (Huszczo, 1983; Youngblood, et al., 1984).

Nevertheless, parents' attitudes toward unions, as opposed to their membership status, do influence childrens' attitudes toward unions (Nicholson, Ursell, and Blyton, 1981; Gallagher, 1999). Because of the influential role of attitudes in voting in union elections, and because attitudes may not be readily amenable to change following adolescence, obtaining an understanding of the early development of attitudes toward unions is important (Krosnic and Alwin, 1989).

Several studies of university and high school students illustrate the family's influence on childrens' general attitudes toward unions and their willingness to vote for union representation. In these studies, students were asked about the extent to which they see their parents as being involved in union activities, about their perceptions of their parents' attitudes and beliefs toward unions, and about their own attitudes toward unions.

The results of these studies indicate that young peoples' perceptions of their parents' attitudes toward unions are positively influenced by the extent to which they see their parents participating in union activities. When parents are perceived as being involved in their union, children infer that they must hold positive attitudes toward unions, that their workplaces must be exploitive, and that they must need protection from their employers.

Students' own attitudes toward unions, absent any direct experience, closely follow their parents' attitudes. Young peoples' willingness to join a union in the future was strongly influenced by their self-reported attitudes toward unions in general (Barling, Kelloway, and Bremermann, 1991; Kelloway and Watts, 1994). In addition, the effects of parents' perceived attitudes and beliefs are magnified when children identify strongly with their parents (Hershizer and Wilson, 1995).

This phenomenon can often be seen in speeches by labor leaders at all levels. For instance, John Sweeney, president of the AFL-CIO, often refers to his upbringing in a union family and quotes his father about the value of a union (Quaglieri, 1989). Richard Trumka, the secretary-treasurer of the AFL-CIO, regularly makes reference to his family's roots in the United Mine Workers (UMW), an organization he served as president. This phenomenon is also a common theme in labor songs. For example, the ballad "Which Side Are You On," begins, "My daddy was a miner and I'm a miner's son, and I'll stick with the union til' this old body's done."

Union veterans often speak of being brought up in households where the union was an integral part of their families' lives. Retired miners reminisce about a secular "shrine of the holy trinity" often found in UMW homes. This refers to photos of Franklin D. Roosevelt, John F. Kennedy, and the legendary UMW president John L. Lewis, which were given prominent places in miners' homes. Older members often suggest that, in the past, parents taught their children to honor and respect unions as institutions that helped working class families win dignity on the job and economic security in their lives. They lament, with some justification, that today's youth do not seem to get the same introduction to the labor movement.

These findings have important practical implications for the labor movement. Attitudes toward unions in general play a central role in employees' decisions about union representation, and these attitudes are at least partially formed before individuals enter the workforce. This suggests that union success in organizing drives is, in part, decided long before an organizer arrives on the scene. It also suggests that the labor movement needs to get its message out to young people, who will be the next generation of union members, through its current member-parents.

> **I…grew up in a union family. My father was a New York City bus driver and a member of the Transport Workers Union. In fact, I sometimes tell my staff how my father would say, "God bless the union," when we were on vacation in Rockaway Beach. . . .**
> —*John Sweeney talking about his father (Quaglieri, 1989, p. 221).*

It is sometimes said that the best union organizer is the boss who, through a lack of respect and concern for employees, points up the need for collective action. Perhaps it should be said that the best organizers are parents who pass on to their children the important role unions can play in their lives.

By stressing to their members the important roles they play as parents and family members in shaping the attitudes toward unions of the next generation, unions can improve their chances of winning organizing elections down the road. Increasing the involvement of members' families in union functions can make a similar contribution. This might include designating one regular union meeting a year as family night, scheduling more union-sponsored social events for members and their families, or simply encouraging members to share union publications with their families.

It is also reasonable to assume that other attitude-shaping influences such as schools, peers, the media, and popular culture have an effect on young people during these formative years. Strategies for helping unions maximize these opportunities are detailed in Chapter 8.

Voting for Unions: Some Conclusions

The issue of how to gain a better understanding of why people vote for or against union representation can be looked at from two perspectives. From a short-term perspective, research has demonstrated that the single factor pervading all individuals' decisions about unionization is the issue of perceived effectiveness. Whether it be the perceived effectiveness of the union or the perceived effectiveness of one's vote in a representation or decertification election, unions need to get this message out.

From a long-term perspective, union organizers and activists can improve their chances of winning elections by recognizing that an individual's decision in this regard is shaped, in part, by general attitudes toward unions. Unions need to recognize the importance of image-building activities that can influence these attitudes. Particularly important in this regard are family members and peers, the media, and schools. Unions should consider how they might make family members, particularly parents, more aware of the importance of sharing the union message with their children, spouses, and other loved ones. Unions should consider ways (written materials, videos, children-focused union activities) to help family members pass on this message.

Unions also should consider how to get their message out to the media and into the schools more effectively. Changing individuals' attitudes toward unions makes it much easier to organize them down the road. Chapter 8 discusses strategies for doing so in more detail.

The research reviewed in this chapter, in large part, reinforces the basic model of union effectiveness outlined in Chapter 2. This model argues that attitudes shape behaviors. In this chapter, the behavior of interest involved voting in union representation and decertification elections. Influencing potential voters' attitudes is the key to success in these elections. Gaining insight into exactly what attitudes unions should focus on and what strategies should be used can make unions more effective.

The case study that follows illustrates the successful use of the principles discussed in this chapter.

CASE STUDY

Bottom-Up Organizing in the Building Trades: New England Regional Council of Carpenters

One of the key findings reported in this chapter is that the way unions conduct their organizing campaigns matters a great deal. The research on which this chapter is based suggests that unions are most effective in organizing when they employ an aggressive, grassroots, rank-and-file strategy. This bottom-up approach differs significantly from the strictly top-down approach employed by many unions in the past. It is particularly far afield from the traditional strategy employed by building trades unions.

This case study examines an innovative organizing program adopted by the New England Regional Council of Carpenters. The program described was developed and is administered by the Regional Council, but it is consistent with a national membership organizing initiative being undertaken by the United Brotherhood of Carpenters and its president, Douglas McCarron.

The New England Regional Council of Carpenters brings together Carpenters locals in the six New England states—Connecticut, Rhode Island, Massachusetts, Vermont, New Hampshire, and Maine. The percentage of the local construction labor markets that are unionized varies a great deal across and within these states. In Boston, for example, roughly 85–90 percent of construction carpentry work is done by union carpenters, whereas in Maine, Vermont, and New Hampshire 85–90 percent of such work is performed by nonunion carpenters.

The Carpenters Union in New England, like most building trades unions, traditionally employed a reactive, top-down approach to organizing. The union's approach was reactive because it did not normally engage in organizing unless a nonunion employer began to operate in an area in which most of the carpentry work was being done by unionized employers. And it could be accurately characterized as top-down because the organizing strategy involved Carpenters Union officials approaching an employer and attempting to convince him to sign a union contract. If the employer agreed, the employees then would have no choice but to become union members.

The nonunion sector of the construction industry has been consistently growing, while the unionized sector has been steadily shrinking. In the postwar period, unionization in this sector has declined from about 80 percent to 30 percent (Allen,

1988; Grabelsky, Pagnucco, and Rockafellow, 1999). Spurred by this fact, the national Carpenters Union and its regional bodies have reexamined both the emphasis they place on organizing and the strategies they employ to bring new members into the union. The result has been the development of programs to recruit and train rank-and-file union carpenters as organizers. In 1999, the Carpenters Union announced plans to spend $25 million on new organizing programs. In addition, the union has plans to build a $12 million training center in Las Vegas to support its efforts.

The New England Regional Council has been a leader in this area. Beginning in 1997, the Regional Council began to organize volunteer organizing committees (VOCs), which previously existed in only some of units, in each of its local unions. It also began to run periodic three-day organizer training and evaluation programs modeled after the AFL-CIO's Organizing Institute. These programs were advertised throughout the council and were open to any interested Carpenters Union member. The purpose of the programs was to introduce members to organizing techniques and strategies and to identify members with particular potential for organizing work. Individuals with organizing potential, including all new organizers hired by the union, were sent to an intensive fourteen-day training program sponsored by the national union.

The council's organizers, who just weeks before were full-time carpenters, were put to work visiting carpenters on nonunion job sites. The organizers would follow up these visits with house calls. Members of the local's VOCs would be enlisted to accompany the organizers to the homes of the nonunion carpenters.

The Regional Council has found this approach to be very effective. The idea that working carpenters are in the best position to relate the benefits of union membership to other working carpenters has proven to be right on target. In the year and a half since the council began its program it has experienced an 11 percent increase in membership. Even more impressive is that the number of employers under contract with the council has increased by three hundred. The new organizing program has even allowed the union to break the nonunion contractors' stranglehold on the residential construction market, in which it recently signed up twenty contractors. Finally, the union credits its new approach, along with the hiring of five minority organizers, with the inroads it is making in organizing minority carpenters, an area in which the union had not previously experienced much success.

While the experience of the New England Regional Council of Carpenters may be exceptional, rank-and-file organizing is taking place across the Carpenters Union with positive results. Even more significant is that unions throughout the building trades are incorporating greater membership involvement and participation in organizing, as well as in other aspects of their work. This movement has been spurred in large part by an educational program called COMET (Construction Organizing Membership Education Training) (Grabelsky, 1995). COMET is designed to generate membership participation and support in organizing. It has been endorsed and used by virtually every building trades union with great success (Grabelsky, Pagnucco, and Rockafellow, 1999). Although its long-term impact on the ability of building trades unions to recapture a significantly greater share of the construction market remains to be seen, COMET and rank-and-file organizing programs like that of the New England Regional Council of Carpenters are changing the face of construction unionism.[3]

3. Much of the information in this case study was provided by Mark Erlich of the New England Regional Council of Carpenters and Jeff Grabelsky of Cornell University's Construction Industry Program.

4

Union Member Orientation and Socialization

Key Points

- First impressions can play a big role in shaping an individual's attitude toward an organization.
- Unions can build loyalty and commitment to the union by creating positive formal and informal orientation/socialization experiences for new members.
- The quality of an orientation program is important in influencing the attitudes of new members.
- The distribution of information should be an important part of every socialization program.
- Unions should not ignore the opportunity to build union commitment among part-time and temporary employees.

Most people are familiar with the saying that "first impressions are lasting impressions." It may be the first fish you caught, the first school dance you attended, something or someone you fell in love with at first sight (a person, a cherry-red 1965 Mustang convertible, a piece of antique furniture), or your first impressions of the union you were asked to join. In any case, most everyone has first experiences that linger in their memory.

If the cliché about first experiences is true, then this phenomenon certainly should be taken into account in considering how to positively influence members' general and specific attitudes toward their union. But how do we really know that first impressions are important? Is there evidence beyond our own limited experiences? Is there scientific proof to support this principle? And if it is true, how can unions use this knowledge to build stronger organizations?

Theory and Research

Organizations ensure their continued existence by passing on their values, beliefs, traditions, and accepted behaviors to new members through a process called socialization. And while the socialization process continues throughout one's membership in an organization, research has concluded that the process is most influential when one is new to the organization. Behavioral science has confirmed that first impressions are, indeed, influential (Van Maanen and Schein, 1979; Trice and Beyer, 1993).

A particularly well developed body of literature specifically addresses the important role that people's early experiences, or first impressions, have on shaping their attitudes toward organizations to which they belong (Van Maanan, 1976; Van Maanan and Schein, 1979). Many organizations have recognized this fact and have attempted to use it to their advantage.

The period of time in which a person is first exposed to an organization, a period during which the individual learns about the goals, values, customs, rituals, and practices of the organization, is known as the initial socialization period. By actively shaping the kind of experience a new member has during this initial contact period, the organization influences the socialization experience of the newcomer. By making a good first impression, the organization is, to an extent, making a lasting impression.

The socialization process has been studied in a variety of different settings—among new recruits to an urban police department (Van Maanan, 1976), beginning students at college (Schein, 1968; Cohen, 1973), newly hired managers at AT&T (Bray, 1978), and inductees into the U.S. Army (Bourne, 1967). In these and other settings, research has demonstrated that the more positive a member's early socialization experience, the stronger and more positive that member's attitudes toward the organization will be.

In studying the early experiences of new members, researchers have also learned that, in most settings, individuals are exposed to two types of socialization experiences—formal socialization and informal socialization (Van Maanan and Schein, 1979; Gordon et al., 1980).

Formal socialization is associated with organized, structured experiences that usually occur on a group level. Army boot camp and a formal initiation ceremony into a club are two examples of this type of socialization. In this setting the organization is attempting to instill in the new members a loyalty or commitment to the organization, to teach the new recruits about the rules and procedures of the organization, and to inform them about the formal expectations of the group.

Informal socialization experiences occur in a less structured, more spontaneous format. They also tend to occur on an individual, as opposed to a group, basis. To a degree, this means that every new member is going to be exposed to a different informal socialization experience. Sometimes this informal experience will reinforce the information received in the formal orientation. It might also serve to convey the expectations of individual members, which may or may not differ from the expectations of the organization. Finally, the one-on-one experience that occurs during this informal socialization process may provide information to the new member about customs, traditions, and practices that occur outside the formal rules of the organization. Examples might include the way that members communicate with one another ("the language of the shop"), expectations of deference in certain matters to more senior members, and informal dress and appearance codes.

Socialization Research on Unions

In a 1980 study, researchers examined the socialization experiences of union members (Gordon et al.). This research looked at the experiences of several hundred union members in four local unions representing the employees of a large utility company. The study focused primarily on the informal socialization process in these four locals. The study found a relationship between the informal socialization process and the members' commitment to the union. The researchers concluded that the more positive a member's informal socialization experience the greater that member's level of commitment to the local union.

Building on the general research on socialization and on the 1980 union study, a larger, national study of early socialization experiences in a union setting was conducted in the early 1990s (Clark et al., 1993). In this study, members who had joined the union during the past four months were surveyed in an effort to gather information about their early formal and informal socialization experiences. Information was also gathered about their levels of commitment to the union. Among this group of new union members, formal socialization experiences were defined as organized orientation programs conducted by union officials and designed to introduce the new members to the union. Informal socialization experiences included contacts or experiences with more senior members of the union that were not organized by the union but provided information to the new member about the organization, its values, goals, and customs, as well as its expectations of the membership.

The results of the study indicated that simply having a formal socialization experience (an organized new member orientation program in this case), by itself, did not lead to higher commitment on the part of the new member. Rather, it was the quality of the formal socialization experience that shaped the commitment level. Specifically, the study indicated that the range and amount of information presented, both verbally and in written form, had an influence on members' commitment.

Informal socialization, measured by a checklist of informal experiences the member may have had (i.e., were you invited to participate in branch activities?), was also found to be related to union commitment. In this case, it was the frequency and intensity of positive, informal socialization experiences that dictated the commitment level of the member. The more frequent and the more positive the informal socialization experiences of the member, the greater the level of commitment.

One last finding of this study was that formal and informal socialization experi-

> The great French Marshall Lyautey once asked his gardener to plant a tree. The gardener objected that the tree was slow growing and would not reach maturity for 100 years. The Marshall replied, "In that case, there is no time to lose; plant it this afternoon!"

ences each made an independent contribution to membership commitment. In other words, formal orientation sessions and subsequent informal socialization experiences each had a separate and unique impact on the members' commitment to the union. This suggests that the union can have the maximum effect on commitment by providing both positive formal and informal socialization experiences (Clark et al., 1993).

An additional study, conducted by the University of Minnesota's Labor Education Service, suggests that exposure to unions well before an individual becomes part of a bargaining unit can have a significant effect on attitudes toward unions. This study found that children who are made aware of their parents' activism and involvement in unionism are far more likely to feel positive about unions than children who had no such exposure. It is reasonable to assume that these feelings will stay with individuals as they grow up and become part of the workforce. Such early socialization can make a union's efforts to build commitment and participation much easier. And though parents' efforts to introduce children to unions are not directly within a union's control, union leaders can encourage their members to engage in such early socialization efforts (AFL-CIO, 1999d).

Socialization Strategies

Formal Socialization

Formal socialization activities differ from informal ones in that they are usually planned, systematic, and consistent for each new member (that is, each individual in a group will have the same formal socialization experience). The union setting provides several opportunities for formal socialization. Perhaps the most important is the initial orientation of new employees as they enter the bargaining unit.

New Member Orientation

Studies have suggested that new members' attitudes toward unions have, in many cases, already been influenced before they gain employment for the first time. Their attitudes can be influenced in a positive or negative fashion by family members, friends, the media, and the schools. The first direct opportunity, however, that most unions have to influence an individual's opinions about the union occurs when the person is hired into the bargaining unit.

Many employers have long recognized the need to provide a preemployment orientation for new hires. Depending on the sophistication of these sessions, the employer can use the opportunity to inform the new employee of its rules and customs, the expectations the employer has of the individual, and the many benefits the company will provide to the employee (usually neglecting to mention that many of these benefits were reluctantly granted at the union's urging during the collective bargaining process).

Generally, the employer will use this opportunity to build commitment and loyalty to the organization that provides the job and pays the wages and benefits. Some employers will conduct extensive orientation programs in which efforts are made to paint the company as a caring parent, inviting the employee to become a "member" of the corporate "family."

It is extremely important for the union to make its case in these early stages of employment, when the new employee is the most impressionable. The union should not let the company define the union for the new hire. It should assert the important role the union has played in creating the conditions and benefits the new employee will enjoy and the role it will play in protecting the employee's rights in the future. The single most important mechanism through which the union can accomplish this is its own new employee or new member orientation program.

In a union shop situation (where the employee is required to join the union), the main goal of the session or sessions will probably be to build commitment and loyalty to the union among its new members. In an agency or open shop setting, getting the new employee to join the union is added to the goal of building commitment and loyalty. In meeting both these goals, often a union's best shot is its first shot. For this reason, the time and resources invested in these programs can generate a very good return.

Since the local union is the part of the union closest to the new employee and the workplace, responsibility for orienting a new hire will usually fall to that level of the organization. The nature of the orientation experience provided by a local union will depend somewhat on the hiring practices of the employer. Probably the most efficient situation occurs when an employer hires new employees in groups, as opposed to one new hire at a time. In this case, the employer will often hold a group orientation. This presents the union with an opportunity to "piggyback" on the employer's program, either by gaining access to the new employees during the employer orientation or by holding a completely separate orientation during the period in which the new employees are entering the workforce.

If employees are not hired in groups but on an individual basis, the union could hold a group orientation session once several individuals have been hired. Research on this issue, however, suggests that the more time that goes by before an organization attempts to socialize a new member, the more influence other groups or individuals will have in shaping that new employee's impressions and opinions (Van Maanan and Schein, 1979).

Employers almost always have the first crack at any new workers. One effective way to minimize that advantage is to get an employer to agree to let the local union share some of the time set aside by the employer to orient the new hire. It is reasonable for the union to propose this because the employee will now be a part of the ongoing union-management relationship. For that reason it is to everyone's advantage for the incoming employee to be aware of the role the union plays in this relationship.

Before proposing to the employer that the union should be part of the orientation program, the local should consider what it hopes to accomplish during this session and how much time will be required to accomplish its goals. This can then be weighed against how much time the employer devotes to its orientation program (for example, the employer is unlikely to give the union one day of a two-day program).

Gaining access to new hires during the employer's orientation program will most likely mean that the incoming workers will be paid by the employer to spend time getting to know the union. Logistical problems and costs will also be reduced if the session is held in the same facility as the employer's orientation. The local does not have to schedule or pay for a meeting place, and because the orientation is mandatory, all new employees will be present.

Finally, while there might be some valid reasons for conducting the union's session away from the employer's turf (i.e., at a union hall or some neutral site), seeing the union come on to management's territory may impress upon the member that the union is on equal ground with the employer or at least is an important part of the workplace.

Many unions have negotiated these arrangements directly into their collective bargaining agreements or they have signed memoranda of understanding concerning this issue. In other cases, while the arrangement is not formally reduced to writing, the parties have a specific unwritten agreement or management simply extends this opportunity as a courtesy to the union.

Some employers refuse to give the union access to new hires, taking the position that keeping the new employees ignorant about the union will work to their advantage. In this case, it is important that the union schedule its own formal orientation separate from the employer's program. The evidence suggests that however it is accomplished, holding a formal orientation session for new employees is a very good investment of time and resources.

The research on this issue indicates that it is the *quality* of the program, and not simply participation in such a program, that is important in influencing the attitudes of new recruits. Simply put, if a union does a good job at planning and im-

> **Model Contract Clause**
> **Sioux City Municipal Hospital**
> **and United Workers Union**
> **Collective Bargaining Agreement**
> **Section 8.** The employer agrees to notify the union whenever a new employee is hired into the bargaining unit. The employer also agrees to set aside two hours of the new employee orientation program for the union to meet with the new hire.

plementing a new member orientation program, the new member is likely to see the union in a positive light. If the program is perceived negatively by the new member, that experience is likely to have a negative influence on the member's attitude toward the union.

Here, again, the research to date provides some guidance in terms of what makes a positive impression on new employees. The key factor found to influence the employee's view of the orientation program was the amount of relevant information acquired by the newcomer during that program (Clark, et al., 1993). This suggests that one of the keys to successfully socializing new employees is to get as much information as possible to them in the short period of time the union has for its session.

It stands to reason that the individuals who conduct the orientation session will have a great impact on the program's success. For this reason, locals should give serious consideration to who they choose to perform this function. In most cases, this individual will be an officer of the local union. Officers are, or at least should be, among the most knowledgeable people in the organization. And having them involved in the program allows the members to get to know their representatives.

While local officers might be the obvious candidates to lead an orientation program, unions should be certain that whoever takes on this assignment gives it the time and effort needed to ensure a successful program. Ideally, the individual would not only be knowledgeable and committed to the union but would be able to convey that knowledge and commitment clearly. It is also important that the person who represents the union emphasizes the positive. The union may face challenges and difficulties, but they should not be the focus of the initial orientation program.

The local union should also give careful consideration to the topics to be covered in the course of the session. Time constraints will certainly limit the subjects the union is able to cover. For that reason it is important to make the best use of the time available. An examination of the agendas of new employee/member programs conducted by several unions identified the following general issues as frequently included in such sessions:

- Introduction of union officers
- Brief history of the union
- Discussion of the union's structure
- Contractual rights and benefits
- Other services provided by the union (social and recreational activities, consumer discounts, and the like)
- Dues obligation
- Workplace issues, including safety and health and training opportunities
- Status of probationary employees (Clark et al., 1993).

The presentation of information on these issues can be accomplished in a number of ways. Speakers, chosen in part because of their public-speaking skills, can make short presentations and then conduct a question and answer segment that gives the newcomers an opportunity to get information on issues of particular concern to them.

Written materials should accompany any presentation. A survey of new members found that they appreciated receiving publications on issues of relevance (Clark and Gallagher, 1992). Some national unions have put together publications specifically designed for new members. These "Welcome to the Union" materials can often reinforce the messages presented verbally.

Other written materials commonly given to new employees and new union members include collective bargaining agreements, union by-laws, brief histories of the union, lists of union officers and their phone numbers, and material explaining the benefits and services provided by the union. Many unions put these materials into a folder or binder called a "New Member Kit." These kits are sometimes available from the national union and ensure that all new employee/members get the same materials, while minimizing the amount of time local union leaders need to spend on acquiring, or in some cases even creating, material.

In addition to oral presentations and written materials, unions are now making greater use of video as a convenient means of presenting information. Many local unions either own their own video players (VCRs) or have access to one through their employer or a video rental store. Many national unions have produced videos on a variety of topics, and some unions maintain a video library from which affiliates can borrow tapes. Playing a video during an orientation session offers a nice change of pace from speakers or written material.

Tapes specifically produced to welcome the new employee/member to the union are very useful. Other tapes that might be played include those focusing on the services the union provides or that depict the history of the union and what it has achieved for its members. While most tapes are produced by national unions, some larger locals have produced videos tailored to their own local unions.

In addition, many new employee/members have video cassette recorders in

Courtesy of IBT.

their homes. Tapes can be made available to the new hires to take home and watch at their leisure or perhaps to view with their family.

Varying the means (written, verbal, video) by which unions deliver information to new members can significantly increase the degree to which that information is comprehended. This is a basic behavioral science principle drawn from learning theory (Bandura, 1977).

While research to date suggests that a onetime orientation is the most common format used by most unions, some locals have more extensive programs that include additional sessions. New employees, once on the job, frequently are confronted with issues or develop questions that were not covered in the initial orientation session. Bringing new members back together after a period of time in the workplace, whether it be after a month, six weeks, or three months, provides them with a chance to have these questions answered. It also gives the union an opportunity to reinforce the message presented at the initial session. This practice has the additional advantage of showing the union's concern for the new employee. Almost always, these follow-up sessions are conducted on the workers' own time and away from the employer's premises.

Another part of a new employee/member orientation program that some local unions have found useful is to give members a small token or gift at the conclusion of the orientation program. Some unions present membership pins to those who join; others pass out T-shirts, mugs, refrigerator magnets, or bumper stickers (Clark and Gallagher, 1992). Although some might view this practice as an empty gesture or a waste of money, this simple act can accomplish several useful things from the union's point of view.

First, most people like to receive these "freebies." Second, depending on what is presented, the gift serves as a reminder to the new employees that the union is now a part of their lives. If the magnet does indeed end up on the refrigerator, it can serve as a reminder of the union every time the door is opened! This benefit may also extend to a new hire's family (in fact, some unions make a point of giving the employee something for each family member at the end of the session, even if it is an inexpensive coloring book for the kids). Third, if the new employee/member wears the T-shirt or puts the bumper sticker on the car, that member is engaging in a small but possibly meaningful act of participation in the union. This may make the member feel more a part of the organization; it also provides free advertising for the union in the community.

Finally, in settings where it is necessary for the union to sign up new members individually (i.e., in the absence of a union shop clause), the formal orientation session provides the first, and possibly the best, opportunity to get new employees to join the union. Systematic new member orientation programs give the union a chance to talk about the many services it provides to members. If done early enough, the orientation session will be the new employee's first exposure to the union. In this setting, the union and its leaders can ensure that the member's first impressions are favorable. Using this opportunity to shed the best possible light on the union can go a long way toward getting the new employee to sign a membership card.

Another important lesson regarding the socialization process learned from behavioral research is that unions need to be very careful not to overstate what they can deliver to their members. Organizations that create unrealistic expectations on the part of their members often experience a high degree of dissatisfaction and turnover. Hence unions should strive to strike a balance between being positive and being cautiously realistic regarding what they can do for their members (Wanous, 1980).

The New Member's First Meeting

Building a positive attitude toward the union is an ongoing activity that should continue beyond the completion of a new employee/member orientation program or the signing up of a new member. One way to make a new member feel a part of the organization is to have that member attend a local union meeting. The first step in making this happen is to invite the new member to the meeting; the more personal the invitation, the better.

The local might send a member a written invitation, followed by a verbal invitation from the steward or a local officer. To ensure the new member's attendance, some locals assign an "escort" who might, for instance, offer the new member a ride to the meeting. In some cases, local unions have someone take the new recruit to dinner, either before or after the meeting (at the union's expense, of course).

Once at the meeting, the local's officers should introduce and welcome the new member. In years past, most unions had a formal swearing-in ceremony in which the new member took the oath of membership; in some unions the new recruit was presented with a membership card and pin. This ritual served as a rite of passage in which the person symbolically took the step of becoming a union member. It could be argued that psychologically this ritual helped commit the member to the organization (it is no accident that kings and queens are crowned, military officers are commissioned, and fraternity and sorority members are initiated). Certainly this act of joining would make a greater impression on the member than signing a dues check-off card in the employer's personnel office.

The simple act of bringing a member to a local meeting in itself will not necessarily influence a member's loyalty or commitment to the organization. This strategy assumes that the local undertakes a real effort to make meetings as dynamic and informative as possible. Dragging a new member to an uninteresting meeting, attended by a handful of unenthusiastic officers, will likely do more damage than good to a member's perception of the union.

Once the recruit is formally a member, the local should continue its efforts to make him or her feel a part of the organization. A short article about the new member in the local newsletter and the posting of a photograph on the union bulletin board are two inexpensive ways to accomplish this goal.

Involvement in Other Membership Activities

Previous research has determined that there is a link between the degree to which the member participates in union activities and the member's level of commitment to the union (Gordon et al., 1980; Gallagher and Clark, 1989; Fullagar and Barling, 1989). Sometimes members do not participate in union activities because they are not asked or encouraged to do so. Getting a member involved in some aspect of the union during the first six months of membership can help shape that member's view of the union.

Matching a member's interest with an activity is one of the best ways to get the new member involved. As a matter of course, the local union might attempt to find out about the interests or talents of the new member. If that individual expresses an interest in bowling, golf, or softball and the local sponsors a league or a team in that area, the new member should be invited to participate. If the member expresses an interest in charity work, the local should get that individual involved in the union's community service program.

If nothing else, the local should consider inviting and encouraging the new member to attend the next union social activity, whether it be the annual Christmas party, summer picnic, or dinner dance. The member should be encouraged to bring a spouse or a guest. An effort should be made to introduce new members and their guests formally at these occasions.

Informal Socialization

Formal socialization or orientation activities differ from informal activities in that they are planned and controlled by the organization, and each new employee/member has a very similar experience. Informal activity occurs on a more spontaneous basis, in many cases leading to individuals having different informal orientation experiences. The uneven nature of informal orientation experiences suggests that if unions want to maximize the positive effect of these experiences they must try to formalize or structure them.

One area in which the union might attempt to structure an experience that, in the past, may have occurred on an informal basis involves the steward's initial contact with the new employee. Sometimes stewards are not notified when a new employee comes into the part of the workplace assigned to them, thereby missing a chance to introduce themselves to the newcomer. Research has suggested that a union member's perception of the steward has a significant influence on their perception of the union (Barling, Fullagar, and Kelloway, 1992). If first impressions are indeed important, failing to greet an employee who is new to the workplace, probably anxious about a new job, and without acquaintances to help learn the ropes, is a lost opportunity.

This problem was borne out in one study that found that new members with negative attitudes toward the union frequently were the same members who complained that they rarely saw their union steward or representative. One such new member suggested that his attitudes toward the union had been greatly influenced by the fact that "it was six months before I even found out who the union steward was in my part of the plant" (Clark and Gallagher, 1992).

Local unions can ensure that this does not happen by establishing a standard procedure whereby the steward assigned to a newcomer is automatically notified when that employee will be joining the steward's department. Stewards should be informed of the importance of the socialization/orientation experience and be clearly instructed that it is their responsibility to introduce themselves to the new employee on his or her first day on the job, at the beginning of the workday if possible. Stewards might also be given a suggested list of things to go over with new employee/members. These might include introducing them to co-workers and giving them a business card that tells how the steward can be contacted. To ensure that the steward completes these tasks, the union can create a checksheet that the steward must return within a specified period of time. If the checksheet is not returned, a reminder would automatically be sent to the steward.

Like the formal orientation process described earlier, to be effective informal orientation needs to be an ongoing process. Toward this end, the union should make an effort to keep in regular contact with the new employee/member, especially in the early months of employment when the new hire may require the most guidance and experience the most stress. This is important because behavioral research shows that newcomers to any organization are not passive receivers of information. They are, in fact, active seekers of information, particularly in areas where they have specific personal concerns or interests. For this reason it is important that the union have someone available to deal with the members' concerns as they arise (Morrison, 1993).

One way for the local union to structure the ongoing socialization/orientation of newcomers is to create a mentor or buddy system. Behavioral scientists have done a fair amount of research on the mentoring process. This research has shown that mentoring, if done effectively, can have a significant impact on new members' attitudes toward their organizations (Kram, 1985).

In such a system, a member, carefully chosen by the local or the steward, is assigned to each new employee. This mentor or buddy could be given a checklist of activities to undertake with the new employee. These could include talking with the new worker at least once a day, making himself or herself available to answer any questions, inviting the new employee out for a drink or something to eat after work, and introducing the new employee to others in the workplace. The mentor might be the individual responsible for bringing the new member to his or her first union meeting. By assigning a mentor, the union is structuring and formalizing an activity that, in the past, happened on a more ad hoc, less consistent, basis.

At least two valuable things can occur in the informal socialization/orientation process that are likely to have a positive influence on a new employee's attitude toward the union. First, by being exposed to individuals who are active and committed to the union (a steward or an assigned mentor), the newcomer is likely to hear the union discussed in a positive light. The attitudes that a new employee encounters early in his or her experience in the workplace will have a significant effect in shaping the newcomer's attitude. In an effort to fit in, most new members of any organization will attempt to discern what the prevailing opinions and attitudes are when they first become members of an organization. Again, first impressions are of great importance.

Second, as the model outlined in Chapter 2 suggests, there is a relationship between the level of information an individual has about the union and that person's attitude toward the organization. The more informed an individual is, the more positive his or her attitude is likely to be. Despite orientations by both the employer and the union, a new employee still has a great deal to learn about the workplace. A steward or co-worker is in a very good position to answer a newcomer's questions about the union (who do I ask if I have a question about the contract? can I bring a guest to the union picnic?), about the employer (am I allowed to use the rest rooms between breaks? who is the guy in the tie who comes through every hour?), and about the workplace itself (where am I allowed to smoke? how is the food in the sandwich machine?). If the new employee feels the steward or co-worker is well-informed and helpful about these issues, the union and its representatives will appear in a positive light.

Influencing Part-Time and Temporary Employees

Part-time and temporary employees constitute a substantial part of the workforces in the United States and Canada. As the numbers of these employees continue to increase, their share of total employment will grow (Callaghan and Hartmann, 1991; Rogers, 2000). There are a multitude of reasons why employers have been increasing the mix of part-time and temporary employees in their workforces. Clearly, some employers are moving in this direction as a means of reducing that part of the workforce that enjoys union representation. Even if this is not the intention, hiring temporary workers to do work formerly done by bargaining unit members has this effect (duRivage, 1992).

For this reason, part-time and temporary workers may be resented by full-time, permanent employees. This resentment may cause these employees, and their union, to exclude, ignore, or express open hostility toward part-timers and temps. For many part-time employees, this may be their first exposure to a union. This treatment is likely to have a negative influence on the part-timer's attitudes toward unions. The negative reception they receive from union members creates a "we against them" situation, and the union can quickly become the part-time or temporary worker's enemy.

This does little to advance labor's cause. It is not unusual for a temp to end up as a permanent, full-time worker down the road, either in the same workplace or somewhere else. That worker may become a part of the bargaining unit, or he or she might become part of workforce that is the focus of an organizing drive. When the union tries to convince that employee to join the union (in an open shop situation), participate in union activities (where there is a union security clause), or vote for the union in the election, the chickens are likely to come home to roost. The member's initial negative experiences with unions could be enough to turn him into a disinterested employee, at best, or an openly antiunion employee, at worst.

This would be unfortunate. Behavioral studies of unionized workers in the retail food and health care industries indicate that, absent such treatment, part-time workers are no less committed, on average, than full-time workers (Gallagher and Wetzel, 1988).

Research on members' attitudes toward unions suggests that the early period of employment presents unions with a critical opportunity to shape attitudes. This chapter has discussed research focusing on the new member socialization/orientation process. It has also suggested practical strategies that unions can employ to make both the formal and informal socialization experiences of new member/employees more positive.

New members are the future of the labor movement. If unions work to socialize these individuals early in their union careers, these efforts will likely have a significant impact on the attitude of the next generation of union members.

The case study that follows spotlights a systematic and successful new member program developed by Branch 3 of the National Association of Letter Carriers (NALC) in Buffalo, New York, in the late 1980s. Branch 3 still conducts a modified version of this program and continues to have an almost 100 percent success rate in signing up new members. The program incorporates many of the principles discussed in this chapter.

CASE STUDY

Bringing New Members into the Union:
National Association of Letter Carriers Branch 3

Branch 3's new-member program involves three elements: orientation, the mentoring program, and new-member classes. Each element works effectively on its own, but when the three are put together, the branch's appeal to new carriers rises exponentially.

"We're trying to make the union an essential part of each carrier's life," says Branch 3 president Robert McClellan. "People may come into the job thinking that a union is just an insurance policy, something that would only affect them if they received discipline. We want to turn that attitude around so carriers see NALC as something they simply couldn't do without—the union is there for them every day that they are on the job."

For new hires in Buffalo, the first socialization experience is the union's orientation session. Branch 3 leaders have spent a lot of time evaluating their orientation practices and determining what a positive orientation should look like.

The first decision branch leaders made concerned the timing of orientation. As required by the National Agreement, Postal Service management must provide an opportunity for local NALC leaders to talk to new hires about the union. Usually management offers time to the union during the carrier's first day on the job. After careful thought, Branch 3 leaders decided not to take management up on this offer. Says McClellan, "We decided that the carrier would be overwhelmed by too much information at that point to really take in our message." Instead, the branch waits until new hires have begun training at the Carrier Academy.

"After a few days of training, new hires have had a chance to get their feet on the floor, so to speak," McClellan says. "They've also been around knowledgeable and helpful union members—carriers who do the actual training." McClellan notes that the union members who are trainers do not attempt to inform new hires about the union. However, most new hires get the message that the professional, dedicated people who are in charge of their training are also committed NALC members, which gives the union a subtle advantage. Around day four or five, McClellan comes to the Academy for a formal orientation session, which lasts about an hour. McClellan covers basic information about NALC, including a bit of history, the gains that the union has achieved for members, and other benefits including the health insurance plans. "We make it clear that carriers can make a choice about joining the union—but we also give them the numbers, that out of about fifteen-hundred active letter carriers in Buffalo, all but thirty-nine are union members. For most people, those figures stand as reason enough to join. McClellan notes that his presentation at orientation is as succinct as he can make it so that the bulk of the time can be devoted to questions from new hires. "We want to get out the message that the union is here to listen to carriers' concerns," he says. "So we encourage questions and spend time on the issues that people seem most concerned about."

Like many branches, Buffalo's standard practice is to notify stewards when new hires at their stations are due to begin work. As part of their union duties, stewards are expected to touch base with these new carriers during their first few days on the job. However, recognizing that stewards are often overloaded, branch officers recently decided to institute an additional program to maintain informal contact with new hires.

"As each new carrier signs up, we assign that carrier to one of our fourteen officers who will act as the carrier's mentor throughout the probation period," explains Peter Priziotte, who is chair of the branch's Education and Information Committee. "We do this because we noticed that a lot of times new hires would have problems, but they were reluctant to speak up at meetings or in front of a bunch of people." By giving each new carrier a personal mentor, the carrier can share difficulties in a much more relaxed private atmosphere. "We figured that if we made the effort to seek out these people, they would feel comfortable saying more about what's happening to them," Priziotte adds.

Each officer has the flexibility to develop such mentoring relationships in whatever way seems appropriate. McClellan himself makes a point of phoning his mentoree either at home or on the job within a couple of days of orientation.

"Some of these people have been in other work situations where they were told that the union would be in touch with them, but that contact never happened," McClellan says. "Here, we make contact right away, instead of making promises about some indefinite 'someday' that never comes. People really seem to appreciate that personal touch."

McClellan also makes a point of stopping to say hello to his new hires when he visits the stations. "I try to get a few private minutes with new carriers, unobtrusively so they don't feel singled out. But I also want to give them the opportunity to share any problems or questions they may have. And if I don't have an answer right then, I make sure I get back to them as soon as I can."

Mentors also call new hires in advance of regular branch meetings to encourage attendance. "We stress that the union meetings are a great opportunity not only to learn more but also to meet other people," Priozotte says. "There's always a social time both before and after the meetings when we try to make it easy for new people to get to know some of the more experienced carriers."

By paying attention to the needs of new hires and being available as resources, Branch 3 leaders usually succeed in helping new carriers get through probation. "We're there to tell the carriers what to watch out for," McClellan says. "And if they get in trouble, we try to find a way to help."

The final contact between Branch 3 mentors and new hires comes when the carriers reach the end of their probationary period. "We always make sure to call the carriers when they get through their ninety days to congratulate them," McClellan says.

Passing probation successfully also qualifies Branch 3 new members for another formal education and socialization experience—a new-member class that is offered only to union members. These classes, which have been a part of Buffalo's new-member program for more than fifteen years, are eagerly anticipated by new carriers. "The word seems to have gotten out that these classes can really help," notes Priziotte, who conducts most of the classes. "We started out with only about five or six carriers, but now we routinely get twenty or more for each session."

McClellan kicks off the three-hour class, which is usually held on a weeknight in the union hall. "I take the opportunity to stress the importance of the union, what we do, all the activities that carriers can get involved in," he says. "And I make sure people understand the grievance procedure and the role of the steward."

After McClellan's talk, members of the Education and Information Committee facilitate a discussion with the new hires. "Originally we would go through the manuals, covering the basic stuff," Priziotte says. "Then we discovered that people got more out of a question-and-answer format." Commonly asked questions concern seniority, how long it takes before PTFs become regular carriers, the Family Medical Leave Act, and carriers' rights to union representation in discipline situations.

"Every session is a little different," Priziotte notes. "But we make sure that we cover what's most important—the rights and responsibilities that carriers have. Safety is a big concern, and we make sure everyone understands the procedures when they believe they are being asked to perform unsafe work." In many ways,

Branch 3's new-member class remains a work in progress. "Every group seems to have its special concerns," Priziotte says. "So we have to be flexible and ready to revise and update what we offer."

For many carriers, the new-member classes add another layer of bonding between members and the union. "It's like another drop of glue helping cement the relationship," comments Priziotte. He notes that in a number of cases, new members who had so far resisted coming to branch meetings will begin regular attendance, and may also volunteer to take on some responsibilities within the branch. "The classes help people recognize their common bonds," McClellan explains. "Then it starts making sense for them to be more active in the union."[1]

1. This case study appeared in the Winter 2000 edition of the *NALC Activist*. This edited version is used here with the permission of the NALC.

5

Political Action

Key Points

- Unions should systematically determine political issues of greatest importance to members.
- It is necessary to provide evidence to members that their support for union-supported candidates and political activities will lead to desired outcomes.
- An effort should be made to create a culture in the union in which member support for, and involvement in, the union's political activities is encouraged.
- Where possible, unions need to provide evidence to members that people whose opinions they value support the union's political programs and positions.
- Unions should encourage members to share their political beliefs with family members and get them involved in the union's political activities.

In the late 1800s, the labor movement in the United States was deeply divided over the issue of whether unions should be involved in the political process. Over time, public policy became one of the most critical factors affecting the success of American unions and political action was recognized as the vehicle for influencing public policy. Today, American labor organizations are united in their belief that labor must be involved in the political process. In fact, recent elections have seen American unions involved on an unprecedented scale, and the results have been impressive. While the need to be involved politically is an article of faith in the American labor movement, there is less unanimity concerning the political strategies unions should employ to maximize their effectiveness in the process.

Unions are involved in politics in two primary ways. First, they attempt to influence who is elected by rewarding their political friends and punishing their political enemies. Second, they work to shape public policy through active involvement in the legislative arena. Because unions are collective organizations, any success they have in cither of these areas is directly proportional to their abilities to convince their members to contribute time and, to a lesser degree, money to political action.

Members' support for labor's political agenda and strategies is, however, neither universal nor automatic. Evidence suggests that a significant portion of American union members do not agree with their union's political positions and activities

(Delaney and Masters, 1991; Clark and Masters, 1996; Freeman and Rogers, 1999). This issue should be of fundamental concern to all labor organizations.

This chapter will examine behavioral research that provides insights into the political attitudes and behaviors of union members. Some of the most useful work in this area identifies the factors that determine member support for political activity, in general, and support for union-endorsed candidates, in particular. This work will be examined along with research that looks at the impact union members have on the voting behavior of relatives and friends. The chapter will conclude with a discussion of strategies for increasing members' participation in election and lobbying campaigns.

Member Support for Union Political Involvement

Studies of American unions have found evidence that a majority of members support their union's involvement in the political process. These same studies, however, have also found that 20 to 45 percent of a union's members typically oppose their union's participation in these activities (Delaney and Masters, 1991).

If union political action programs desire to enlist members' support for union-endorsed political candidates and union-supported legislation, they must first convince their members that involvement in politics is a legitimate and important endeavor for the union. Maximizing membership support in this area is also important because of efforts by labor's political opposition to pass legislation limiting the use of union funds for political purposes. (See the case study at the end of this chapter.)

As the model outlined in Chapter 2 suggests, attitudes shape behaviors. This framework can be extended to include the notion that political attitudes shape political behaviors. And as will be argued in Chapter 7, attitudes can be influenced by information. Thus one way unions can influence attitudes about union involvement in politics, and ultimately members' participation in union political action programs, is by providing members with relevant information.

Among the most important information that can be presented to members in this regard is the message that union political action efforts do make a difference. Many of the labor movement's past political achievements still have important ramifications for American workers. Labor's efforts to help pass the Occupational Safety and Health Act in 1970 is one such example. Labor's successful efforts to periodically increase the minimum wage is another.

Unions can influence members' attitudes about the appropriateness of a union's involvement in the political process by providing evidence that their peers in the workplace are supportive of, and involved in, the political work of the union. The most effective means of accomplishing this is to create a culture in the union that includes political involvement as an integral part of the life of the organization (see

Figure 5.1 Two Factors Influencing Member Support for Union Political Involvement

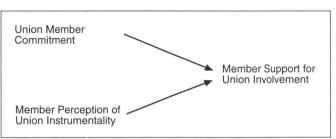

Chapter 9). In this scenario, political action would not be something that is "done" by the union or a few select individuals at election time. Rather, it would be an on-going activity that is part of most, if not all, union functions. It would also include the expectation that members have a responsibility to be involved. This grassroots, rank-and-file approach is consistent with the strategy recommended for effective organizing campaigns in Chapter 3.

Research has yielded further insight into members' support for union political involvement. A 1987 study found that a member's level of commitment to the union directly affects that member's beliefs about the propriety of the union's involvement in politics. This study also found the same relationship between the member's perception of his or her local union's instrumentality (influence on economic and noneconomic issues in the workplace) and support for union involvement in politics (see Figure 5.1). Finally, the research found that female members are more supportive of union political involvement than are male members.

The findings concerning union commitment and union instrumentality, again, suggest the importance of influencing members' general and specific attitudes about unions. It is quite possible that both union commitment and union instrumentality may facilitate a member's receptiveness to union information. Thus efforts to build union commitment and enhance the union's effectiveness in representing members in the workplace will have the additional benefit of building acceptance for the union's political action program.

The finding that female members are more supportive of the union's involvement in politics than males suggests that female members would also probably be more supportive of the particular political positions of the union. Women members might, therefore, be a particularly valuable political resource for unions. The growing number of women in the labor movement may have some very positive benefits for labor's political action program (Fields, Masters, and Thacker, 1987).

As Chapter 4 suggests, behavioral research provides strong evidence that one of the most important opportunities unions have for shaping the beliefs of their members is when an individual is first exposed to the union. This clearly argues for unions to organize systematic socialization/orientation programs for new hires. Such programs should include a discussion of the union's political action program, its rationale, and the benefits it provides to the new hire.

Unions need to give a great deal of thought to how detailed and how aggressive this presentation should be. Most individuals will come to the workplace with some general political orientation and with some positions on at least some political issues. If during this important early socialization period, the union strongly promotes an orientation or a position that is different from those of the new employee, it may make a negative, rather than a positive, impression. Because perceived instrumentality and union commitment are related to an individual's support for union political involvement, the prudent course of action might be to focus socialization efforts on informing the new hire about what the union does in the workplace and on building commitment. Specific discussions of the union's political action program can come later.

Support for Political Candidates

Numerous studies have shown that a majority of union members vote for union-endorsed candidates. One such study suggests that, on average, American union members vote for endorsed candidates at a rate 15 to 20 percentage points higher than nonmembers (Delaney, Masters, and Schwochau, 1990). Although this is encouraging news for unions, it is balanced by the knowledge that a significant number of members ignore their union's endorsement, sometimes providing the margin of victory for candidates opposed by labor. As Figure 5.2 illustrates, in only two of the last ten presidential elections has union member support for the union-endorsed candidate risen above 65 percent.

The 1984 U.S. presidential election, in which 43 percent of union members voted for labor's political archenemy Ronald Reagan, is a dramatic example of the independence of union voters (AFL-CIO, 1984). A more recent example occurred in 1994, when many union members across the country ignored their union's recommendation and helped vote in a solidly Republican Congress. That year union voters in Pennsylvania, a relatively strong union state, contributed to the election of a conservative governor and an even more conservative senator by giving them 50 percent and 36 percent, respectively, of union member votes cast for the two major party candidates (Clark and Masters, 1996).

Most American union leaders today realize that their membership represents a relatively small, and diminishing, percentage of the electorate. Most are also aware that there has been a gradual but ongoing decline in union members' support for endorsed candidates that began in the late 1960s (Axelrod, 1972, 1982). This scenario suggests that the potential for the election defections described above is always present.

Further underscoring the somewhat weakened political clout of the U.S. labor

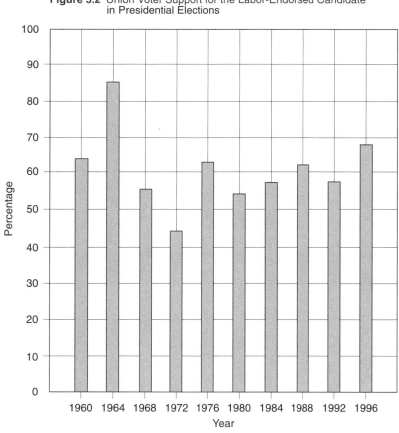

Figure 5.2 Union Voter Support for the Labor-Endorsed Candidate in Presidential Elections

Source: Sousa, 1993; Hart Research Associates, 1996.

movement is research suggesting that even when union members vote for union-endorsed candidates, many do not do so because of the union endorsement. In fact, two studies suggest that a significant percentage of union voters either are not aware of the union's endorsement or, if they are aware, indicate that the endorsement was not a factor in their voting decision (Patton and Marrone, 1984; Patton, Marrone, and Hindman, 1986). A third study found that only 72 percent of union members in Pennsylvania were generally or always aware of which candidates their union endorsed (Clark and Masters, 1996).

The need for unions to generate support for union-endorsed candidates and the less than hoped for impact of union endorsements suggest that to improve their overall political performance, unions need to be more effective in influencing members' voting decisions. There is little doubt that virtually all unions recognize this fact and strive to have greater impact in this area. There is also probably no consensus among unions as to how to accomplish this goal.

Behavioral science provides some important insights into the decision-making process individuals go through in casting their votes. Research in this area suggests that, in making a decision, individuals consider whether voting for a union-endorsed candidate will lead to positive and desirable outcomes regarding issues of interest to them. Central to this determination is the attitude that individuals hold toward unions in general and the attitude they hold toward the union that represents them (general and specific attitudes). They will also consider how other people they view positively will vote and how those individuals think they should vote (normative beliefs).

The Role of Information

The relationship of information to voter behavior has long been of interest to political scientists. One of the more well-accepted findings of research in this field has to do with voter turnout. Researchers have found significant evidence that turnout grows as voters become increasingly informed and knowledgeable about candidates and issues (Neuman, 1986). This finding suggests that voter education should be a key component, if not the primary focus, of labor's get-out-the-vote efforts.

More union-specific research suggests that information also plays a significant role in who union members vote for. These findings suggest that if unions are going to influence members' voting decisions they need to provide members with information beyond the names of candidates endorsed by the union. Research further indicates that unions have the most impact on members' voting decisions when they focus on workplace-related issues that members value highly (Delaney and Masters, 1991; Clark and Masters, 1996). The further unions move away from these issues and toward broader social issues, the less receptive members are to the union's influence.

The 1996 study of Pennsylvania union members' political beliefs asked members to rank ten economic and social issues according to the influence those issues had on their voting decision. The members ranked wages and standards of living, jobs, and workplace health and safety first, second, and fourth respectively (see Figure 5.3). These findings suggest that if unions are going to maximize their political influence over members they need to provide convincing information that positive and desirable outcomes regarding workplace-related issues are likely to result if members vote for the union-backed candidate (Clark and Masters, 1996).

A 1990 study further illustrates this principle. This research examined an experimental union phone bank strategy that emphasized worker-relevant issues and that ultimately had a positive effect on members' voting decisions in congressional elections. The study was conducted in Illinois, where AFL-CIO unions have relied on phone banks as a means to generate support for union-endorsed candidates. Before 1988, the phone bank strategy involved calling members, informing them which candidate labor had endorsed, and asking them to vote for that candidate.

In the 1988 elections, unions in three Illinois congressional districts employed an

Figure 5.0   Issues Influencing Union Members' Voting Decisions

1. Wages and Standards of Living
2. Jobs
3. Welfare Reform
4. Workplace Safety and Health
5. Balancing the Federal Budget
6. Abortion
7. Gun Control
8. Affirmative Action
9. School Vouchers
10. Free Trade with Mexico

Source: Clark and Masters, 1996.

experimental phone bank strategy developed by the AFL-CIO. The new approach involved polling members about which candidate they intended to vote for and which issues they viewed as most important. Different follow-up strategies were then employed for supporters and nonsupporters of the union-endorsed candidate and for undecided members. Supporters were encouraged to participate in campaign activities ranging from talking with their families and friends about the election to distributing campaign literature and working phone banks. This involvement made a positive contribution in two ways. First, it helped solidify the members' support by offering ongoing positive reinforcement of their voting decision and by increasing their investment in that decision. Second, it expanded the resources available to run a successful campaign.

Nonsupporters were contacted again, and if they still expressed an intention to vote against labor's candidate, they were not contacted further. The program devoted the greatest amount of attention to undecided voters. These members were the focus of a get-out-the-vote campaign and were sent letters from the candidates and from union representatives that specifically addressed the key issues identified by that voter in the polling process.

In each of the three congressional districts the percentage of union members voting for the labor-endorsed candidates increased significantly from the 1980 and 1984 elections. An analysis of the returns concluded that union voters played a decisive role in the successful campaigns of all three union-supported candidates. A follow-up survey of union voters in those districts found evidence that the experimental union phone bank program contributed significantly to the elections' outcomes. It also concluded that the program's focus on work-related issues singled out by members as particularly critical played an influential role in those members' voting decisions (Leroy, 1990). These results demonstrate the importance of relevant information in voters' decision making.

Information provided in the context of individual political decision making should try to convince voters that their vote for a particular candidate will lead to positive and desirable outcomes on issues of interest to them. Traditionally, American unions have limited their political involvement to public policy issues that affect an individual's workplace, worklife, or standard of living. These issues range from collective bargaining and employment to worker safety and health. In virtually every political campaign, however, these largely economic issues compete for voters' interest with social and cultural issues. Although issues such as abortion rights, gun control, and crime are not directly related to the workplace, they are nonetheless of great importance to many union members.

There is some evidence that a sizable segment of union members in the United States are somewhat liberal on economic issues but somewhat conservative on social and cultural issues (Clark and Masters, 1996). One example of this phenomenon was the considerable support American unions gave to the Vietnam War (a conservative position on a social/cultural issue) at the same time the labor movement was championing the passage of the Occupational Safety and Health Act (a liberal position on an economic issue). Of more immediate relevance is that in recent decades, many union members have simultaneously opposed gun control and supported expanded collective bargaining rights. Union members may very well hold membership in other groups (e.g., the National Rifle Association [NRA], the Christian Coalition) that influence their politics as much as, or more than their union.

In contrast, candidates are often either consistently liberal or conservative on both economic and social/cultural issues. In these situations, union members may face the difficult choice of voting for the union-endorsed candidate who shares their beliefs on economic issues but opposes them on social/cultural issues or voting for the candidate who shares their beliefs on social/cultural issues but opposes them and their union on economic issues (Clark, 1998).

This dilemma of conflicting beliefs presents unions with a couple of strategic options. One option is for unions to take a consistently liberal, or even moderate, position on both economic and social/cultural issues and attempt to sway dissenting members to their point of view. This approach would appear to be problematic for several reasons, most notably the significant number of union members who staunchly support the more conservative position on social/cultural issues. The 1996 study cited earlier, for example, found that 32 percent of union members in Pennsylvania were either supportive or very supportive of the NRA, the primary anti-gun-control lobbying organization in the United States (Clark and Masters, 1996).

In addition to opposition within their membership, many union leaders appear to be uncomfortable extending their union's involvement in politics to non-work-related areas (e.g., gun control, abortion). There seems to be little support within the labor movement for such an approach.

A second, more feasible approach, involves unions and union leaders clearly pointing out to members the economic consequences of votes based on support for conservative positions on social/cultural issues. Members would need to be con-

place issues) outweigh the positive outcomes related to another set of beliefs (social/cultural issues). Interest group voting records can be used to contrast the records of members of Congress on economic and social/cultural issues.

An analysis of these ratings indicates that while many of the social/cultural issue interest groups do not take positions on overtly economic/workplace issues, the candidates they support do. For the 1993–94 legislative year, there was a positive and significant relationship between the ratings given members of Congress by conservative social/cultural issue lobbying groups like the NRA, the Christian Coalition, and the Family Research Council and conservative economic interest groups like the U.S. Chamber of Commerce and the National Association of Manufacturers. There was a negative and significant relationship between the ratings of each of these groups and the AFL-CIO (Clark, 1998) (see Figures 5.4 and 5.5).

As interest groups use these ratings to decide which candidates to support, this analysis suggests that a candidate supported by the NRA, for example, is also likely to be supported by the Chamber of Commerce and opposed by the labor movement. Unions need to let their members know that a vote based solely on a conservative social/cultural issue is often a vote for the employers' candidate and against their own economic interests (Clark, 1998).

When union members hold conflicting beliefs, unions need to provide information about the economic consequences of their vote. The AFL-CIO's campaign in

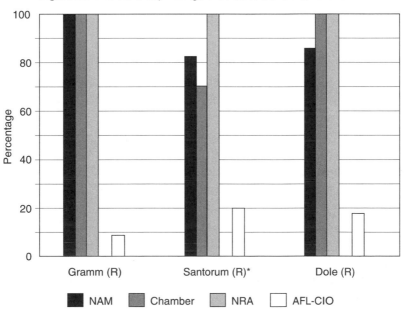

Figure 5.4 Interest Group Ratings of Selected Senators, 1993–94

* Rating based on votes in House before election to the Senate.
Source: Clark, 1998.

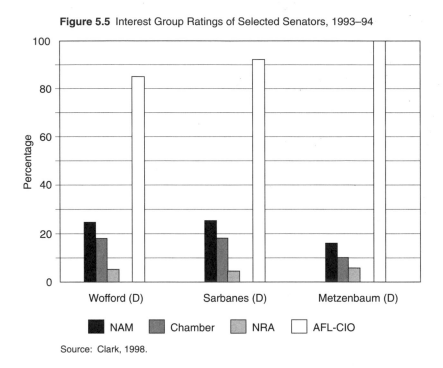

Figure 5.5 Interest Group Ratings of Selected Senators, 1993–94

Source: Clark, 1998.

the 1996 elections was consistent with this approach as it focused attention on pensions, health care, and educational opportunities. The "Labor '96' " program included a massive television and radio ad campaign that hammered home the economic outcomes members could expect by casting their vote one way or another.

The success of this strategy can be measured in a number of ways. Labor's 1996 get-out-the-vote campaign helped increase the number of union voters by 2.3 million above 1992 levels. Union households in 1996 accounted for 23 percent of the overall vote, up from 19 percent and 14 percent in 1992 and 1994 respectively.

Labor's efforts also gave boosts to its endorsed candidates. Sixty-four percent of union members voted for President Clinton in 1996. In congressional races, union members and their families helped the Democratic party rebound from the debacle of 1994. Sixty-eight percent of union members and 62 percent of union households voted for Democrats in these races. Only 35 percent of union households voted Republican in 1996, down from 40 percent in 1994. This represented a switch of one million votes (Hart Research Associates, 1996).

The survey of union political views in Pennsylvania provides one small but significant insight that suggests that members' support for conservative social issues may be diminishing. The survey results clearly indicate that there is greater support for the NRA among older, white, male union members than among members who are young, female, or people of color (Clark and Masters, 1996). As the membership of the labor movement is becoming younger, increasingly female, and more racially diverse, the problem of members holding political views at odds with their union, while remaining significant, may diminish.

The Role of Normative Beliefs

In addition to information, an individual's voting decision is influenced by the beliefs of people whom that individual values. These beliefs are called normative beliefs, and the theory behind their impact on voter behavior is called the theory of proxy voting. This theory suggests that when people are committed to voting but lack sufficient information or the motivation to become informed about the candidates or the issues, they often follow the advice of an individual they trust (Neuman, 1986).

One way unions can maximize their impact on union voters is to influence their members' normative beliefs. Toward this end, unions could direct their efforts toward a couple of areas. First, unions should recognize that the attitudes of individuals joining a union have, to a great extent, been shaped by persons who have been significant in their lives up to that point, most notably family members. They should also be aware that with age and experience family influence fades. As discussed in Chapter 4, it is also clear that day-to-day interaction with the local union and its representatives can significantly influence new members' attitudes toward the union (Fullagar et al., 1995; Heshizer and Wilson, 1995). This influence can extend to voting decisions.

Second, labor organizations need to create a culture, both in the union and in the workplace, that accepts, values, and encourages political involvement. To build such a culture, unions should involve as many members as possible and should make members' involvement visible. As more and more members are seen to be supportive of, and involved in, the political work of the union, more reticent members will be motivated to participate. Political action then becomes something that members are encouraged, or even expected, to do, rather than something done by the organization.

Third, unions need to consider taking advantage of the opportunities for directly influencing members' attitudes that this increased visibility provides. Unions can have an impact on these attitudes by seizing every opportunity to convey to members that others support the union's endorsed candidates. Many of the traditional ways of publicizing support for candidates—public rallies, pins, bumper stickers, T-shirts—make this support visible to uncommitted members. In some unions and workplaces, newer methods of communication like websites and e-mail can be employed.

To address the finding that individuals' voting decisions are particularly influenced by people they consider important in their lives, unions can encourage one-on-one contact between supporters and members who have not declared their support. Friends, individuals viewed as workplace leaders, and people working in close proximity potentially can have the most impact on undecided voters. The simple declaration of support for a union-endorsed candidate a member makes by wearing a pin, a T-shirt, or a hat or by engaging a fellow member in conversation about a candidate sends an important message to undecided members. The message that "I intend to vote for the union's candidate; you should too" goes to the heart of normative beliefs. Television, radio, and print ads, while also potentially effective, are less likely to have an impact on normative beliefs because they customarily lack the direct tie-ins to the people voters consider important in their lives.

While all of these strategies involving the interaction of members provide ways to influence normative beliefs, they also provide opportunities to convey information on the potential outcomes that result from casting a vote for the union-endorsed candidate, thus helping simultaneously to influence general and specific attitudes toward unions.

Extending Labor's Influence to Families and Friends

The findings of related research in this area suggest an additional way the labor movement can extend its influence in the election process beyond its membership. This research has found that relatives of union members vote for union-endorsed candidates at a rate greater than nonmembers (Delaney, Masters, and Schwochau, 1990). This is consistent with the theory of proxy voting discussed earlier.

At a time when the percentage of the workforce that is organized continues to decline, the families of union members constitute an underused resource for labor's political action efforts. While union programs aimed at influencing the voting decisions of members and the general public both have some influence on union family members, the number of voters in these families may justify the development of systematic strategies designed to reach this voting bloc.

The model of union member behavior discussed earlier suggests that, to the degree union family members vote for labor-endorsed candidates, they do so because of some combination of general and specific attitudes toward unions and normative considerations. These family members may share the same view of unions as the union member. Because the union member is someone of importance to the family, that person's opinions could influence the voting decision of others in the family.

In planning their political strategy, unions should consider ways to influence the beliefs of union family members. Simple steps such as including a suggestion that members share any union publications they receive with their families, asking members to speak to their families on behalf of the union's candidate, addressing mailings to the members' families, or encouraging members to bring their families to union political functions may have an effect.

Finally, though little research has been done on the subject, the same behavioral and normative principles that cause family members to vote for union-endorsed candidates also are likely to apply to friends and neighbors. Union members are presented with numerous opportunities every day to influence the voting behaviors of people they know. If people believe that voting for labor's candidates will result in positive and desirable outcomes, they should not be reluctant to share these beliefs with others.

Members' Participation in Political Campaigns

In addition to gaining members' support for the union's involvement in the political process and for candidates endorsed by the union, the success of union political action programs is also related to the level of participation a union is able to generate among its members. Virtually all union political activities, including voter registration and voter turnout drives, election campaigns, and lobbying efforts, rely on the voluntary efforts of union members. One of the problems union leaders face is how to mobilize the membership in the face of an important election or a critical legislative vote.

Although little of the research on union participation focuses specifically on political activities, it is reasonable to assume that a general increase in members' participation in union activities will result in an increase in political participation. Again, recognizing the relationship between attitudes and behaviors, it makes sense for unions to focus their efforts on shaping members' attitudes to achieve increased participation.

Toward this end, many of the strategies discussed for influencing members' support for union political involvement and for influencing their voting decisions should also influence members' willingness to participate in union activities. Such active participation requires more effort from the member than simply believing in the appropriateness of union political involvement or casting a vote. It seems logical, therefore, that participation may be a function of the strength or intensity of a member's attitudes.

This suggests that the stronger a member's belief that the election of a candidate will result in desirable outcomes, the more likely the member is not only to vote for that candidate but to campaign actively for the candidate as well. In terms of normative considerations, the more strongly members believe that a person or group important to them thinks they should vote for a candidate, the more likely they will be both to vote for the candidate and to contribute time and effort toward the candidate's election.

A member's beliefs are shaped, in part, by the belief that the consequences of supporting a candidate or program are both positive and significant. Effective information addressing a member's most relevant concerns can have a big impact on these beliefs. Unions can influence a member's normative beliefs by increasing the visibility of the union's position on a candidate or an issue and increasing the visibility of supporters of the union's position. These strategies are consistent with behavioral research on "resource mobilization" that suggests that individuals will participate in the work of an organization only if

1. they believe the issues involved are important to their lives,
2. they believe that their participation will make a difference,
3. they know that opportunities to participate exist, and
4. they have the capacity to participate. (Klandermans, 1984a, 1984b)

The earlier discussion in this chapter addressed the need to convince members that the issues involved are relevant to them and that their efforts are needed. This research, however, underscores two other necessary conditions for participation that are sometimes overlooked. One of these is that people need to be informed that opportunities exist for them to participate. Sometimes people do not participate in the work of an organization simply because they are not asked. Another condition is that people need to have the capacity to participate. This suggests that unions may need to invest in educating and training their members before they can participate in certain kinds of work on behalf of their union.

Finally, it is also necessary to consider that some union members will face barriers to participation. Family obligations are one such significant obstacle. Unions can assist members in overcoming these barriers by taking them into consideration when planning union activities. Scheduling meetings at times less likely to conflict with family commitments, making provisions for child care, and planning political activities that include a member's family are three means of reducing barriers to participation.

Outcomes of Union Political Action

Political action has, in the past, played a critical role in the fortunes of the American labor movement. There is ample evidence that public policy, by defining employee and union rights, constructing the framework for negotiations, and policing the system, has influenced the effectiveness of unions in organizing, bargaining, and administering contracts. There is every indication that union effectiveness in politics will play an equally important role in labor's future.

One final area of relevant research has focused on the outcomes of union political action. This work suggests that union efforts in this area not only influence overall union success on an organizational level, but they also have significant ramifications at the individual level. A study published in 1987 found that a member's perception of union political instrumentality plays a role in the decision to join a union. This research suggests that in organizing drives, employees, in addition to evaluating the potential effectiveness of a union to raise wages and benefits, also look at the potential influence a union might have in the political process (Fiorito, 1987).

By extension, this research also suggests that a union's instrumentality in politics, that is, the degree to which it accomplishes what it sets out to do, affects members' levels of commitment and participation. Success in the political arena, by increasing commitment and participation, can be a great union-building tool. Unions should also bear in mind that the reverse is also probably true. When union-endorsed candidates or union-promoted legislative issues are defeated on a regular basis, members' perceptions of their union's instrumentality is eroded, as is their confidence that their own involvement can make a difference. This scenario could, in the long run, make it more difficult for unions to mobilize their members.

In sum, behavioral research provides significant evidence that an individual's political attitudes and beliefs directly shape his or her political behavior. Convincing members to vote for union-endorsed candidates and participate in union political and legislative campaigns are two of the central goals of union political action programs. Research suggests that this behavior can be encouraged by influencing, in various ways, the views members hold toward their unions and toward their unions' political efforts and positions. The discussion suggests that many of the same strategies identified in the organizing (Chapter 3), socialization/orientation (Chapter 4), and information and communications strategies (Chapter 7) chapters have relevance in the political arena as well.

In pursuing these goals, unions and union leaders need to be realistic. Given the diversity of political opinion among labor's membership and the fact that unions are only one of many potential groups attempting to influence the political attitudes of their members, the American labor movement will never begin to approach unanimity in politics. The findings presented in this chapter, however, suggest that there are plenty of areas in which labor can improve its political performance.

Finally, the AFL-CIO has adopted a set of guidelines called the "Ten Rules for Union Political Action" (see below) that contain many of the principles addressed above. Like the principles discussed, these rules were distilled from research on union attitudes conducted by a professional polling organization. These "Ten Rules" have been widely publicized across the labor movement and are distributed at most AFL-CIO COPE training programs. They serve as an example of how behavioral research can be put to practical use (Garin and Molyneux, 1998).

The case study that follows is an example of what the labor movement can accomplish with a largely member-based, issue-focused, informational campaign. Proposition 226, also known as the "Paycheck Protection Initiative," was a 1998 California ballot initiative or referendum that would have required unions in that state to obtain advance written authorization from their members before their dues could be used for political purposes. The defeat of Proposition 226 may have been

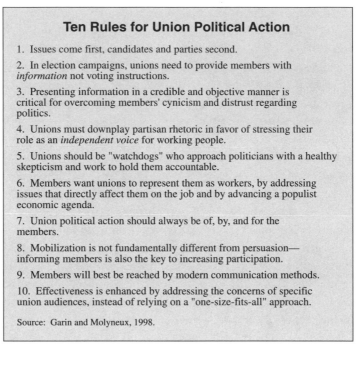

Ten Rules for Union Political Action

1. Issues come first, candidates and parties second.

2. In election campaigns, unions need to provide members with *information* not voting instructions.

3. Presenting information in a credible and objective manner is critical for overcoming members' cynicism and distrust regarding politics.

4. Unions must downplay partisan rhetoric in favor of stressing their role as an *independent voice* for working people.

5. Unions should be "watchdogs" who approach politicians with a healthy skepticism and work to hold them accountable.

6. Members want unions to represent them as workers, by addressing issues that directly affect them on the job and by advancing a populist economic agenda.

7. Union political action should always be of, by, and for the members.

8. Mobilization is not fundamentally different from persuasion— informing members is also the key to increasing participation.

9. Members will best be reached by modern communication methods.

10. Effectiveness is enhanced by addressing the concerns of specific union audiences, instead of relying on a "one-size-fits-all" approach.

Source: Garin and Molyneux, 1998.

one of the most significant and historic victories in labor's long history of political involvement (Clark, 1999). It provides a model for future efforts.

CASE STUDY

The Defeat of California Proposition 226

Four months before election day, the prospects for defeating California's Proposition 226—an anti-union initiative designed to silence the voice of working families—looked daunting, even inside the labor movement. In February 1998, polls indicated the initiative had wide support—71 percent of union members supported Prop 226, and only 26 percent said they were against it.

On election day, those numbers were reversed. On June 2, 71 percent of union members and a total of 53.5 percent of all voters cast their ballot against the measure. Support for Prop 226 had dropped 17 points, and opposition to the initiative increased 28 points. In short, unions scored a pick-up of 45 points in just a few months. AFL-CIO President John Sweeney called the victory "a modern political miracle," and he was not alone.

Lessons learned in this victory are not just crucial to future legislative and political battles—they are pivotal to the future growth of the labor movement. If unions are able to involve as many workers in future battles as they engaged in the campaign against Prop 226, they may be able to activate workers on an unprecedented scale in the political and organizing battles of tomorrow.

Not in 16 years as a community and labor organizer had I seen with greater clarity just how powerful the most basic forms of member communications can be. Nuts-and-bolts organizing isn't an exciting topic. Essential member contact programs—from leaflets to phone calls to one-on-one discussions—seem simple, obvious tactics. Yet, if there is one clear lesson from the 226 experience, it is that unions need to rethink their approach to membership mobilization and one-on-one contact. This is what distinguished the Prop 226 campaign from other campaigns.

These days, it is clear that no modern campaign is complete without direct mail and advertising. Winning public opinion requires broad outreach on a scale not currently possible through organizing alone. But it was the grassroots component of the Prop 226 campaign that catapulted labor to victory. A quick look at the numbers tells much of the story. The campaign against Prop 226:

- Recruited 28,000 new political activists.
- Made 65,000 volunteer phone contacts.
- Walked 5,005 precincts reaching more than 600,000 union members.
- Visited 18,000 worksites.
- Organized 8,000 volunteers to work the weekend before the election.
- Sent more than 4 million pieces of mail.
- Made 800,000 get-out-the-vote calls.

Labor set out to win 67 percent or 550,000 "No" votes from union members and 46 percent of the public vote. The extraordinary budget was crafted accordingly, and the field operations were designed to build the California Labor Federation's internal mobilization capacity for this and future campaigns, including recruiting 20,000 new political activists.

The core labor strategy was a creative and massive outreach program focused on member education and contact, primarily at the worksites, but also at union hall leadership meetings and in more generic communications through precinct walks and phone banks. We bridged the gap between the rhetoric and the reality of member education, and we successfully used worker education to mobilize.

There was no one-size-fits-all approach. Educational efforts varied by union, location, audience and educator. Some unions, like the Teamsters, developed a specific framework for educating their members, including a discussion of key issues, the role of political action, and how big business attacks on unions impact wages and benefits. They coupled this discussion with action plans and developed basic member education tools, such as talking points specifically tailored for their members. They used training programs to promote the idea of Teamsters talking to Teamsters on the shop floor.

Public sector—and many private sector—unions secured release time from their employers to hold worksite meetings. One county gave the American Federation of State, County and Municipal Employees (AFSCME) several half-hour segments to conduct 226 meetings. The Communications Workers of America connected with their members at midnight in the worksite of one of their largest employers.

The Carpenters and Painters unions used their apprentice classes to teach apprentices about the relationship between politics and labor. The Ironworkers used their hiring hall to recruit activists, and the Sheet Metal Workers used their retirees council to organize retirees.

Programs varied in length from 20 to 40 minutes at worksites to several hours in union halls. Some of the strongest educational work was conducted in one-to-one meetings. In many instances, there were no pre-developed education models for field organizers to use—no formal course in membership education—no formal course in pedagogical techniques were necessary. The worker education initiatives in the 226 campaign were rooted in basic day-to-day communication skills. They simply provided members an opportunity to raise questions and discuss issues.

But if there was a diversity in how and where the issues were discussed, there was also an important consistency in message. Organizers were armed with polling and focus group-tested messages that resonated with the rank-and-file. This information saved precious time in trial-and-error presentations, confirmed gut suspicions about what worked, and opened new ways of thinking about how to connect with union members.

Starting up worksite meetings was as easy as identifying workplaces to meet and determining how much time and opportunity existed for discussion. In some cases, both union members and non-members had access to these informational meetings. Workers were interested to see and hear from their leaders. By taking time to travel to worksites, union leaders sent a message to their members about the importance of the issue and signaled a change in their way of doing business.

In many of the meetings, rank-and-file members were stunned to learn how they had been deceived by the opposition's disinformation campaign, and angered by how the "Yes on 226" committee manipulated the message on television spots. That combination of education and anger produced militant activists and engaged new volunteers on a historic scale. Unions recruited 28,000 volunteers from among their ranks.

The breadth and effectiveness of the member contact, education, and mobilization program was revealed in election day exit polling and post-election polls commissioned by the AFL-CIO and the California Labor Federation. Pollster David Binder found member contact was fairly extensive. He reported that 75 percent of union members said they received mail on Prop 226, 50 percent were contacted by phone and 31 percent received some information at the worksite. Measuring the effectiveness of the worksite meetings, one-on-ones, and phone contacts, he found:

- Of those who received union handbills and leaflets, 73 percent voted "No."
- Of those who attended worksite meetings, 83 percent voted "No."

- Of those who received a phone call *and* had a one on one discussion, 90 percent voted "No."

The biggest influence on union members, they said in a survey conducted by Peter Hart and Associates, fell into four distinctive areas: 35 percent of the "No" vote was attributed to literature and mail from the union or AFL-CIO, 19 percent to TV and radio ads, 9 percent to personal contact from the union, 19 percent to a combination of all of these reasons and 18 percent to other reasons.

What the Hart numbers reflect is the breadth and penetration of labor's outreach to union members. They do not indicate the efficacy of one medium over another but rather the necessity to include mail and advertising to complement member-to-member contact. Phone trees, leaflets, phone banks, worksite meetings, public action, and other forms of communication through religious and community organizations are not adequate to reach hundreds of thousands of voters and offset opposition advertising. Neither the unions nor the community has developed the infrastructure enough to make this scale of communications possible. Still the Binder results reinforce, in extraordinary terms, how effective direct member contact programs can be, particularly at the worksite.

A key lesson in the fight against 226 was that to engage members, unions must organize around issues, not just political parties or candidates. While there is great disenchantment and outright hostility toward partisan politics, union members hold critical views on a wide range of issues, and they expect unions to advance their interests to counter corporate money. Indeed, a Peter Hart poll found that 68 percent of union members think unions should invest in politics and legislation to counter the influence of corporations and the wealthy. When asked, 86 percent of union members said they approved of unions fighting to increase the minimum wage and to protect Medicare from large cuts.

Another lesson that can be drawn from this battle: As critical as worksite-based strategies were, community outreach and education and building alliances with non-labor organizations were also key to victory. There is much work to be done to rebuild community ties, similar to the work the AFL-CIO has begun with academics and intellectuals, or their newly reinvigorated effort to strengthen the federation's civil rights program. To advance a broad social agenda, from the right of workers to organize to confronting proposals to privatize the Social Security system, it is critical for unions to expand their work with a wide range of non-labor organizations. The 226 experience illustrates the need to find new ways to make our voices heard, to strengthen direct communications with members, to use worksites as organizing platforms, and to develop strategies to engage unionized workers to help organize the unorganized and organize for economic and social justice.[1]

1. This case study was excerpted from Ken Grossinger's "How Labor Defeated California's Proposition 226" published in the September-October 1998 issue of *Working USA*. It is used with the permission of M.E. Sharpe, Inc.

6

Grievance Procedures

Key Points

- The establishment of grievance procedures in most organized workplaces is one of the most important achievements of the modern American labor movement.
- Members' attitudes toward the grievance procedure can have a significant influence on their attitudes toward the union.
- Members' attitudes toward the union are influenced more by how they view the grievance *process* itself than by the *outcomes* of the process.
- There are many things unions can do to ensure that their grievance procedures are functioning as effectively as possible.

More than 96 percent of collective bargaining agreements in the United States include a grievance procedure ending in arbitration (Skratek, 1997). The establishment of such procedures in most organized workplaces is one of the less heralded but most important achievements of the modern American labor movement. Grievance procedures are the primary mechanism through which unions can bring fairness, consistency, justice, and equity to the workplace on a day-to-day basis. By providing due process, grievance procedures give members a means to challenge the unilateral actions of the employer. Grievance procedures, in essence, provide employees their "day in court" when they feel they have been unfairly treated or wrongly accused. Unions are not shy about proclaiming the value of this mechanism, describing it in various publications as "the most important article in the contract" (IBT, 1984, p. 24) and "the key element in our system of industrial democracy" (NALC, 1983, p. 7).

The results of research in this area confirm the perception that union members value grievance procedures, particularly when they feel the union and its representatives are doing an effective job in administering the process (Gordon and Fryxell, 1993; Clark, Gallagher, and Pavlak, 1990). Because grievance procedures operate in the workplace, they are often visible to members. Seeing the union "in action" can have a positive impact on members' attitudes toward their union and toward unions in general.

This is particularly true if the member perceives the grievance procedure as contributing to greater workplace justice. Such a perception has been found to increase members' commitment to the union (Clark, Gallagher, and Pavlak, 1990; Eaton,

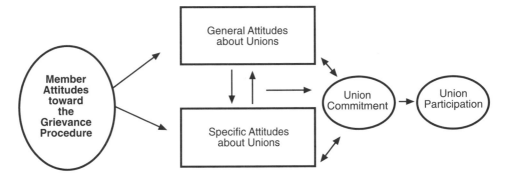

Figure 6.1 Relationship between Attitudes toward the Grievance Procedure and Participation

Gordon, and Keefe, 1992). In Chapter 2, evidence supporting the link between general and specific attitudes toward the union, union commitment, members' participation in union activities, and, ultimately, union effectiveness was presented (see Figure 6.1). Now members' attitudes toward the grievance procedure can be added to that model. Clearly, the grievance procedure can be a valuable tool for building more effective unions.

This chapter will discuss the various roles grievance procedures play in the workplace and the insights that research in this area provides as to how unions can most effectively use this process as a union-building tool.

The Role of the Grievance Procedure

Grievance procedures serve many important functions in the workplace. One of the most important involves the "policing," or enforcement, of the provisions of the contract. If the employer (or the union, for that matter) fails to comply with the terms of the collective agreement, the grievance procedure can be invoked as a mechanism to force compliance (Thomson, 1974).

A second function is the grievance procedure's role in the day-to-day interpretation of the contract. One observer of the process has suggested that "every labor agreement contains a certain amount of unintentional ambiguity which may give rise to questions of interpretation" (Briggs, 1984, p. 11). For example, both the union and the employer think a funeral leave clause granting employees three days of paid leave upon the death of an "immediate relative" is clear when it is agreed to in negotiations. Only later do the parties learn that they interpret the phrase in very different ways. Honest disagreements over the interpretation of contract provisions are inevitable. Grievance procedures serve as a mechanism for the fair and efficient resolution of such disputes.

A third, and related, function involves the adaptation and extension of the agreement to meet changing circumstances and unforeseen situations (Chamberlain and

Kuhn, 1965). A contract cannot directly address all of the situations that might arise while it is in effect. Contracts, therefore, often are couched in general language. In resolving the intentional ambiguity present in most contracts, the grievance procedure serves as a forum for the continuous bargaining of workplace issues. This process gives the collective bargaining process a dynamic quality.

A fourth function of the grievance procedure involves the management of conflict. Grievance procedures serve "to channel conflict into an institutional mechanism for peaceful resolution, thus preventing minor misunderstandings from being blown into major problems" (Thomson, 1974, p. 1). In this regard, grievance procedures also act as alternatives to strikes as a means of resolving disputes.

The grievance procedure also plays a fifth role that is important to both parties. As a means of communication in the workplace, it "provides a vehicle for individual employees to express themselves" (Briggs, 1984, p. 12). This chance to "complain with dignity" gives employees a voice in their on-the-job life and, by giving unhappy employees an alternative to quitting, can contribute to lower turnover, higher skill levels, and improved productivity (Hirschman, 1970; Freeman and Medoff, 1984).

Perhaps the most valued function of the grievance procedure, from the union point of view, is in bringing due process and justice to the workplace (Briggs, 1984). The formalized nature of the process, specifically the opportunity it affords to appeal decisions to higher authorities, provides the individual with due process rights not present in workplaces that lack a grievance procedure. Coupled with an arbitration provision, it allows employees to challenge unilateral decisions made by management in a wide range of areas and provides employees with a chance to tell their side of the story regarding workplace disputes.

Unions understand that workers value this "voice" function of the grievance procedure. It is not surprising, therefore, to learn that in a 1979 study of approximately fifteen-hundred workers, grievance representation was considered the most important of all union activities (Kochan). In a different study of thirty-three organizing campaigns, the establishment of grievance procedures as a means of preventing unfairness in the workplace was brought up by the union in 82 percent of the campaigns, more than any other issue including improved wages (Getman, Goldberg, and Herman, 1976).

Clearly, given these many functions, the grievance procedure is a central part of a union's presence in the workplace. Not surprisingly, it also is central to a fundamental debate that has taken place in recent years about how unions should perform their representation functions. This debate has focused on whether a "servicing" model of unionism (in which the union helps members by solving problems for them) or an "organizing" model (where members are actively involved in the solutions) is the best way to represent members (Diamond, 1988; Banks and Metzgar, 1989; Conrow, 1991).

A union that adopted the servicing approach would view a grievance as an individual problem that the union's staff or officers should endeavor to solve. In contrast, a union operating under the organizing model would be more likely to see a grievance as a group issue around which the membership could mobilize, rather than an individual issue to be resolved by union professionals. The grievance procedure, in this context, would serve as a mechanism for increasing participation in the union (Conrow, 1991; Fletcher and Hurd, 1998).

Whether a union employs one or the other or some combination of these models, the effective operation of the grievance procedure remains important. Given the emphasis placed on member participation throughout this book, the insights research on grievance procedures provides may be of particular interest to those unions that have moved, or would like to move, toward the organizing model of union representation.

Members' Attitudes toward the Grievance Procedure

Grievance procedures should generate a certain degree of goodwill among a union's members, given the numerous functions they perform. Still, any benefits that might accrue to a union from the grievance procedure will do so only if the process operates effectively. Toward that end, studies have attempted to measure the effectiveness of the grievance procedure from the points of view of unions and employers. Several criteria have been used as measures of effectiveness. The most commonly cited measures are the grievance rate, speed of settlement, extent of arbitration usage, and equity of settlement.

Ultimately, from a union standpoint, effectiveness is in the "eye of the member." The commonly cited measures of effectiveness are somewhat ambiguous and subjective when used to shed light on how members view the grievance process. For example, are members going to view the grievance procedure and the union positively if unions settle all grievances in a speedy fashion? Certainly members will not be happy if most grievances are simply dropped, thereby ensuring a quick settlement. Thus none of these criteria, taken alone, accurately measure members' perception of grievance procedure effectiveness.

To shed more light on members' views of the grievance procedure, a scale was developed that incorporated several issues thought to be important to union members, including some of those described above (Clark, 1986; Clark, Gallagher, and Pavlak, 1991).

This scale is based on the notion that a member's attitude toward the grievance procedure (ATGP) is made up of four distinct concerns:

1. The EFFECT of the grievance procedure on the workplace and its impact on the way employers treat employees in terms of equity, dignity, and protection from arbitrary action.

2. The level of satisfaction with the PROCESS itself, including the fairness of the procedure and the speed with which disputes were settled.
3. The member's evaluation of union REPRESENTATION in the grievance procedure, in both style and substance.
4. A general sense of IMPORTANCE or value which the individual member attaches to the presence of the grievance procedure in the employment relationship.

In essence, the ATGP scale suggests that union members evaluate grievance procedures by taking into consideration these four dimensions. To get an accurate sense of how members feel about their grievance procedure, it is necessary to consider their feelings toward all four of these dimensions of the process.

Grievance Procedures and Commitment to the Union

In a 1990 study involving over a thousand members from the same union who work for the same employer and use the same grievance procedure, members' attitudes toward the grievance procedure were measured in each of the four areas described above—EFFECT, PROCESS, REPRESENTATION, and IMPORTANCE. Members' levels of commitment to the union were also measured in an effort to determine the degree to which their feelings toward this process were related to their overall feelings toward the union.

The results clearly indicated that members' commitment was shaped, to a significant degree, by three of the four dimensions. PROCESS, REPRESENTATION, and IMPORTANCE all appeared to play a role in determining how a member viewed his or her union. Interestingly, the members' view of the EFFECT of the grievance procedure in the workplace played a less important role in shaping union commitment (Clark, Gallagher, and Pavlak, 1990).

These results suggest that a union can positively influence the membership's level of commitment to the union by ensuring that the grievance procedure is viewed positively by its members. Specifically, as PROCESS and REPRESENTATION focus largely on procedural concerns—did I get a fair hearing? did the union do a good job in representing me?—the union should pay particular attention to these issues. Unions should, of course, also be concerned with the outcomes (EFFECT) of grievances, but the research suggests that exposure to the process can still have a positive impact on members' attitudes, regardless of the outcomes.

These findings are consistent with at least two other major workplace studies on this issue (Gordon and Frywell, 1993; Eaton, Gordon, and Keefe, 1992). They are also consistent with behavioral research on justice in settings other than labor-management relationships. Much of this research has also found a distinction between the process/representation aspect of justice systems and the effects/outcomes aspect. This literature has come to refer to the former as "procedural" justice

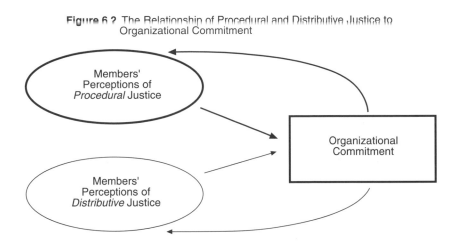

Figure 6.2 The Relationship of Procedural and Distributive Justice to Organizational Commitment

and the latter as "distributive" justice (Tyler, 1986; Greenburg, 1990; Ambrose, Harland, and Kulik, 1991).

While this research has found a relationship between procedural and distributive justice and commitment to the organization, at least one study also suggests that commitment, itself, may have an influence on a member's view of procedural and distributive justice (Konovsky, Folger, and Fogel, 1990). In essence, this means that organizational commitment and views of procedural and distributive justice reinforce one another.

One explanation as to why members' attitudes toward their union might be influenced more by the process itself (procedural justice) than by its outcomes (distributive justice) is that the union has more control over how the case is handled and presented than over how it is decided. Whereas the union, alone, decides how it will investigate and present a grievance, the outcome is a joint product of the union, the employer, and, quite often, an arbitrator. While some members will always blame a union for the outcome of a grievance, this research suggests that more will judge the union based on the process itself.

Practical Strategies

The research described above does not conclude that outcomes are unimportant. Clearly, they are. It does, however, suggest that unions should concentrate on what they can control—the establishment of effective grievance procedures and the representation of members. Realistically, this is all that unions can do. As simple as this sounds, too often grievance procedures and the performance of union representatives in those procedures are not up to par. In every union, improvement is possible. Grievance representation is a benefit that is available to all members of the bargaining unit. It is one of the basic reasons that workers want unions and, as shown earlier, it can be a very useful tool in building commitment to the organization. Some crucial areas involving the grievance procedure that unions should consider are discussed below.

The Structure of the Grievance Procedure

In their efforts to make grievance procedures more effective, union leaders sometimes fail to address the most fundamental problem with the process—its structure. In many cases, grievance procedures are one of the first articles included in a collective bargaining agreement. Often the language concerning the grievance procedure dates back to the original contract. That language is sometimes seen as carved in stone. Bargaining over the form and structure of the grievance procedure is a mandatory item of bargaining; it can be addressed at the bargaining table long after the language was first agreed upon. If a bargaining unit decides its grievance procedure is broken, it should take steps to fix it.

Local leaders should periodically reexamine the structure of their current grievance procedure. Special attention should be given to the following issues:

Is the grievance procedure accessible? Is the language in the contractual grievance procedure provision too restrictive? Does it discourage grievances? Is the statute of limitations unreasonable?

Are the time limits reasonable? Do they provide adequate time for investigation, while also providing incentives for the speedy resolution of disputes?

Does the contract provide the union with reasonable access to information it needs to process grievances?

Can new innovations such as grievance mediation improve the handling of grievances?

The Steward's Role in the Grievance Procedure

Labor organizations sometimes make the case that "the position of steward [sometimes called 'representative' or 'committeeperson'] is the most vital in the union" (AFSCME, 1987, p. 8). Although this assertion is questionable in a union that employs the service model of representation, it is undoubtedly true in those unions that follow the organizing model.

The importance of the steward is usually tied to the fact that those serving in this position are the "link" or "bridge" between the union's members and its officers. Many in the labor movement believe that the steward personifies the union in the eyes of the member, arguing that what the member thinks of the steward will determine the member's perception of the union. This view is suggested by the title of the USW handbook for stewards, "The Union Is You" (USW, n.d.).

While the steward's job may involve many functions, including political action, organizing, counseling, and education, the premise that the steward occupies a critical role in the union hierarchy is largely based on the steward's responsibilities in the grievance procedure. Union publications aimed at stewards consistently stress that a central responsibility of stewards in most unions other than those in the building trades is to handle grievances (Nash, 1984).

The level of training, preparation, and support concerning the steward's role in the grievance procedure varies greatly across national unions and even across locals in national unions. This is one area related to the grievance procedure over which unions have a great deal of control. While labor organizations may have little influence over management's actions and attitudes related to the grievance procedure, there is much they can do to ensure that their front-line representatives in the process—stewards—perform as effectively as possible.

Grievance Handling Skills

To perform their jobs competently, stewards must know how the grievance process operates. They must be familiar with the steps of the process, including who is involved at each level, what the time limits are, and the correct procedure for filing a grievance.

Stewards are the union representatives most accessible to members. For that reason they must be prepared to answer members' questions about the contract. To do so they need to know the contract. They must be knowledgeable enough to determine whether a management action constitutes a violation of the labor agreement.

Beyond knowledge of the grievance procedure and the contract, stewards must know how to investigate a possible grievance and build a case. Stewards are the union representative closest to the problem; they must be skilled at gathering evidence and organizing that evidence into a case the union can pursue at higher levels of the grievance procedure.

Member Relations

Handling a member's grievance presents an opportunity for the union to demonstrate the important part it plays in the workplace. By standing up for a member's contractual rights or challenging an unfair management action, the union demonstrates its unique role as the only party willing, and hopefully able, to represent members' interests and bring due process and justice to the workplace. As the research on procedural justice discussed earlier suggests, however, to make a positive impression on the member the grievance process must actually bring a sense of fairness and due process to the workplace. In addition, the union must demonstrate that it is an effective representative of the members' interests. If it does, members are likely to evaluate the union positively.

Interestingly, there is a less strong relationship between the members' perception of the effectiveness of the grievance procedure and satisfaction with the employer.

This suggests that "the union's reputation among workers is more closely staked to the performance of the grievance system than is management's" (Gordon and Fryxell, 1993, p. 248).

One way to help ensure that the union is an effective and visible advocate in the workplace is for a representative of the union always to be available to the members. The union should make sure that it has adequate representation in each part of the work location and on each shift to guarantee that someone will be available to assist a member. A well-publicized backup system should be devised so that members will know who to contact if their steward or representative is unavailable. A business card is one way to make sure all members know who their representative is and how to contact that individual.

Members should be informed of their rights to representation under the law and under the contract. Unions and stewards should not assume that members know their contractual rights, their right to use the grievance procedure, or their right to representation in disciplinary hearings under the *Weingarten* doctrine. Some unions use the flip side of their business card to inform members of their *Weingarten* rights.

Once members file a grievance they should be kept informed of the status of that grievance. In many situations, grievants have an emotional stake (fear, anger, anxiety) in their complaint. To a steward, an individual grievance may be only one of many. To the grievant, it may be the one and only grievance he or she has ever filed. Stewards and other representatives must try to put themselves in the member's shoes if they wish to positively influence that member's attitudes toward the union.

Under the National Labor Relations Act, when a union wins an organizing election, it wins the right to exclusive representation in that workplace. This means that no other union can represent any member in that bargaining unit. It also bestows on the union the obligation to represent all employees in that unit, including

Union Steward's Business card

Bettina Davis
Steward, Local 1234
Warehouse Division

Ph. 234–1223   Beeper 23

Courtesy of UAW.

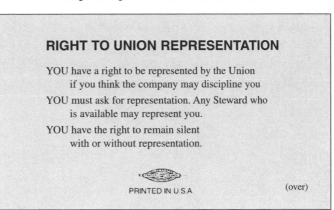

Weingarten rights on back of steward's card

those who voted against the union and those who choose not to join the union. This responsibility extends to the grievance procedure.

Unions must represent nonmembers in the grievance procedure. And according to the law, they must provide the same quality of representation that they provide to members or, potentially, face duty of fair representation suits. Stewards often balk at expending time and energy on these "free riders." Unions should, however, emphasize the need for stewards to do so. Toward this end it might be helpful for union leaders to emphasize that grievances provide a real opportunity to demonstrate to nonmembers why a union's presence in the workplace is so important.

The behavioral research referred to earlier makes it clear that most workers, whether they are members or not, value procedural justice in the workplace. Few situations have more potential for changing a person's attitudes about unions than the processing of a grievance. Grievances are often very personal and highly charged emotionally. Giving employees a chance to have their grievances heard and representing them in an efficient and professional manner, regardless of the outcome, can be an effective way of influencing nonmembers' attitudes toward the union and, ultimately, bringing them into the union.

Finally, because the grievance procedure has significant potential for influencing the general and specific attitudes of members, unions should consider taking advantage of every opportunity to inform people about the process. Certainly, a discussion of the role the grievance procedure plays should be a central part of every new member orientation program. Union newsletters and local union meetings should highlight successful grievances. Such publicity reminds members and nonmembers of the value of the process and underscores the union's representation skills. Of course, this strategy assumes that the union is providing effective representation.

Raising the profile of the grievance procedure may raise a concern on the part of local union leaders that such publicity will invite more grievances and overload the process. This is certainly a legitimate concern, but part of a properly functioning grievance process is the screening out of problems that should not be filed as grievances. If done sensitively, even this act of turning down a grievance can help educate members about the proper role of the process. When a decision is made that a grievance cannot be taken forward, a union representative should clearly explain to the member why their particular concern is not a grievance. If appropriate, the representative should also help the member resolve the problem through other channels.

Training

One of the keys to ensuring that stewards are skilled at handling grievances and sensitive to the concerns of members using the grievance procedure is to provide adequate training. Stewards, whether elected or appointed, should not have to learn the skills required of them entirely on the job or by trial and error. Ideally, a new steward should take part in a training program as soon as possible after accepting the position. Some local unions have the capability to provide this training to their stewards in-house; other locals seek and receive assistance from their national unions in setting up such programs or work with a university labor education program to expose their stewards to the basic information they need to carry out their duties.

Another means by which new stewards can learn the ropes is to assign an experienced steward as a mentor. A significant body of behavioral research suggests that this is a very effective way to pass on leadership skills and values (Davies and Easterby-Smith, 1984). A mentoring relationship can range from a kind of apprenticeship, in which the new steward spends time actually observing the mentor performing his or her responsibilities, to a less formal arrangement in which a beginning steward is assigned an experienced steward to call on for advice on an as needed basis. Ideally, mentoring would be used as a supplement to, not in place of, formal training.

While an introductory training session on some scale is vital for a new steward, local unions should, when possible, engage in a systematic and ongoing education process for stewards. This may involve advanced steward training programs or holding stewards' meetings at periodic intervals. These sessions can review the fundamentals of grievance handling, address specific problems stewards are having, or update stewards on relevant changes in the contract or law.

Reducing Steward Turnover

One problem local unions sometimes encounter in developing an effective steward system is the frequent turnover of individuals in these positions. While training can help a steward become more effective, there is little question that experience is a great asset in handling the typical problems a steward faces. If stewards quit before they can develop this expertise, the union is prevented from accumulating the collective experience that marks an effective steward system. Many stewards re sign because they see little reward for what is sometimes a very demanding job. Local unions can take action that might lower the turnover rate of stewards. Most of these actions involve making the stewards' position more attractive.

In many workplaces, unions negotiate superseniority clauses into the contract. These clauses provide that stewards jump to the head of the seniority line in a department or a workplace, ensuring that they will be among the last individuals to be laid off. This is done for several reasons. First, it guarantees that as long as there are employees in the workplace, there will be experienced stewards to represent them. Second, it makes it much more difficult for employers to retaliate against stewards by laying them off. Third, by giving them greater job security, it provides members with an additional incentive to volunteer to serve as stewards.

Local unions can also increase the rewards stewards receive by working to raise the status of stewards in the organization. Stewards can be given special jackets, shirts, hats, or notebooks that designate them as stewards. These items can serve as tangible rewards for their work and, simultaneously, give them some standing and recognition in the workplace. International Association of Machinists and Aerospace Workers (IAM) Local 933 in Tucson, Arizona, holds an annual Stewards Appreciation Day to recognize its stewards.

Local unions can also ensure that stewards do not feel overwhelmed by the job by providing greater support services. Ensuring that there is someone always available whom they can call for advice and assistance is a first step. Some unions also provide training for stewards in stress management. Systematic training in the technical aspects of their job, as discussed above, can also help stewards feel better equipped to handle the problems they deal with on a day-to-day basis.

Meetings with other stewards facing the same pressures and problems is an additional means of providing a support system. Interaction with other stewards facing the same problems assures stewards that they are not the only ones experiencing the stress and frustration that accompanies their work.

> IAM Local 933 in Tucson, Arizona, holds an annual Stewards Appreciation Day. In 1999, in addition to other activities meant to recognize the contributions of stewards, the local arranged for Tucson mayor George Miller to issue an official proclamation. The proclamation praised stewards as "unsung heroes" who "address concerns of their fellow employees" and uphold collective bargaining by assuming the roles of "educator, organizer, communicator, and political activist"
> (AFL-CIO Work in Progress, July 19, 1999).

The organizing approach to grievance representation, by its very nature, addresses the issues of turnover and burnout. By encouraging more members to participate actively in the work of the union, the organizing model may take some of the pressure off the small number of individuals who would be expected to handle most of the work under the servicing model (Conrow, 1991).

Finally, if a local union succeeds in making the steward's position more appealing, it will attract better equipped individuals to the job. Conversely, if the steward's position is perceived as a job to be avoided at all costs, the local will get "stewards of last resort." Members will quickly recognize this problem. Their lack of confidence in their stewards will be reflected in their perceptions of, and attitudes toward, the union.

The Organization's Role in the Grievance Procedure

Most local, regional, and national unions have insufficient resources, both financial and in numbers of personnel, to both adequately represent existing members and organize new ones. As external organizing has become a higher priority, many local unions have reassigned responsibility for handling grievances from full-time staff to rank-and-file representatives. This frees staff from their day-to-day servicing obligations and allows them to concentrate on organizing new members. While this would seem to be a reasonable strategy, the labor movement's experience with this practice has been mixed (Fletcher and Hurd, 1998).

One of the problems with this restructuring of responsibilities is that rank-and-file representatives can effectively assume grievance handling duties only if they are given adequate training and support. This, in itself, consumes staff time and financial resources which the union may want to devote to external organizing. The end result sometimes is unconstructive tension between the external organizing and internal servicing functions of the union (Fletcher and Hurd, 1998). If unions continue to emphasize both internal and external organizing, they must reconcile these two often competing functions. While organizing is, indeed, critically important to the labor movement, unions must not lose sight of the fact that few services they provide are as visible, touch as many members directly, and influence commitment to as great a degree as the grievance process.

Ideally, this restructuring can be a win-win situation for the union. If members who become more involved in the union through work as grievance handlers are given adequate training and support, they should become more committed to the union. Adding more members who actively participate and who are committed to the union can only strengthen an organization. Unfortunately, such restructuring has not always had such positive outcomes (Conrow, 1991; Fletcher and Hurd, 1998).

This chapter has suggested several strategies that unions can employ to make their grievance procedures work more effectively, thus ensuring that members see the process in a positive light. Specific suggestions are presented concerning the structure of the grievance procedure and the steward's role in the process. The list of strategies presented here is not exhaustive. The resources a local union has at its disposal, the local's relationship with management, and the individuals representing the union in the process all differ from workplace to workplace. Local union leaders must adapt these strategies to fit their particular circumstances. There is a great deal of room for creativity and innovation as unions think about how to make their grievance procedures function more effectively.

The case that follows describes a model steward system that incorporates many of the issues and strategies discussed in this chapter.

CASE STUDY

Building an Effective Steward System in a Statewide Local

The Oregon Public Employees, SEIU Local 503, is a statewide local union of approximately twenty-thousand members.[1] Most of Local 503's members work for state government, some work for local governments, and a small number are employed in the not-for-profit service sector.

Local 503 has gradually been moving from a servicing model of representation toward an organizing model. One part of this transition has been the reassignment of responsibility for the first three steps of the grievance procedure from staff to the local's stewards.

The local has an extensive steward system consisting of over six hundred stewards in units across Oregon. Sixty-one chief stewards, one in each sublocal, assist and support the stewards in their work. The chief stewards hold periodic stewards' meetings, coordinate training for stewards, and maintain the unit's grievance records. The local's stewards are further tied together by a statewide Stewards Committee, a representative group of stewards from across the local who meet periodically to discuss issues of mutual concern and who also sponsor a local-wide stewards' conference every two years.

At the heart of Local 503's steward system is a systematic, multilevel, training program that equips stewards to carry out their duties effectively. Because handling grievances is a central part of their responsibility, the first level of the training program focuses heavily on the grievance procedure. At this level, stewards learn the basics of handling grievances (e.g., the legal framework; what is a grievance and what is not; how to investigate, write, and present grievances). This training also focuses on building the local union through internal organizing. As part of this discussion, instructors emphasize the important role the grievance process can play in building a stronger and more effective union.

1. The information in this case study was provided by Jesse Bostelle, former education director and field services coordinator for the Oregon Public Employees Union, SEIU Local 503. She now serves as assistant director of education for SEIU in Washington, D.C.

While Local 503's training program is designed, in part, to help stewards become effective grievance handlers, the local views the steward as having a leadership role that extends beyond handling grievances. The local believes that stewards should be involved in a range of other internal and external organizing functions. For this reason, the second level of the training program focuses on issues and skills that go beyond the traditional representation function of stewards. These issues and skills include listening to members and learning to identify workplace problems, identifying and recruiting potential leaders from the membership, and planning and conducting an internal organizing campaign.

Each level of the program involves twelve hours of classes. Depending on work schedules and other logistical considerations, classes might run three hours a night, one night a week, for four weeks. Alternatively, the classes might be scheduled on weekends. Consistent with its commitment to the organizing model and maximum membership participation, the classes are open to any member who wants to get involved in the union.

Local 503 believes that its steward training program not only equips stewards to be more effective in handling members' grievances, but also helps build a stronger union by broadening stewards' interests and skills beyond the grievance representation process.

It is interesting to note that Local 503 does not see burnout, and the subsequent turnover, of stewards as a problem. As discussed earlier, the steward's job can be so stressful that union members will often serve only a short time in the position. This represents a real problem for many unions as they constantly lose the cumulative experience that stewards gain with time. Since experience is an effective teacher, turnover acts to reduce the accumulated wisdom, knowledge, skill, and, ultimately, the effectiveness of the unions' corps of stewards. Turnover also forces unions to devote more and more of their limited resources to training and developing new stewards.

There may be several reasons why Local 503 does not experience these problems with its stewards. First, a systematic, ongoing training program, like the one 503 conducts, helps to equip stewards to handle the many demands placed on them. Feeling ill-equipped and unprepared to meet their responsibilities is a key reason why stewards step down. Effective training that prepares stewards well can help alleviate these feelings of inadequacy.

Second, by its very nature, the organizing approach requires a local union to have a significantly greater number of members actively involved in the work of the union than would be required in a service-oriented local. Local 503 has expanded the number of leadership positions at all work sites in its jurisdiction, thus increasing the level of membership involvement. The greater involvement of the membership has had the effect of reducing the need for the stewards to "do it all." The consequent reduction in stress felt by stewards might well contribute to the relatively low turnover experienced by the local.

And third, the organizing model adopted by Local 503 has resulted in an active and energetic organization that is fully engaged in a range of organizing, political, legislative, and community activities. There is, in short, a great deal going on in the local. Many opportunities are available for stewards to get involved in the union beyond their responsibilities as stewards. And since these are areas of the union's work in which the stewards have chosen to be involved, stress is less of a problem. These opportunities very often deepen a member's commitment to the union and their willingness to get involved. Sometimes this may result in a steward moving to another position involving work in which he or she has become interested (such as organizing or political action). This, however, is a form of turnover unions can live with.

In sum, Local 503 has developed a steward system that has resulted in more effective and more involved stewards than had been the case in the past. The local credits its systematic, ongoing training program, in part, for the effectiveness of its stewards. This, combined with the other steps the local has taken to move toward an organizing model, has caused the local's stewards to be more engaged, both in their role in the grievance procedure and in the many other programs with which the union is involved.

7

Information and Communication Strategies

Key Points

- Unions can influence attitudes and beliefs by effectively communicating relevant information.
- Union leaders should be aware of the three steps of effective communication—attention, comprehension, and acceptance.
- An effective communicator will consider how the source, the message, the channel, and the receiver will influence attention, comprehension, and acceptance.

Each of the chapters in this book addresses key activities central to the success of a modern labor organization. These range from convincing members to vote for union representation to socializing new members into the union to generating support for union-endorsed political candidates. Despite the varied nature of these activities they all have one thing in common—they involve mobilizing the union's membership in pursuit of its goals and objectives. And the primary tool unions have to mobilize their members is information.

Unions, like all organizations, use information in countless ways. They use it to account for their finances, to track the status of the economy, and to document their past and illuminate their future. But most important, they can use it to persuade their members and prospective members to engage in behavior or activities that will move the union in the direction it needs to go.

This chapter focuses on the important role that information plays in this process of persuasion. The relationship of information to members' attitudes and behavior will be examined in the first part of the chapter. The second part of the chapter will discuss how unions can effectively communicate information to bring about behavioral change. The chapter concludes with a case study of the AFL-CIO's "America Needs a Raise" program.

The Information-Attitude-Behavior Relationship

Much of this book is based on the premise that unions can become more effective by changing the attitudes and beliefs of that portion of the membership or prospective membership that is not supportive of, or active in, the organization. This, in turn, can lead to a change in members' behavior.

The model discussed in Chapter 2 was developed to help provide insight into human behavior. As described in that chapter, this model argues that behavior has its roots in the underlying attitudes of individuals. Information, effectively communicated, is, perhaps, the most important means through which unions can influence attitudes. Most behavioral scientists interested in effective organizations inevitably look at the role played by information and communications strategies. Some of the earliest research in this area remains among the most useful. In the 1950s, a research team known as the Yale Group identified the components of effective communications in a useful, straightforward model (Janis, 1959; Hovland, Janis, and Kelley, 1964). Their work suggests that individuals will be persuaded to change their attitudes and behavior depending on the degree to which communications garner their *attention*, the degree to which they *comprehend* the communication's content, and the degree to which they *accept or yield* to what is comprehended. To communicate effectively, unions, therefore, need to present information in a way that will address the issues of attention, comprehension, and acceptance. Subsequent research in this area identifies specific strategies toward these ends.

Two-Way Communications

The most imaginative and innovative communication strategy addressing the issues of attention, comprehension, and acceptance will have little impact on a desired behavior if it targets attitudes irrelevant to that behavior. For that reason, to be effective any communications strategy must first identify the attitudes underlying the behavior it is designed to change or reinforce. Communication must, for this reason, be a two-way process.

It is vital that leaders in any membership organization be attuned to the messages the membership sends to them. For this reason, individual leaders need to develop good listening skills. Unions, as organizations, can develop systematic means of improving two-way communications. This might involve conducting periodic polls or surveys of members, holding "town meeting" or "rap session" forums where members can express themselves, or simply establishing a genuine "open door" policy that encourages members to stay in touch with their leaders.

Identifying members' attitudes can help unions be more effective in many areas, including political action, collective bargaining, and contract administration. It is a particularly useful, even essential, tool for bringing new members into the union. In organizing drives, unions employ various communications strategies in an effort to get bargaining unit members to engage in a desired behavior—voting for the union on election day. Identifying attitudes is the first step in this process.

Chapter 3 discussed research that identified some of the attitudes and beliefs underlying people's voting behavior in the context of an organizing campaign. This research indicates that when employees are involved in a representation election, how they vote will be determined by the three types of attitudes included in the model of union effectiveness presented earlier—their attitudes toward their jobs (satisfaction), their attitudes about the potential effectiveness of the union trying to organize them (instrumentality), and their attitudes about unions in general (Brett, 1980).

Unions can assess their chances of success in a potential organizing drive by identifying voters' attitudes in these three areas. If a sufficient number of employees in a bargaining unit are dissatisfied with their workplace experiences and hold positive attitudes concerning the organizing union and unions in general, the organizing effort will probably go forward. If the employees are satisfied with their situation and hold negative attitudes about the organizing union and unions in general, the organizing drive probably should not occur. And if the employees' attitudes are mixed, as is more likely, the union can use this information to target its organizing efforts.

Unions should, in particular, consider the findings outlined in Chapter 4. These findings suggest that attitudes toward unions in general are often formed early in an individual's life and are, therefore, difficult to change in the short term. Although unions may have no choice but to address these general attitudes in an organizing campaign, a much broader, long-term, image-building strategy can significantly enhance the labor movement's prospects for organizing. This issue and strategies for image-building will be discussed in Chapter 8.

In virtually every organizing drive, a union will need to make the case that it can effectively address the workplace issues of concern to potential members. Organizing efforts will be greatly aided if the union can identify as specifically as possible these workplace issues early in the campaign. A 1997 study found that organizing strategies that provide the union with specific information about workers' priorities (i.e., what they value), such as surveys and systematic house calls, greatly increase the union's chances of winning an election (Bronfenbrenner).

Identifying the relevant attitudes underlying employees' decisions to vote for or against the union is something many successful organizers do instinctively. Yet the link between attitudes and behaviors is so significant that it should be done carefully and systematically.

While the identification of relevant attitudes is an important step in the organizing process, this same behavioral principle also applies to the relationship between a union and its members after the union is in place. Unions continually work to generate member participation in, and support of, the programs of the union. Unions require the active support of their membership when they sit down at the bargaining table, when they engage in a strike or are targeted by a lockout, when they back candidates for political office, and when they challenge management actions through the grievance procedure. In attempting to build this support, unions need to systematically identify the attitudes underlying the behaviors they wish to encourage.

Identifying such attitudes could, for example, be a routine part of any union's preparation for bargaining. It is important for union leaders to recognize that members' attitudes are not static. They can change in reaction to economic, political, social, and cultural developments. A union that finds out six weeks into a bitter strike that, over time, its members' attitudes have changed in regard to bargaining priorities will be in a very weak position.

As more unions and their members are presented with the opportunity to get involved in nontraditional relationships with employers (e.g., employee involvement, cooperative union-management programs), unions need to have a clear sense of members' attitudes about such programs.

Changing Beliefs through Effective Communications

In most cases, the process of identifying relevant attitudes will reveal that at least some individuals hold attitudes that are incompatible with desired behaviors. For example, during an organizing drive unions will sometimes encounter individuals who believe that unions exist only "to protect the lazy and incompetent worker." Individuals who hold this belief are unlikely to vote for the union. The challenge unions face in this situation is how to change that belief. The answer, in part, is information, effectively communicated.

A number of models of effective communications have been developed based on the behavioral research conducted in this area. These approaches identify several components or variables that an individual or organization should consider when developing or delivering a message designed to influence beliefs and attitudes (Janis, 1959; Hovland, Janis, and Kelley, 1964; McGuire, 1985, 1989). Four of the most important variables are the *source* of the message, the *message* itself, the *channel* by which the message will be delivered, and the *receiver* of the message. Another, and perhaps more straightforward, way of articulating these variables is "*who* says *what* to *whom*, and *how* do they say it" (see Figure 7.1) (McGuire, 1985, p. 172).

This model also suggests that in changing attitudes, and ultimately behavior, an individual goes through a series of steps or stages. To bring about the desired

Figure 7.1 Components of an Effective Message

Figure 7.2 Model of Effective Communications

		Components of the Communication Process			
		Source	Message	Receiver	Channel
Steps in the Communication Process	1. Attention				
	2. Comprehension				
	3. Acceptance				

change, the union must take an active role in each of these steps. Specifically, the union must ensure that the message garners the *attention* of the individual, that the individual *comprehends* the content of the message, and that he or she *accepts,* or yields to, what is comprehended (Janis, 1959; Hovland, Janis, and Kelley, 1964). In doing so, the union must consider each of the variables described previously. Figure 7.2 brings the elements of the model together.

The simplest way to think about this approach is to take the three steps in the communication process—attention, comprehension, and acceptance—and to consider, for each step, the four variables or concerns that are part of an effective message. The following discussion draws on the research in this area to suggest some ways to address each of these concerns. The first step involves getting an individual's attention.

Attention

There is an old story that points out the importance of this first step. It involves a farmer who once sold a mule to his neighbor. The mule was described as extremely cooperative and a good worker. "Just treat him well," the farmer said. "Tell him what to do, and you will never have a problem." The neighbor took the mule home, harnessed him to a plow, and said "Giddyup." There was no response from the mule. The neighbor, becoming increasingly angry, uttered several variations of the command. He swore, jumped up and down, and swatted the mule with his reins. The mule remained unaffected. The neighbor rushed back to the farmer and complained. The farmer remarked calmly that the neighbor must not be treating the mule properly and volunteered to try his luck. Arriving at the neighbor's, they found the mule exactly as he had been left. The farmer looked about, picked up a stout two-by-four, and hit the mule squarely between the eyes. The mule shook his head slightly and then in response to a mild, "Now, git along please," the mule set to work with good speed. In departing, the farmer simply said, "You have to get his attention first" (Anderson, 1978, p. 105).

The current period in history has been dubbed the information age. Each day, for better or worse, we are inundated with hundreds of messages from many different sources, all competing for our attention. It is beyond our capacities to process each of these messages fully. Therefore, we mentally sort the messages we receive, discarding some, giving others a brief notice, and turning our full attention only to those we consider to be highly relevant or important.

To change someone's attitudes, a union or a union representative must first get that person to turn their full attention to the message being communicated. In sorting messages, the *source* is the first factor that influences the level of attention we give to the message. One researcher has suggested that an individual will consider three factors when evaluating the source of a message—credibility, familiarity/attractiveness, and power (Kelman, 1961).

Credibility will increase the likelihood that a message will gain an individual's attention. People innately want to get the "right" information. They will consider whether the source of the message or information is credible and whether the source has appropriate expertise related to the subject of the message. If so, the receiver is likely to give the message more attention. Familiarity is also a source consideration that will affect attention. People are much more likely to pay attention to a message that comes from someone similar to them, someone they know or with whom they feel comfortable. The same basically holds true for attractiveness. Last, an individual will consider whether the source of the message has the power, or represents a group that has the power, to help the individual get something he or she wants (McGuire, 1985).

Examples of how credibility is established in union settings are commonplace. At formal union gatherings such as conventions or education programs a considerable amount of time and effort is often spent introducing a speaker. The speaker's efforts on behalf of the organization will be detailed, as will offices held and awards received. This may seem a mere formality, but these introductions serve a very useful purpose. By recounting the speaker's achievements, the introduction serves to establish the credibility of the speaker as a source of information (Bettinghaus and Cody, 1994). John Sweeney's introduction of the United Farm Workers (UFW) founder and president, Cesar Chavez, at the 1988 SEIU Convention is an example of such an introduction (see below).

Attractiveness and familiarity are also qualities that garner attention (McGuire, 1985). Advertisements often feature pictures of celebrities or other attractive men and women, sometimes in bathing suits or other revealing attire. Clearly, these visual images are designed to attract one's attention to the ad. Even if a union organizer happens to look good in a bikini or a muscle shirt, such attention-getting devices have no place in an organizing drive or other union context. Familiarity, however, can be equally effective in encouraging a union member to pay attention to a message the union wishes to communicate.

Assigning organizers who match the demographic characteristics of significant

> ### Introduction of Cesar Chavez by President John Sweeney at the 1988 SEIU Convention
>
> It's a privilege to introduce to you a long-time friend of the Service Employees, Cesar Chavez, founder and president of the United Farm Workers.
>
> Cesar was born in 1927 on a small farm near Yuma, Arizona. He began his life as a migrant farmer when he was ten years old. Outraged by the exploitation of farm workers by agribusiness giants and propelled by his dream to create an organization for farm workers whose suffering he had shared, Cesar founded the National Farm Workers Association in 1962.
>
> The Farm Workers Association and the Agricultural Workers Organizing Committee merged in 1967 to form the UFW, which affiliated with the AFL-CIO.
>
> From the earliest years, Cesar and the UFW adhered to the same principles of nonviolence practiced by Gandhi and Martin Luther King. In fact, Cesar conducted a 25-day fast in 1968 to reaffirm the UFW's commitment to nonviolence.
>
> Confronted by relentless hostility from growers, Cesar called for a worldwide boycott of California grapes. By 1975 a poll showed that 17 million U.S. adults were honoring the grape boycott. As a result, former California Governor Jerry Brown signed the historic 1975 collective bargaining law for farm workers.
>
> I would ask each and every one of you . . . to give a warm welcome to labor's living legend, Cesar Chavez. (SEIU, 1988)

portions of the group being organized (young organizers with young workers, an organizer with service sector experience organizing service workers, a Spanish-speaking organizer with Hispanic workers) has clear advantages. A steward delivering a message will likely be better able to gain the attention of his or her members in the workplace than a stranger would. Unions should take this factor into account when communicating with members or prospective members.

Behavioral researchers label this phenomenon "relational demography." Their research provides concrete evidence that people with similar backgrounds (job responsibilities, education) and demographic characteristics (age, gender, race) interact more effectively with one another than do people who have little in common. People are initially more inclined to listen to those who appear to be like themselves because they assume that person's experiences and perspectives may be similar to theirs (Tsui and O'Reilly, 1989; Gramm and Schnell, 1997).

Another strategy that unions sometimes employ in organizing drives finds support in the research literature. The literature suggests that credibility and familiarity are, to some degree, "transferable" (Bettinghaus and Cody, 1994). When union organizers ask a well-respected member of the bargaining unit to introduce them to other members of the unit, the organizers are hoping that the credibility and familiarity of that member will be transferred to them. A speaker who invokes the name of John L. Lewis when addressing a gathering of coal miners, or Martin Luther King when addressing a group of African Americans, is, knowingly (or perhaps unknowingly), drawing on the credibility of those legendary figures. This is a solid behavioral principle that union leaders and activists can use to their advantage.

In addition to the source, the *message* communicated also plays a role in getting an individual's attention. Here, as in much of our previous discussion, relevance is a key concern. People are much more open to a message whose subject is part of their direct experience. A data entry clerk is more likely to pay attention to a message about eyestrain from computer screens than a message about the North American Free Trade Agreement. A young, single worker is more likely to be open to a message about employer educational benefits than about the pension plan.

Another issue that has received a fair amount of research attention is the effectiveness of emotional versus logical/rational messages. Unfortunately, the research to date on this issue provides little concrete advice other than to suggest that every message usually contains some element of both emotion and reason. There is some evidence that increasing the emotional content of a message, up to a point, will increase an individual's attention to that message. Much of the information that unions communicate to members and prospective members has very important implications for people's lives. This information, whether it involves an unfair dismissal, a change in the health care benefits, or a strike strategy, can generate anger, indignation, fear, and disappointment. Unions need to recognize the link between emotion and attention.

Receiver factors involve characteristics of the person on the receiving end of the message that can influence that individual's openness to the message. Receiver factors are intertwined with the other factors previously discussed. The gender, race, age, and ideology of a receiver, for example, will influence how that person views the credibility of a messenger or how familiar or attractive that messenger is. Areas of interest held by the receiver will also influence the attention given to a message (McGuire, 1985).

Unions and union representatives need to be sensitive to the concerns and interests of the members who are on the receiving end of their communications. A democratic system of government, which American unions have, encourages leaders to stay in touch with the membership. If they do not, they are in danger of being voted out. Also, if a union leader is elected, it is more likely that the members will view that leader as credible by right of having won election.

Currently, although all local officers (presidents, vice-presidents, treasurers, and so on) must be elected, unions can choose whether to elect or to appoint their stewards and equivalent first-line representatives. While the unions that fill these positions by appointment undoubtedly see benefits in this method, they should also weigh the advantages that the election of first-line union representatives has for improving the communications process.

The term *channel* refers to the means through which a message is conveyed. Channels range from one-on-one conversations to mass media like television and radio. Certainly the means by which a person receives a message will influence the attention paid to that message. A channel that requires a person to participate actively in receiving a message, including responding to it, will, by necessity, compel that person to pay more attention to the message than one that does not. Face-to-face communication is the most effective means of gaining attention for a message because it involves participation and response. A message received at a meeting which the receiver has made an effort to attend has the potential to be more effective than a radio or television ad because of the investment the receiver's participation represents (McGuire, 1985).

Unions have long recognized the value of face-to-face contact. The structures of many unions encourage communications between the leadership and the membership through the steward system. Stewards are the eyes and ears, as well as the voice, of the union in the workplace. The steward position is also the point in a union's structure at which the membership and the leadership come together on a daily or almost daily basis. The two-way communications that can occur at this level of the union allow information to be passed from the union to the member and for information about members' beliefs and attitudes to be fed back to the union. An effective steward system can facilitate communications by drawing

The AFL-CIO has developed the "1-on-1" program as a structured communications method that local union activists can learn and put to work in their local unions. It is designed to facilitate face-to-face conversations about important issues, hear member opinions, and enlist their support.

The AFL-CIO provides train-the-trainer programs at the Meany Center for Labor Studies.

Courtesy of AFL-CIO.

members' attention to information that the organization deems critical through a channel the membership deems credible and familiar.

Another strategy that research in this area suggests is very important in gaining attention involves changing or varying the channel employed to deliver a message. Any stimulus loses its ability to command attention after continual use (Anderson, 1978). Toward this end, unions might consider varying the means by which they deliver messages. Some unions have implemented this strategy by producing and circulating videotapes to communicate a particularly important message. National and local unions are taking advantage of new technologies such as web sites and electronic mail to draw attention to the information they disseminate (Shostak, 1999; Fiorito, Jarley, Delaney, and Kolodinsky, 2000). Unions need to be aware that the novelty of these approaches will probably wear off quickly if they, too, become commonplace.

Comprehension

As stated previously, effective communications can be used to influence people's beliefs and move them toward a desired behavior. For a message to be effective it must first gain a person's attention. Second, the message must be comprehended or understood. A message that is ambiguous or unclear will have little impact on a person's behavior, regardless of how successful it is in gaining the person's attention.

Most of the behavioral research relevant to the issue of comprehension has focused on the message, the channel, and the receiver. Unfortunately, much of the considerable research on the *message* component provides only vague guidance on how to construct a message that will be understood by the receiver. Rather, work in this area concludes that the organization of a message, the skill and style of the presenter, and the employment of humor contribute to comprehension but that their impact varies greatly depending on the situation.

The research does, however, provide a few useful conclusions on message comprehension. First, emotion, though helpful at gaining attention for a message, may get in the way of comprehension. This finding suggests that an effective message might include an emotional appeal at the beginning to gain the audience's attention, followed by a more rational, logical presentation (McGuire, 1985).

A second conclusion regarding comprehension suggests that messages providing explicit conclusions are more effective than messages that provide information but allow the receiver to draw his or her own conclusions. Several studies have found that this principle particularly applies to the use of statistical information. Statistics presented without argument or interpretation are less effective at achieving comprehension than those that explain the point the statistics are being used to make (Petty and Cacioppo, 1984; Clark, 1984).

A third conclusion suggests that message repetition has a significant effect on comprehension. While the research is clear on this phenomenon, additional evidence suggests that there is a point of diminishing returns beyond which repetition becomes less and less useful (Staats, 1968). Unfortunately, there is no clear rule of thumb as to when this point is reached. Union leaders should consider repeating important messages, perhaps employing different means of delivery. But they also should be aware that, at some point, the repetition of a message may have little effect on comprehension. One can readily envision a scenario in which message repetition can become unproductive.

The second component that should be taken into account when considering the issue of comprehension is the *receiver*. Some researchers who have studied this issue suggest that sensitivity to the receiver is the key to comprehension. The evidence indicates that a person is more likely to comprehend information in which he or she has an interest or a stake. It also suggests that comprehension is much more likely if information relates to a person's experience (Anderson, 1978; Reardon, 1991).

These insights can be applied to many of the labor movement's efforts to communicate with its members. In the area of politics, for example, unions cannot expect their members to take much of an interest in, or learn a great deal about, issues that do not directly affect them.

As noted in Figure 7.2, the *channel* through which a message is delivered is another factor that contributes to effective comprehension. Perhaps the most critical issue addressed by research in this area is the relative influence of face-to-face communication versus mass media (radio and television) and the written word. The results show a good deal of agreement. Face-to-face communications are more effective at achieving comprehension than are mass media and written forms of communication.

The explanation for this centers on the fact that a receiver's attention is compelled to a much greater degree by a human communicator than it is by radio or television or by a book, a letter, or an electronic message. This is not so much a matter of gaining the receiver's attention as it is of holding it (McGuire, 1985). In addition, face-to-face communication provides an opportunity for feedback, or two-way communication, in which a receiver can seek clarification of the message sent. Such communication also allows the receiver to pick up visual cues (facial expressions, arm gestures) that can enhance comprehension. These findings provide further evidence that initiatives like the AFL-CIO's One-on-One program have a great deal to offer. Finally, written communication becomes an increasingly effective means of achieving comprehension as the complexity of the message increases (Anderson, 1978).

Acceptance

Ultimately, to influence a person's beliefs, a message must gain acceptance. The communications process is cumulative so that, strictly speaking, anything that contributes to attention and comprehension contributes to acceptance.

Acceptance can be influenced by each of the variables of the communications process discussed previously. For example, in deciding whether or not to accept a message, an individual might consider the credibility, the familiarity or attractiveness, and the power of the *source*. Certainly there are situations in which the source becomes an important, if not the main, element in an act of persuasion. Very credible, attractive, or powerful individuals can be highly effective in getting people to change their beliefs.

Some figures in labor's history have had this kind of presence. John L. Lewis is probably the foremost figure in this regard. His forceful, charismatic personality helped win the devotion of his members. Jimmy Hoffa and Walter Reuther also come to mind as leaders with charismatic personalities. This is not to say that the messages these individuals communicated were not important or valid. Rather, it seems apparent that at some point in their careers these leaders developed sufficient credibility, familiarity, and power that their persona had as much, and in some cases, more impact on changing people's beliefs than their message.

Another example of this phenomenon is the effect Ronald Reagan had on American workers in the 1980 and 1984 presidential elections. Despite his arguably pro-business, antiunion policies and philosophy and the active opposition of almost all major unions, Reagan enjoyed significant support from union voters, winning 45 percent and 43 percent of the labor vote in 1980 and 1984 respectively. Although it is difficult to prove, many political observers attribute the acceptance of his message by union members more to his personal charm, wit, and sincerity than to his political agenda. One could argue that the inability of George Bush, a far less charismatic figure, to garner that same support in presidential elections (Bush won only 37 percent of the labor vote in 1988) while running on a similar political platform is evidence of this principle (Sousa, 1993).

Except in unusual situations, like those detailed above, the *message* itself usually plays a very critical role in changing an individual's belief. Some of the message issues mentioned in regard to improving comprehension, such as drawing explicit conclusions and repetition, will also affect acceptance. Research in this area suggests several other acceptance-related issues that should be considered.

The order in which material is presented, for example, has been shown to have an influence on acceptance. It is most effective to present material that will be viewed most positively by the receiver first, the less positive material next, and the least positive material last (Anderson, 1978; McGuire, 1985).

Another question that has been studied is whether a speaker, in trying to win support for one side of an argument, should present the opposite side of the argument as well. The research suggests that it probably is not necessary to present both sides of an issue when communicating with an individual or group that is already generally supportive or is unlikely to encounter the opposition's argument on a regular basis. When the receiver is hostile to one's position or the receiver will be consistently confronted with the other side of the issue, however, it is more effective to address and refute the opposition's position (McGuire, 1964; Zimbardo and Ebbeson, 1970).

This is a finding that union organizers and political activists should consider. For example, if an organizer finds herself in a difficult campaign with a vocal and aggressive employer, ignoring the employer's arguments against union representation would probably put the union at a disadvantage. It is strategically more effective for the union to refute those arguments with well-supported arguments of its own. In some cases, it may even be advantageous for the union to bring up the arguments the employer is likely to make before the employer makes them. By preempting the employer's arguments and refuting them, the union can significantly reduce their impact. Organizers call this technique "inoculation."

A final message-related acceptance issue that should be considered is the finding that negative messages are less likely to gain acceptance than positive messages. These messages can be very effective but should be used with great care. In particular, excessive and unfair labeling can cause a backlash against the message and sympathy for the object of the message (Anderson, 1978). This dynamic may, at least in part, explain the high approval ratings President Bill Clinton enjoyed in the midst of the Whitewater, campaign financing, and sexual misconduct investigations.

To maximize the effectiveness of a communications effort, the relationship between the *receiver* and message acceptance should be considered. Sensitivity to the receiver is as significant for the acceptance step as it is for the attention and comprehension steps. Acceptance, and ultimately the change in belief and behavior that might result from acceptance, is most likely to occur if receivers see the message as being in their self-interest. If receivers perceive the message and the subsequent change as moving them toward something they want, acceptance is more likely.

The interrelationship of the receiver and the source can also influence acceptance. The more the receiver identifies with the source in demographic characteristics, interests, and culture, the greater the chance of acceptance. A source who is considered to be "one of us" will be more likely to gain acceptance than a source who is seen as "different." This perhaps explains research findings that organizing campaigns are much more effective when unions employ rank-and-file organizing committees that are representative of the workforce (Bronfenbrenner, 1997).

Ignoring the potential of this relationship between the receiver and the source can have negative consequences. An example of how problematic a mismatch in this regard can be is found in the efforts of an industrial union to organize the clerical workers at a large state university in the late 1980s. Many employees who were active in that campaign now argue that the union made a serious error when it sent in a male organizer whose work and organizing experience were largely in an industrial/factory situation and who was from an urban/industrial area to organize employees whose work experience was almost exclusively in an office setting and who were from a rural region of the state.

Evidence that the labor movement is becoming more attuned to this behavioral principle can be found in its efforts to recruit women, young people, people of color, and speakers of a second language into their organizing ranks. The primary vehicle for doing so is the AFL-CIO sponsored Organizing Institute, which is working to develop a corps of organizers who better reflect the workers expected to be the target of recruitment efforts in the years ahead.

Language can play a particularly important role in increasing a receiver's identification with the source of a message. Where the organizing effort involves workers who speak English as a second language or who do not speak English at all, unions need organizers who can communicate effectively in the workers' native tongue. The labor movement is currently wrestling with this issue as it increasingly tries to organize workers with Hispanic, Asian, or other backgrounds.

Regional accents and dialects can also increase identification. Generally, the research in this area demonstrates that when a receiver perceives the source of a message as someone who "speaks my language," broadly defined, chances of the message being accepted are improved.

Last, when considering the *channel* component of a message the factors found to increase comprehension will also usually facilitate acceptance. Face-to-face communication, for example, has been singled out as the most effective delivery method for gaining acceptance. Significant research has found this to be particularly true in the organizing process (Hurd, 1989). One-on-one verbal exchanges from a distance (telephone calls) would probably be next in order of effectiveness, followed by the mass media (radio and television) and written communications.

On the basis of research to date, communications experts suggest that delivering a message through more than one channel can improve its persuasiveness. Combining a face-to-face conversation with written materials, for example, reinforces the message through repetition and may allow greater comprehension by providing more in-depth information (Anderson, 1978).

The use of new technology in the delivery of messages should also be consid-

---

THE MEDIUM IS THE MESSAGE

When Khan Tran, an organizer for UFCW Local 428 in San Jose, hosted a radio program on workers' rights over a local Vietnamese radio station, the message reached workers at high-tech Supracor Systems. The workers contacted Tran and asked for help in forming a union. After a tough campaign, the workers—mostly immigrants from Mexico, Bosnia, Vietnam and Samoa—voted to join the union.

Source: AFL-CIO, 1997-98.

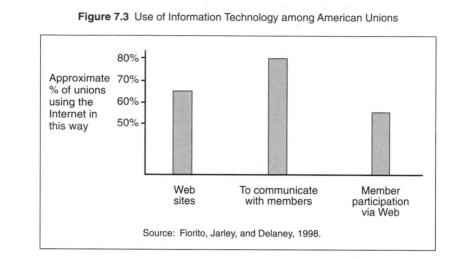

Figure 7.3 Use of Information Technology among American Unions

Approximate % of unions using the Internet in this way

Web sites

To communicate with members

Member participation via Web

Source: Fiorito, Jarley, and Delaney, 1998.

ered. Advances in technology continue to expand the number of delivery mechanisms available. These include electronic mail (e-mail), simultaneous electronic message exchange (chat groups), web-based information delivery, and videoconferencing, among others. These channels have significant potential for rapid information distribution. They can help increase attention, comprehension, and acceptance by tailoring messages and message delivery to the interests of receivers and taking advantage of the benefits of message repetition (Lee, 1996; Shostak, 1999).

A 1999 study commissioned by the AFL-CIO estimated that 57 percent of all unionized workers have home computers (Hart Research Associates, 1999). As Figure 7.3 suggests, the labor movement is beginning to take advantage of this new technology to communicate with its members. Most national and international unions now have web sites where members can obtain a wide range of up-to-date information about the organization, its policies, and its programs. An increasing number of local unions, central labor councils, regional union bodies, and state federations are constructing such sites to give their members rapid access to information.

In addition, an increasing number of unions are using electronic mail to facilitate communications among officers, staff, and members. The United Food and Commercial Workers (UFCW) put the Internet to good use in a 1997 organizing campaign at a Borders Book and Music store in West Des Moines, Iowa. UFCW members organized an e-mail link between the workers in West Des Moines and UFCW members at Chicago's Lincoln Park Borders store, the first Borders store to organize. A longtime Borders employee in West Des Moines noted how helpful this interchange was: "Acting as an organizer for my store, I found it cathartic to talk to people who knew what it was like to go through this union experience" (UFCW, 1997, p. 4).

The UFCW went on to use e-mail in a successful organizing effort at a Borders store in Lower Manhattan. That organizing effort was aided by a "How to Unionize" website set up by a former Borders employee from another city (Mendels, 1999).

Internet technology also played a critical role in the IAM's successful 1998 campaign to organize United Airlines ticket agents and cargo workers. This campaign used e-mail and a constantly updated website to keep nineteen-thousand workers located around the country in touch with their union and each other. This experience should be instructive to groups of workers who desire to organize but are spread across large geographic regions (Lazarovici, 1999).

An organizing drive among engineers at a Pratt and Whitney factory by an independent union raised questions about the right of a union to use an employers' e-mail system to contact workers. In 1997 the Florida Professional Association (FPA) sent messages to Pratt and Whitney's two-thousand engineers at their company e-mail addresses. After the company suspended two employees working with the union for misuse of company property, the union filed unfair labor practices with the NLRB. Two years later the FPA withdrew its unfair labor practices in return for limited use of the company's system. But because the NLRB has not ruled on the issue, the right of unions to use employers' e-mail systems remains unsettled (Cohen, 1999).

Several labor information networks for union activists have also sprung up. These networks allow members who have the necessary computer equipment and a minimal amount of expertise to post questions, inquiries, and opinions that can be read and responded to by members across the United States, Canada, and beyond. News reports have attributed the success of labor's protest against the World Trade Organization in Seattle in late 1999, at least in part, to such electronic networks.

And an increasing number of unions are mounting "cybercampaigns" to get information out about, and mobilize support for, their disputes with employers. Cybercampaigns use websites and e-mail to put pressure on employers by urging supporters to contact company officials, politicians, retailers, stockholders, and the media. In doing so, the labor movement is "transforming the Internet from a tool for information to a weapon of struggle" (Lee, 1999).

The International Federation of Chemical, Energy, Mine, and General Workers (ICEM), a federation of unions from around the world, has pioneered the use of such campaigns in disputes with multinational corporations. One example is a cybercampaign it conducted in 1999 with the U.S.-based United Steelworkers union (USW) in support of a strike in Charlotte, North Carolina, against General Tire. General Tire is owned by Continental AG, a multinational corporation based in Hanover, Germany that manufactures tires worldwide. The ICEM-USW campaign was able to bring together Continental employees and union supporters around the globe in support of the General Tire strike (ICEM-USW, 1999).

In an effort to take advantage of this new opportunity to communicate with its members, the AFL-CIO announced in 1999 that it was creating its own Internet service called Workingfamilies.com. The purpose of this America Online-type service was to make the Internet more affordable for union members, while giving the

AFL-CIO and its member unions a means to inform and mobilize their members. As part of this program, the AFL-CIO is also negotiating with major computer manufacturers such as Dell and Gateway to create a discount program through which union members could purchase computers for as little as $600 (McKay, 1999).

Labor organizations should be aware, however, that while these new technologies facilitate communications among people at a distance, they cannot replicate face-to-face communications. Their ease of use and potentially lower costs should not allow them to replace or reduce opportunities for face-to-face interaction.

To review, unions and union activists can influence members' attitudes by effectively communicating relevant information. Several models of effective communication have been developed based on the behavioral research conducted in this area. These models identify three steps in an effective communication process—attention, comprehension, and acceptance. Each of these steps is influenced by the source of a message, the message itself, the channel communicating the message, and the receiver.

In communicating with members, unions and union leaders should consider the source to be used to deliver a message. The source should have immediate credibility with, and be familiar to, those receiving the message. To be as effective as possible, the message itself should have two dimensions—an emotional dimension and a logical or rational one. The emotional dimension helps to gain the receiver's attention; the rational part promotes comprehension and acceptance of the message. Repetition of a message has also been found to be a part of effective communication. Also, in communicating information, unions and union leaders need to be sensitive to the characteristics and backgrounds of those on the receiving end.

Finally, the channel by which a message is communicated is also important. A two-way channel of communication has been proven to be more effective than a one-way channel, especially if it involves face-to-face contact. Using more than one channel and varying the channel has also been demonstrated to increase communication effectiveness.

The next chapter will focus on labor's image problem and what unions can do to improve the way their members and the public at large perceive them. This is an area in which the principles discussed in this chapter can be put to use.

The case study that follows is an example of a successful union communication program that incorporates many of the principles discussed above. The results were remarkable and, possibly, historic.

CASE STUDY

The "America Needs a Raise" Campaign

Communicating effectively is not an easy task because the factors on which the process depends—the source, message, channel, and receiver—will vary in almost every situation. Labor organizations and their representatives need to be able to adapt and implement the principles of effective communication at the national, regional, local, and individual levels.

The AFL-CIO's "America Needs a Raise" program is a good example of a national-level program designed to change behaviors by identifying and changing individual attitudes. This program had its roots in the congressional election of 1994, when many friends of the labor movement were defeated and Republicans took over both houses of Congress for the first time in many years. After that debacle, the AFL-CIO and many of its member unions made an effort to reconnect with their rank and file by identifying the membership's main concerns and beliefs. Meetings, polls, and focus groups were used to gather information on what these concerns and beliefs were (Kusnet, 1998).

The "America Needs a Raise" program was kicked off in March 1996 at a special convention of the AFL-CIO. At this meeting the AFL-CIO's political and organizing plan for the year ahead was presented. This plan was, in large part, based on the results of the member surveys conducted by the national unions (Byrne and Parks, 1996).

The stated purpose of the campaign was fourfold:

- Build a powerful grassroots movement against cuts in federal, state, and local programs working families depend on and push for a quick and big increase in the federal minimum wage.
- Create a strategic campaign center to give maximum support to 16 million workers and their unions as they attempt to pry long-overdue compensation increases from the tightened fists of multi-billion-dollar corporate giants.
- Persuade employers to practice corporate responsibility for their employees and the communities they serve as well as for their stockholders and executives.
- Energize a nationwide organizing campaign to bring wages and benefits to millions of workers who need and deserve them (AFL-CIO, 1996a).

The convention was followed by a series of town meetings held from March to May that were hosted by the top officers of the AFL-CIO and the national presidents of numerous unions. These meetings provided an opportunity for union activists around the country to learn about the positions and strategies the labor movement was proposing for the upcoming election and to provide feedback to their leadership. It also presented a chance, through the press coverage these meetings received, for labor to get its message out to unrepresented workers who might later want to organize. Held in twenty-six cities, these town meetings were highly publicized events that helped to raise the profile of the "America Needs a Raise" program.

The labor movement's message concerning the 1996 elections was also widely disseminated by a $35 million political education program using radio and television ads (Byrne and Parks, 1996). Some of these ads focused on the need for a raise in the minimum wage, which was subsequently passed in July of that year. In November, President Clinton, the labor-endorsed candidate, won reelection and the Democrats made substantial gains in Congress.

While limited in the strategies it could employ because of the national nature of its campaign and the millions of individuals it was attempting to communicate with inside and outside the labor movement, the "America Needs a Raise" program, when evaluated by the principles discussed above, did many things right. First, it made a systematic effort to identify the beliefs of its audience. It then used these findings to tailor its message to the issues and concerns of its members. The town meetings were used to gain attention for the program and to communicate its message, face to face, to its most active members, while providing an opportunity for two-way communication between the leadership and the rank and file. Finally, the labor movement used the most effective channel available to it to spread its message and explain its positions to the widest possible audience (Kusnet, 1998).

In the end, the program was modestly successful in electing labor's friends and defeating its enemies but very successful at getting members involved and putting the labor movement back on the map as a force to be reckoned with in American politics.

8

Union Image-Building

Key Points

- The labor movement has an image problem.
- This image problem directly influences attitides of members and nonmembers toward unions.
- This image problem, in part, stems from myths and misconceptions about unions.
- Many of the myths and misconceptions concerning unions involve strikes, violence, corruption, and greed.
- All levels of the labor movement must actively challenge these myths and misconceptions in order to improve labor's image.
- Image-building efforts should focus on labor's own members, the community, the news media, and the schools.

Over the last two centuries, the American labor movement has made significant contributions to the economic, social, and political life of this country and its citizens. Unfortunately, labor's story is not widely known beyond its own membership. Often, union members themselves are unaware of the great contributions made by their unions. Even more of a problem than the lack of information are the many misconceptions that abound about unions and their members. In short, the labor movement has an image problem. It is a problem that has implications for all aspects of labor's work, including organizing, bargaining, and political action.

Image is defined as a mental picture, a conception, or an impression that a person has of something. It is, therefore, an integral part of the attitudes that individuals develop toward a person, a place, or an organization. Union members who picture the labor movement in less than positive terms are likely to hold less than positive attitudes toward their specific union and toward unions in general. Members with less than positive attitudes are unlikely to participate actively in their union.

The labor movement has clearly recognized the importance of this image problem. In 1985, the AFL-CIO formed a blue-ribbon panel to study and evaluate the state of the American labor movement. In its report, *The Changing Situation of Workers and Their Unions,* the panel identified labor's public image as an issue of fundamental importance to labor's future (AFL-CIO, 1985b). The leadership of the AFL-CIO elected in 1995 has made changing labor's image an important part of its program to revitalize the American labor movement (Sweeney, 1996).

Chapter 7 focused on general information and communications strategies. This chapter will examine a specific challenge facing the labor movement that can be most effectively met by putting those strategies into practice. That challenge is improving labor's image among union members and the general public.

The chapter will focus on the factors that have shaped this image and that influence members' attitudes. It will conclude with a discussion of strategies for developing a more positive public image that incorporates many of the elements of effective communication previously discussed.

Labor's Image Problem

A great deal of empirical evidence exists to support the contention that labor, as an institution, has an image problem. One example is a periodic Gallup opinion poll that attempts to determine what percentage of the American public "approves" of unions (see Figure 8.1). When the survey was first conducted in 1957, 76 percent of the representative sample of the public indicated they approved of unions. In 1967, this figure dropped to 66 percent. The figure fell further to 59 percent in 1978, and by 1981 only 55 percent stated they approved of unions. Although this figure rose to 58 percent in 1985, labor's public approval rating remains well below the level of past years (Heshizer, 1985; AFL-CIO, 1985a).

Another national Gallup poll conducted periodically asks individuals, "How much confidence do you have in the following institutions?" and provides the fol-

Figure 8.1 Public Approval of American Unions

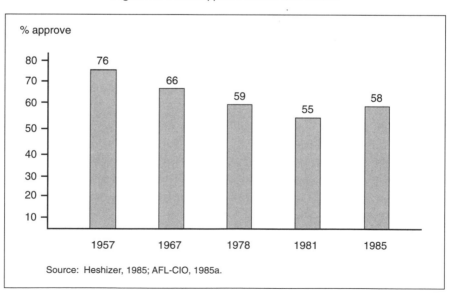

Source: Heshizer, 1985; AFL-CIO, 1985a.

Table 8.1 Confidence In American Institutions

Institution	Percent responding "a great deal" or "quite a lot" Year					
	1975	1979	1983	1987	1991	1993
Military	58	54	53	61	69	76
Organized religion	68	65	62	61	56	63
Public schools	NA	53	39	50	35	39
Banks	NA	60	51	51	30	38
Newspapers	NA	51	38	31	32	31
Organized labor	**38**	**36**	**26**	**26**	**22**	**26**
Big business	40	34	28	NA	18	23
Congress	40	34	28	NA	18	19

NA = not available.
Source: Gallup Poll, 1994, pp. 55–67.

lowing responses: a great deal, quite a lot, some, and very little. As Table 8.1 indicates, only 26 percent indicated that they had a great deal or quite a lot of confidence in organized labor as an institution. Labor placed sixth out of eight institutions, well behind the military, organized religion, public schools, banks, and newspapers and just ahead of big business and Congress. The figure also indicates that the public's confidence in organized labor has fallen significantly since 1975.

Labor's Image: The Role of the Media and Popular Culture

From the labor movement's point of view, at least some, if not a significant portion, of the negativism about unions stems from myths and misconceptions. To develop an effective strategy to improve labor's image, it is important to consider the nature of these misconceptions and the way they are perpetuated.

The discussion of the sources of union members' attitudes in Chapter 2 suggested that, in addition to people's own firsthand experiences, their attitudes are shaped by information they receive from family and peers and from other sources. Because only about 14 percent of the workforce is organized, most people do not have actual firsthand experience with unions. The majority of the public gets their information secondhand.

The major nonfamily/peer sources that disseminate information about unions are the news media (television, radio, newspapers, magazines, and more recently the World Wide Web) and popular culture (chiefly movies and television programs). Even what individuals hear from family and peers may have its origins in these sources. Clearly, the manner in which the media and popular culture depict unions plays a significant role in shaping labor's public image.

Many in the labor movement believe that the news media is a major cause of labor's public image problem. The 1985 Report of the Committee on the Evolution of Work criticized the media's coverage of unions by suggesting that "too often, only the bad news about organized labor gets publicized; successes are ignored, and efforts made by unions to further the interests of workers and the general public go unnoticed" (AFL-CIO, 1985b).

There is evidence to support these charges. A 1979 study found that in the 1950s 34 percent of the space devoted to unions in the two largest-selling American newsmagazines, *Time* and *Newsweek*, was unfavorable (Freeman and Medoff, 1979). During the 1970s the percentage of labor stories that were negative in tone and substance rose to 50 percent. One of the negative issues that the media tends to fixate on in regard to unions is strikes. The results of a 1982 study support the impression that this one issue accounts for a very significant part of the coverage unions receive in the media (Chermish, 1982).

In addition to strikes, a content analysis of media reporting about unions found a heavy emphasis on corruption and violence (Clark, 1989). This study also found that reporting about economic gains tended to portray unions as greedy. Because so many union-related stories focus on strikes, violence, corruption, and greed, labor's image problem is easier to understand.

The news media undoubtedly shapes people's general attitudes about unions, but it is not the only source that influences how people view labor organizations. Popular culture, specifically movies and television programs, also has an impact. Among high school and college-age young people, whose interest in traditional news sources is limited, popular culture's influence may be particularly great (Gallagher, 1999).

Unfortunately, movies and television generally either ignore the role that unions play in American society or they portray unions and union leaders in a negative light. Many, if not most, films that include some reference to unions do so in connection with organized crime, violence, or both. From early films such as *On the Waterfront*, through the *Godfather* and *F.I.S.T.*, up to more recent movies like *Hoffa* and *Casino*, the labor movement is portrayed in an ugly light. There are rare exceptions to this rule (*Norma Rae* for one), but on balance, Hollywood's portrayal of the labor movement has, historically, been less than flattering (Clark, 1989; Puette, 1992).

It can be argued that even popular music has, in a small way, contributed to the declining public image of the labor movement. Whereas a generation ago, young people listened to folk singers such as Peter, Paul, and Mary; Joan Baez; and Bob Dylan sing about social justice issues (e.g., racism, sexism), today's popular music rarely focuses on such substantial issues. As the lyrics to his pop hit *Allentown* suggest, even when a major pop star like Billy Joel writes a song about a social ill such as deindustrialization he suggests that unions are part of the problem, not part of the solution.

Common Myths and Misconceptions about Labor

People's attitudes toward unions, identified throughout this book as critical in shaping union-related behavior, can be greatly influenced by the myths and misconceptions that exist about the labor movement. Any effort by unions to address their image problem and ultimately influence people's attitudes toward unions will need to address these myths and misconceptions.

Union activists at the local level can make a significant contribution by challenging and correcting these myths whenever the opportunity arises. Union members, in their day-to-day contact with other members and the general public, have many opportunities to set the record straight.

To confront these misconceptions effectively, members should consider the elements of effective communication outlined in Chapter 7. At a minimum, members themselves must be equipped with accurate and convincing information when formulating a message. Unions can assist in this process by providing members with information they can use in this role. Identifying the myths and misconceptions about labor and being familiar with possible responses to this misinformation is a useful first step in turning labor's image problem around. The following section identifies some of these myths and suggests responses that can be useful in addressing them.

Strikes

Public Perception

Most people closely associate unions with strikes. Perhaps because of the attention paid to strikes, the public seems to have the impression that unions strike often and that strikes are tremendously disruptive, both in the workplace and in society at large. There also appears to be an impression that strikes are a common part of every union member's experience. And because strikes, particularly long and dramatic strikes involving many members, are given extensive coverage by the news media, many people conclude that strikes are a uniformly negative phenomenon that should be strictly limited or even in some instances (as in the case of government employees) entirely banned.

Response

In fact, strikes are a much less disruptive influence in the workplace than many other factors. Statistics suggest that the common cold, for instance, causes more absences among workers each year than do strikes (UAW, 1986). According to the U.S. Department of Labor, the percent of work time lost because of strikes annually averages less than 1 percent and the number of strikes has been falling consistently. For example, the number of strikes involving one-thousand workers or more fell from fifty-one in 1989 to a record low of twenty-nine in 1997 (Bureau of Labor Statistics, 1999).

In addition, work stoppages are not a common or frequent occurrence in the life of the average union member. Many members never experience a strike during their working careers. While the threat of a strike is necessary as a deterrent, unions employ them only as a last resort.

In response to the argument that strikes should be banned, the case can be made that the right to strike (in essence, the right to withdraw one's labor) is a fundamental human right, no less important than freedom of speech and freedom of the press. In addition, the right to strike is a vital and necessary part of the system of collective bargaining, a process based on the democratic principle that workers should participate in determining the conditions under which they will work. As one union publication puts it:

> Free collective bargaining is the only instrument that workers have to protect and promote their interests in the economic system. Without that ultimate right to withdraw their labor, they would have no strength to bargain, and would have to accept whatever wages and working conditions their employer decided to impose on them.
>
> The only thing workers have to bargain with is their skill or their labor. Denied the right to withhold it as a last resort, they become powerless. The strike is therefore not a breakdown of collective bargaining—it is the indispensable cornerstone of that process. (Canadian Labor Confederation, 1979)

Greed

Public Perception

A second charge often leveled against unions is that they are responsible for excessively high wage levels won at the expense of nonunion workers and the efficient operation of the economy (Freeman and Medoff, 1984). These high wage levels, the argument goes, cause high prices and inflation. The news media sometimes help to fuel this fire by presenting confusing information concerning the wage and benefit levels of unionized workers. For example, news reports sometimes present the total hourly compensation of a worker (hourly wages plus the hourly value of benefits) in a manner that leads people to misinterpret that figure as hourly wages alone.

The difference between union and nonunion wages and benefits also can lead the public to label unions and unionized employees as greedy. The median weekly earnings of full-time unionized wage and salary workers in 1997 were 33 percent higher than those of nonunion workers (AFL-CIO, 1999b). Many people see this difference and assume that union workers really do not earn this higher pay.

Another example sometimes seen in the media is the reporting of bargaining proposals made by unions in negotiations, without noting the context in which these proposals are made. Most people familiar with labor negotiations recognize that proposals made by the parties early in the process tend to be exaggerated. The parties do this, not because they believe there is much chance of achieving those early demands, but to leave themselves room to compromise later in the process. Many people, however, are not familiar with how bargaining works. If a union's early position is made public without being put in the context of bargaining strategy, it can lead people to believe the union is being unreasonable.

Response

There is evidence to suggest that union wage gains are not a significant cause of inflation (Freeman and Medoff, 1984). In fact, for most of the last twenty-five years, wage increases generated by unions have not kept up with the increasing cost of living caused by inflation. Since the early 1970s, when wages, adjusted for inflation, peaked at $13.60, average hourly earnings fell to a low of $11.82 in 1996 (AFL-CIO, 1998a).

And while much of the public is aware that unionized workers are paid higher wages than nonunion workers, most are probably not aware that, on average, union workers are significantly more productive than their nonunion counterparts (Lynch and Black, 1998). The argument can be made that unionized workers have earned the right to move up the economic ladder based on their productivity. Related to this is the old axiom that "you get what you pay for," both in better productivity from higher paid union workers and in higher union pay attracting better qualified individuals to a given job.

Corruption

Public Perception

A third issue often cited as contributing to labor's public image problem, and one that clearly has influenced people's attitudes about unions in general, is the question of union corruption. Stories about union corruption are front-page news. They create images that tend to linger and are reinforced each time new allegations are raised. Sensational accounts of union ties to organized crime leave indelible impressions on people's minds, even if they refer to events that occurred many years ago. These images are kept alive by Hollywood, which, every year or two, dutifully trots out another film with a union–organized crime connection.

Response

Despite the occasional problems experienced by the labor movement, the level of corruption among unions and union leaders is negligible. The Labor-Management

Reporting and Disclosure Act (LMRDA), the federal law that governs the administration of unions, plays a significant role in maintaining the integrity of American labor organizations. LMRDA lays down stringent financial and administrative guidelines under which unions must operate. All labor organizations are required to file detailed financial reports with the Department of Labor each year accounting for all income and expenditures. These reports are available to the public. In addition, the federal government has the authority to monitor union elections and other aspects of union government. Very few institutions in American society are as closely regulated or as subject to scrutiny as are American unions.

In the past, however, there have been instances of corruption and abuse of power in unions. And there continue to be isolated problems of this nature. It should be stressed, however, that these incidents are, and always have been, isolated occurrences. The evidence is clear that all but a minute fraction of American union leaders are honest and dedicated in the performance of their duties. Supporting this conclusion is an investigation by a former U.S. attorney general that found serious problems of corruption in less than one-half of 1 percent of all local unions (UAW, 1986).

In addition, there is a great deal of evidence to suggest that corruption is a much bigger problem in other major institutions in American society, such as corporations, than it is in the labor movement. For example, it has been estimated that the savings and loan scandal of the 1980s alone could end up costing investors and taxpayers up to $1,000 billion (Brummer, 1990), a figure that dwarfs union losses caused by financial impropriety.

Violence

Public Perception

A final issue that arguably has a negative impact on the public's attitudes toward the labor movement involves the perception that unions often engage in violence in an effort to achieve their objectives. Like the above issues, any violence involving unions is bound to find its way on to the evening news or into the morning newspaper. And the images projected, particularly through television, make a lasting impression on those who see them. One televised report of violence on a picket line, whether provoked or unprovoked, makes a more lasting impression on the public than innumerable stories on union community services or successful contract negotiations.

Response

In fact, in the eyes of the Federal Bureau of Investigation, violent crimes involving unions are such an insignificant problem that it does not have a separate statistical category for such occurrences. It also should be pointed out that violent confrontations involving unions are often provoked or instigated by employers or their agents.

Finally, modern unions do not employ physical force or violence as institutional strategies in pursuit of their goals. When violence does occur on a picket line or in some other union-related context, that violence is usually the responsibility of individuals who have made bad decisions. Those individuals, not their unions, should be condemned for their actions.

Summary—Myths and Misconceptions

The above discussion stresses the prevalence of myths and misconceptions involving unions. It also stresses that these myths and misconceptions can have a significant influence on the attitudes toward unions (particularly general attitudes) of both members and potential members. And since the evidence suggests that there is a direct connection between attitudes toward unions, the behaviors that unions want to encourage, and the effectiveness of unions as organizations, this misinformation is an issue that the labor movement must address.

It also suggests some ideas and arguments that might be employed in countering these myths. This discussion touches on only a few of the facts and arguments that activists can use to set the record straight about unions. It does, however, underscore that to address and correct misinformation, union members need to stay well informed. This does not mean that a member must memorize pages of statistics; it does mean, however, that members should become familiar with the functions and services of their union, as well as with the basic facts discussed above.

More and more resources for staying informed about the labor movement are available to union activists. Such resources include periodicals published by unions and union-friendly organizations, books, and union and university labor education programs and courses. Additional sources are being added every day on the World Wide Web. In addition to union websites, less formal labor-related sites are being organized and run by union activists in the United States and elsewhere. Listservs that bring union supporters together via electronic mail to discuss the latest events and exchange ideas and experiences are also becoming widespread.

Changing Labor's Image—Activities at the Local Level

While union members should be well-prepared to counter the myths and misconceptions that circulate about unions, more needs to be done than just reacting to these assaults on their public image. Recognizing this fact, the AFL-CIO has stepped up its efforts to get its message out through television and radio spots. This is a strategy it successfully employed in its 1996 political campaign. Individual national unions are also investing a great deal of money attacking this problem through the use of sophisticated communications strategies and technologies.

While these efforts should have an impact on how the public views unions, to be effective they must be accompanied by efforts by local unions and individual members. As suggested in Chapter 7, a familiar person delivering a message is often able to establish greater credibility with a listener than is a voice in a video or the writer of an article. For this reason, local union activists, through direct day-to-day, one-on-one contact with individuals, may present the greatest opportunity to tell labor's side of the story.

Any effort to improve labor's image at the national, local, or individual level should direct its efforts toward members, the community at large, the news media, and the schools. As was discussed in the previous chapter on communications and information strategies, any effort to convey a message should first carefully consider the audience toward which the message is directed.

Improving Labor's Image within the Union

Most local union activists recognize that many of their own members hold less than positive views of unions and the labor movement. They would also probably agree that this attitude toward unions is at least partly based on the myths and misconceptions described above. Clearly, the most obvious place for union activists to start to create a more positive image of labor is within their own organizations. Such an effort might include the following activities:

- Because attendance at local meetings is traditionally low, local unions might develop strategies to attract more members to these meetings. At the same time, locals must ensure that their meetings, if attended by more members, will make a positive impression. Meetings should be well organized, both in the physical arrangements and the agenda. An effort should be made to keep the meetings at a reasonable length, while ensuring that members have adequate time to participate. Adding guest speakers or films of interest to the program might make the meetings more attractive. Other means to draw members might be considered—refreshments, door prizes, and the like—but these attractions should remain secondary to the business of the meeting.
- To keep members better informed, locals might initiate, or make better use of, local union newsletters.
- Locals might also consider instituting the One-on-One program. Sponsored by the AFL-CIO, this program creates a systematic communications network to inform less active members about the work of the union.
- Social activities like picnics, bowling tournaments, and family outings should be considered as a means to get inactive members, as well as family members, involved in the union.

- Labor education programs are a means of better preparing officers and active members for their union roles; encouraging inactive members to attend these classes provides an opportunity to inform them about the union.
- Locals should take steps to make sure that new members are welcomed into the union and given adequate information about union activities, services, and responsibilities (see Chapter 4).
- Making more materials on unions (books, publications, videos) available for members' use can positively influence members' opinions.

Local unions and activists should not expect these activities to produce immediate or dramatic results. Unrealistic goals such as involving or influencing 100 percent of the membership only set people up for failure. Realistic objectives need to be set. One example might be to increase attendance at union meetings by 10–20 percent over a few months. Once this goal is reached, a new target can be set. Over time these small steps can have a positive and significant effect on how members view the union.

Changing Labor's Image within the Community

Union groups interested in image-building activities should also consider ways to directly, and positively, influence the general public's perception of the labor movement. This is critical for many reasons, including the fact that the general public is the source of future union members; the need for the labor movement sometimes to call on the support of the public in bargaining, strike, or boycott situations; and the idea that a positive public image contributes to labor's political and legislative work. Efforts to influence the general public's perception of labor will also reach union members. Such a program might consider the following ideas:

- The labor movement's contributions to community charities are substantial, yet it often receives little credit for this work. Although labor's participation in these programs stems from a genuine interest in improving community life, that does not mean that labor's efforts should be shrouded in secrecy. When union members participate in the United Way, Red Cross, Boy Scouts, and other groups, the union should make an effort to have that work recognized. Press releases, for example, should be prepared and sent to newspapers and to radio and television stations.
- Unions might also take advantage of more visible community activities that depict them in a positive light. Examples might include participation in parades, fairs, and other community events; sponsorship of youth athletic teams; and charity telethons.
- Labor groups might create awards for their members who make outstanding contributions to the community. This allows the union to recognize deserving individuals and to publicize individuals' contributions through photos and press releases.

Photo by author.

- When the news media have proven uncooperative, unions have, in recent years, attempted to take their message directly to the public through paid advertising in a variety of mediums. Union ads can be placed in virtually any advertising outlet, from local newspapers and radio and television stations, to billboards and message boards on buses.

Changing Labor's Image through the Media and Popular Culture

A third target for labor's image-building efforts is the media and popular culture. For many people, the primary source of information concerning unions is the news media (UAW, 1986). A strong case can be made that the issues on which the media focuses and the way stories are presented contribute to a negative, and often distorted, perception of labor. If the labor movement wants to deal effectively with its image problem, it must address this problem.

At the national level, unions have attempted to deal with this issue by creating public/media relations departments staffed with individuals possessing knowledge and expertise concerning the media and how to deal with them. Media relations, however, is often ignored at the local level. There are several steps that local unions and labor councils might consider to counter, or even improve, the picture the media create of labor:

- Locals and labor councils can form public relations or media relations committees or appoint individuals to coordinate public relations activities in general and to deal with media relations in particular.
- Individuals charged with dealing with the media and officers who have occasion to act as spokespersons for the local or labor council should attend education and training programs designed to prepare them to carry out these responsibilities more effectively. Such programs are available at the George Meany Center for La-

bor Studies, as well as through individual union and university labor education programs.

- Efforts should be made to develop ongoing, positive, and professional relationships with the local news media. Many times contact with the media outside the context of a story is helpful in building mutual trust and respect. A particular effort should be made to get to know reporters who cover labor issues and events. Some local unions have held "Meet the Media Nights" in an effort to develop better relationships with reporters in the community.

- Efforts should also be made to gain a better understanding of the way the media works and the pressures and needs of individual reporters. In many cases reporters need help that a union officer or spokesman can provide. The relationship should be a two-way street.

- Local labor groups should monitor the coverage unions receive from the local media. When that coverage is unfair, biased, distorted, or inaccurate, it should be brought to the attention of both reporters and editors. If these problems continue, local labor organizations should attempt to meet with newspaper, television, or radio station officials to voice their point of view.

- Letters to the editors can be an effective way to respond to distorted or biased reporting. Letter-writing campaigns can be organized and coordinated for greater impact. Paid advertisements can be used when there is no other way of getting labor's position known.

- Cable and public television have been used by some labor groups as vehicles for communicating their message, both to the general public and to union members. Ads, programs, and shows created by local union members can sometimes be aired on these stations.

Many resources are available to help local unions develop expertise in dealing with the media. Local activists should contact their national union or the AFL-CIO communications or education departments for assistance.

Popular culture, in the form of movies, television programs, and music, also influences people's images of the world around them. Unions are no exception. Unfortunately, this may be one of the most difficult areas for union supporters to influence. Still, there are a few possibilities:

- Locals, labor councils, and labor activists can be aware of how unions are being portrayed in public culture. When a movie appears that paints unions in a negative light, union supporters can write letters to the editor pointing out distortions or inaccuracies and providing positive information about labor's role in society.

- Similarly, when movies that paint unions in a more positive light (*Norma Rae* and *Matewan*, for example) appear, efforts should be made to get letters to the editor or op-ed pieces published that draw attention to the films.

- Union activists should be aware of singers and musicians who write and perform music about the issues of importance to unions. Few of these artists achieve great fame (although Bruce Springsteen is one who did). Most need the support of like-minded organizations. Unions at the local and national levels should help sustain and promote these musicians by giving them opportunities to perform at union rallies, social events, picket lines, and other events.

Changing Labor's Image in the Schools

A special opportunity for influencing the public's perception of unions has been recognized by the labor movement in recent years. That opportunity involves getting labor's message into the schools. As most people think back about their experience in elementary and secondary schools, they conclude that little, if any, attention was given to unions, their history, or their role in society.

Yet today's young people are tomorrow's workers and labor's future. Exposing them, at an early age, to the historical contributions unions have made and the valuable role unions can play in their working lives can pay long-term dividends. It is also a potentially effective way to address the distorted image of labor conveyed by popular films and television shows.

Many labor groups have begun programs to get information about the labor movement into the schools. This is particularly appropriate for classes in American history, social studies, and economics at the high school and college levels. The following are some ideas local labor groups might consider:

- Locals or labor councils should identify individuals willing and able to speak to classes about the labor movement. Individuals need not be experienced instructors or public speakers, but they should have a background in, and commitment to, the labor movement; some knowledge of labor history; and good communications skills that will allow them to make a positive impression on young people.
- An effort should be made, when possible, to provide potential speakers with training, both on subjects like labor history and in skills like public speaking. Union education departments or university labor education programs may offer courses specifically designed to prepare individuals for this role.
- In initiating a "labor in the schools" program, a first step is to determine the appropriate person or group to whom to offer the union's services. Often this might be a principal, a curriculum director, or a teacher. In many cases, the local teachers' union might be a good place to start. If a school district is unreceptive to such offers, the local labor community might consider running one of its own activists for a position on the school board.
- In addition to providing speakers, local labor groups can make films, videos, books, and teaching materials available to the schools. For example, donating books on labor to a school library serves a valuable purpose; it also presents a tai-

Courtesy of CWA.

lor-made opportunity for some positive publicity. When making such a presentation, the local group should not miss the opportunity to involve the media.

- Involving elementary students in such programs should also be considered. Although speakers might not be appropriate at that level, there may be other ways to reach these young people. Some unions have produced material appropriate for this age group.

- Many labor groups sponsor essay contests, awarding prizes to students who write the best essay on a topic relevant to the labor movement. Such contests should be open to all students in an appropriate age group, not just to the children of union members.

- Scholarship programs to help defray the costs of a college education are another useful mechanism for increasing labor's visibility in the schools. Selection could be based on academic performance and promise, essay submissions, or random drawing.

- At the college and university level, unions might contact Scholars, Artists, and Writers for Social Justice (SAWSJ). SAWSJ is a coalition that includes many college and university faculty interested in working with the labor movement on social justice issues.

A first step for local unions and teachers interested in "labor in the schools" programs should be to gather material on how to initiate and conduct such a program. Again, the education departments of national unions and the AFL-CIO are a good source of assistance.

Changing Labor's Image in the Home and the Family

Many longtime union members feel that young people growing up in union households today do not appreciate the importance of the labor movement in the same way that the youth of past generations did. Whether or not this is true, behavioral science has established that a person's early experiences in life can significantly influence attitudes held later in life (see Chapter 4). Additional research (also discussed in Chapter 4) has shown that children who are aware of their parents' activism and involvement in unionism are far more likely to hold positive attitudes about unions than children who had no such exposure. Finally, Chapter 7 cited research that found that people whose opinions an individual values highly (family members and peers in particular) also play an important role in shaping people's attitudes.

These findings suggest that one of the first places union members need to build a positive image of unions is in their own home and family. Children who have grown up in union households and have experienced firsthand how unions can improve the lives of workers and their families should enter the workforce with positive attitudes about the labor movement. But in today's fast-paced world, we cannot expect our children to acquire a sense of labor's contributions through osmosis, and we cannot count on the media, popular culture, or the schools to get labor's message out.

Union parents need to convey this message personally to their children, as well as to their spouses and other family members. While labor's past accomplishments are important, special emphasis should be placed on the relevance unions have for today. Here are some ideas for doing this:

- Union members should bring the union home with them. This might involve talking about union activities with one's family, informing them about how the union contract affects their income and benefits, and making union publications available in the home. Special emphasis should be given to the manner in which unions bring fairness, equity, and dignity to the workplace.
- Members should consider making sure that the family library includes some books about the labor movement. Their presence might generate interest among family members or visitors and can also serve as reference material for school reports and projects.

> ### KIDS' NIGHT IN ST. LOUIS
>
> The St. Louis Central Labor Council sponsors Kids' Night in con-junction with one of its monthly meetings. The purpose is to teach members' children "about unionism and its relationship to the work-a-day world." In the course of the evening a variety of union members show the kids what they do every day. Favorite demonstrations included those by the American Federation of Radio and Television Artists (AFTRA) who put on puppet shows and the Hotel Employees and Restaurant Employees (HERE) who dished up ice cream. Also of interest were the Carpenters who built a workbench and the International Brotherhood of Electrical Workers (IBEW) who talked about electric power generation. A presentation by one of the children about the life of a 10 year-old boy who worked in the textile factory in the early 1900s and how unions fought for his right to go to school rather than work, was also part of the program. (AFL-CIO, 1998b)

- Data gathered by the University of Minnesota's Labor Education Service indicate that young people who are aware of their parents' involvement in unions are far more likely to hold positive attitudes about unions (AFL-CIO, 1999c). For this reason, union members and local unions should make an effort to involve family members in union activities.
- In families with a union activist, spouses or children may see the union primarily as an organization that takes their partner or parent away from them for significant periods of time. Including them in union activities allows families to spend more time together and to see what their loved one does when away from the home on union business. It also presents an opportunity for the union to educate family members about the value of unions in our society. Opportunities to involve the family might range from designating a union meeting as family night; to sponsoring social activities like picnics, parades, and holiday parties; to encouraging families to visit picket lines or union rallies.

Throughout this book, the importance of members' attitudes as a primary determinant of behavior has been stressed. Since the labor movement draws its present and future membership from the public, its public image is directly related to members' attitudes. While attempting to build a more positive image with both union members and the public at large is a formidable challenge, there are clearly many opportunities—in the union, the community, the media, and the schools—for unions and union activists to address labor's image problem. There also appears to be reason for the labor movement to be cautiously optimistic concerning its ability to significantly and positively influence the public's perceptions of unions.

This appears to be an opportune time for labor to mount an aggressive image-building campaign. Labor's public approval rating appears to have bottomed out and to be on the rise. Strike levels, always a factor in the negative perception many have of unions, have been declining. And the reasonable settlements that unions have accepted in the recent past tend to negate the image of unions as greedy and irresponsible. Factors such as these, when coupled with the increasingly negative public perception of the business community, suggest that labor's efforts in building a more positive image may bear fruit. Such efforts could help significantly to build more effective unions.

The case that follows is an example of an activity sponsored by one local union that has significant image-building ramifications. Although improving labor's image is probably far down on the list of reasons why this local sponsors the event, this, ultimately, might be the most important outcome of the day's activities.

CASE STUDY

Influencing Attitudes toward the Union:
The Annual Branch 84 Summer Picnic

The National Association of Letter Carriers' Branch 84 in Pittsburgh has an active social program. The highlight of this program is the annual Branch 84 Summer Picnic. Usually held in August in several pavilions at the County Fairgrounds, the picnic is open to all active and retired branch members and their families. There is something for everyone at the picnic, and the planning committee makes a special effort to ensure that children have a memorable day.

On arrival, each child is given a treat bag filled with toys, candy, and snacks. Children then have the opportunity to ride a pony, have their faces painted, watch a magic show, visit with a clown, or bounce around the carnival-style "moonwalk." Later in the day they have the chance to win prizes in the numerous kids' games organized by the branch.

While the children are making the rounds, parents and other adults also have activities from which to choose. They can watch the Branch 84 Softball League Championship game at a nearby field, dance to the music of one of two bands, or participate in one of the numerous games and competitions held for adults. Among the older crowd, bingo and horseshoes are the more popular pastimes.

Virtually all of Branch 84's officers and many regional and national representatives attend. It is not unusual to find the NALC's national president sitting at a picnic table or strolling the grounds talking to members. For some, the gathering of union representatives presents an opportunity to express themselves on the direction of the union or to seek assistance with a work-related problem.

And no one goes home hungry. The branch serves 450 dozen ears of corn; 7,500 hot dogs, kielbasa, and sausage sandwiches; ice cream; watermelon; and popcorn. The food is washed down by gallons of beer, soft drinks, and buttermilk. All of this is paid for with branch funds; there is no separate charge to the membership.

Approximately twenty-five hundred–three-thousand letter carriers and family members attend the Branch 84 picnic each year. It is hard to imagine anyone leaving this event without warm memories of the day. Children, particularly, are likely to remember this event fondly well into adulthood. And though there is no formal union "program," and speeches are kept to a minimum, it is also likely that the association of these happy memories with the union will have a positive impact on the participants' attitudes toward Branch 84 and toward unions in general.

Will these memories have an impact if a child or spouse in attendance is involved in a representation election or goes to work in a unionized workplace somewhere down the road? The research suggests they very well might.

9

Union Culture

Key Points

- Union leaders need to understand the central role that culture plays in an effective organization.
- Unions need to build a strong culture consistent with their values, goals, and objectives.
- Rituals, ceremonies, rites, heroes, myths, stories, symbols, and language are all elements of organizational culture. Union leaders need to be consciously aware of the role these elements of culture play in labor organizations.
- Most efforts to change an organization's culture will meet with some resistance. A systematic approach to change is most effective in overcoming such resistance.

Slogans, songs, logos, hats, jackets, banquets, parades, and picnics are all parts of the American labor movement. To some, they are simply window dressing, unconnected to the important things that build an effective union. In fact, these things are part of a very important and potentially powerful phenomenon called organizational culture. It is important that unions and union leaders understand the central role that culture plays in an effective organization and work to build a strong culture consistent with their values, goals, and objectives.

Most of the preceding chapters have focused on specific areas and activities that provide unions and union leaders with opportunities to influence *individual* members' attitudes and, ultimately, behavior. This chapter will focus on organizational culture, a topic that, by definition, involves the behavior of individuals *and* groups of individuals. Culture is an important part of the fields of anthropology, sociology, and organizational behavior, all fields that study group behavior.

The field of anthropology, which, for many people, brings to mind the study of ancient civilizations or isolated groups living in exotic climes, may seem to have little relevance to the modern American labor organization. However, cultural anthropology, one of the two leading branches of anthropology, is concerned with the study of patterns of behavior, whether that behavior occurs in tribes living in the Amazon River basin or in groups like unions and corporations.

Culture is an important part of every organization. It consists of the unofficial rules, procedures, and beliefs of an organization (Buono, Bowditch, and Lewis, 1985; Wagner and Hollenbeck, 1998). Organizational culture is, in some ways, like background noise; sometimes you notice it, sometimes it just blends in, but it is always there.

Culture, Commitment, and Participation

Culture serves a very important function in groups. It communicates and reinforces the values, priorities, goals, and objectives of the organization among its members and prospective members. In doing so, an organization's culture gives members a sense of organizational identity, togetherness, and purpose that promotes commitment to, and influences attitudes about, the group. In a sense, culture is the glue that binds members to the organization (Wagner and Hollenbeck, 1998).

Throughout this book, commitment has been cited as an important component in the building of effective unions, and factors, activities, and strategies that contribute to increasing commitment have been identified. Some additional research on commitment not previously discussed in this book provides added insight into this important concept. This research suggests that people have different reasons for being committed to an organization.

First, commitment may be rooted in the positive feelings people hold about the mission or purpose of the organization. Individuals value being associated with, or being part of, organizations. Behavioral researchers call this "affective" commitment.

A second reason why people are committed to a group is because they perceive the cost of leaving it as too high. An example might be when a person stays in a job because of accumulated seniority and seniority-related benefits. This type of commitment is called "calculative" or "continuance" commitment.

"Moral" or "normative" commitment is a third type of commitment. In this case, people are committed to the organization because they "feel they should" or they feel that others expect them to be. Commitment related to peer pressure is an example of this type of commitment (Meyer and Allen, 1997).

In sum, this research suggests that people are committed to organizations, to varying degrees, because they want to be, they need to be, or they feel they should be (see Figure 9.1).

Figure 9.1 Individuals are committed because:

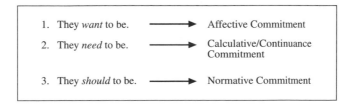

Culture helps to build overall commitment to organizations by building *affective* and *normative* commitment. If a union has a strong positive culture, it will cause people to *want* to be a part of the organization or at least to feel that they *should* be.

Culture also clearly communicates to members the behaviors, including participation, that are accepted or encouraged by the organization. This principle is supported by studies conducted in 1984 and 1986 that focused on resource mobilization theory (Klandermans). These studies found that "participation is inextricably bound up with the group culture, and the individual decision to participate is influenced by the group to which the individual belongs" (Klandermans, 1986, p. 190). They further found that union members' "willingness to participate in collective action appears to be strengthened by the belief that others will participate" (Klandermans, 1984b, p. 591).

Active participation is evidence of a strong organizational culture. In organizations with strong cultures, members will consider the values and expectations of the group when deciding whether to engage or not to engage in a certain behavior (Trice and Beyer, 1993). In organizations with weak cultures, these values and expectations will play less of a role. Whether an organization has a strong or weak culture is important because research has found evidence of a clear link between culture and organizational effectiveness (Deal and Kennedy, 1982). The evidence suggests that if unions are to be effective they need to develop strong cultures that emphasize and reward participation in the work of the union.

Culture and Values

Among organizations with strong cultures are such diverse groups as the U.S. Marine Corps, local bowling teams, and the Boy and Girl Scouts. The commitment and loyalty engendered among individuals who are immersed in the Marine Corps' culture is represented in its mottoes of "Once a Marine, Always a Marine" and "Semper Fi" (short for Semper Fidelis or always faithful). The Marines' many traditions, stories, and heroes are a part of this culture and serve to convey and reinforce the group's basic values.

Although they may exhibit less esprit de corps, bowling teams also engage in behaviors designed to build a sense of group identity, togetherness, and purpose. The team's uniform, rituals and superstitions, and the language the members use to interact with one another are examples of organizational culture at work.

The Boy and Girl Scouts are also examples of organizations with strong cultures. Not only do they have elaborate uniforms and awards that tie members to the group, but they have many rites, rituals, and ceremonies, as well as oaths, creeds, and signs, that create group identity and convey the values of the organizations ("A Scout is trustworthy, loyal, helpful, obedient, etc.").

These groups may also have subcultures within the prevailing culture. For example, officers in the Marine Corps have their own separate subcultures. While they subscribe to the prevailing culture of the group, officers also have distinct rituals and traditions that apply only to them (e.g., only commissioned and noncommissioned officers carry swords on ceremonial occasions). Officers also have codes of conduct that apply solely to them.

The existence of subcultures is normal. In an organization with a strong culture, subcultures do not cause problems because the overall values and beliefs of the group are well recognized and well accepted. If the culture is weak, however, subcultures can override, or compete with, the overall culture, which can be disruptive to the organization (Deal and Kennedy, 1982).

The effectiveness of a culture can be measured by the degree to which that culture and its various elements and subcultures clearly communicate the values of the organization. Unions also have prevailing cultures that underscore their values and norms. Before looking at the way those values are communicated, it is important to identify those values.

One place to look for unions' values is in their constitutions—the governing documents of American unions. Most union constitutions contain preambles or sections that state the objectives and purposes of the union. These statements articulate the basic values of American labor organizations. Common to most union constitutions are terms such as dignity, respect, democracy, social and economic justice, unity, voice, and collective action. These represent the basic values of the labor movement.

One of the core values emphasized by unions is the welfare of the collective group. Toward this end, unions emphasize the principles of solidarity, unity, and togetherness. One common aspect of union culture that helps communicate these values is the use of the terms "brother" and "sister" to refer to other members. Another aspect of union culture that embodies these values is the prohibition on crossing a picket line. The degree to which crossing a picket line violates the values and norms of the labor movement is evident in the fact that this principle is sometimes referred to as labor's "eleventh commandment."

Other values held in high regard by unions are fairness, justice, and equity. Managers often complain about the tendency of unions to challenge, through the grievance procedure, many of the disciplinary actions taken by management. One interpretation is that such challenges simply reflect the value unions and union members place on due process and the fairness it brings to the workplace. Another interpretation is that by challenging any questionable management decision, the union is forcing managers to evaluate the fairness of any action they take, before they take it. Ultimately, if a union is able to create a strong, positive culture, members and managers alike will be more reluctant to engage in actions that are inconsistent with its values.

One might also include member participation as something that is valued by all unions. While this would certainly be the case in a union that operates under the organizing model discussed earlier, it would not necessarily be the case in a service-oriented union.

The Elements of Organizational Culture

An organization's culture is communicated in a variety of ways, including rituals, taboos, rites, and ceremonies (Deal and Kennedy, 1982; Trice and Beyer, 1993). Rituals are the everyday, routine exchanges, gestures, and behaviors that reinforce individuals' connections to the organization or the group. These rituals can be relatively formal in nature (like salutes in the military) or they can be relatively informal (like a handshake, a kiss, or a "high five").

Rituals consist of behaviors that are accepted, and even encouraged, by an organization. Taboos, in contrast, are behaviors that are discouraged or even forbidden. In some organizations, it is well known that facial hair, casual dress, or the use of profanity are considered taboo (swearing in church would be a good example of the latter).

Ceremonies and rites consist of well-accepted group activities. Ceremonies are special events in which the members of an organization celebrate the myths, stories, and heroes of the group. Rites are specific activities that are incorporated in ceremonies. One common example of a ceremony is graduation. Graduations celebrate the accomplishments of group members through a ceremony, part of the purpose of which is to communicate the values of, and build loyalty to, the group. Graduation speeches are one of the main ways of doing this.

Graduation ceremonies also include rites such as the handing out of diplomas, the moving of tassels on the graduate's cap from one side to the other, and the singing of the alma mater. Other examples of ceremonies that include rites are baptism (anointing or immersion in water) and retirement (presentation of a gift).

Heroes, myths, and stories are additional elements of an organization's culture. Anthropologists generally define heroes as people who embody the values of the organization. Within groups heroes serve as role models for the members. Over time, the accomplishments and qualities of a group's heroes may be exaggerated or modified to better fit the values of the group. Our national heroes—Washington, Jefferson, Franklin, Lincoln, Anthony, Roosevelt, Kennedy, King—may or may not have been the absolute paragons of virtue they are sometimes represented to be, but they are effective vehicles for communicating the values of our nation to the next generation of citizens.

Stories and myths are also devices for communicating a group's values and priorities. Stories differ from myths in that the former are more likely to be true than the latter. Sometimes an account lies somewhere between truth and fantasy, story and myth. The stories taught in elementary school about George Washington cutting down the cherry tree, Benjamin Franklin discovering electricity by flying a kite in a storm, and Abraham Lincoln gaining an education by walking great distances each day may or may not be entirely accurate. Whether true or not, they effectively stress the values of honesty, imagination, and perseverance that are important to our culture.

Symbols and language are two other important parts of organizational culture (Trice and Beyer, 1993; Wagner and Hollenbeck, 1998). In the context of culture, symbols are objects or actions that have special meaning and are closely associated with an organization. Some of the most visible symbols in our society represent companies and their products. Golden arches are associated with a fast-food company, mouse ears are synonymous with an entertainment conglomerate, and the "swoosh" is the well-known symbol of a sportswear empire.

Language, whether it be spoken or written, also plays a role in the culture of groups. Like symbols, language can communicate the beliefs and values of organizations. Language, however, is more useful than symbols because it can communicate more complex messages (Trice and Beyer, 1993). Occupational groups sometimes develop their own unique vocabularies that identify individuals as one of their own. Police have such language (for example, "perp" for the perpetrator of a crime and "the house" for the station house or headquarters). Technicians and programmers in the computer industry also have a language of their own. For instance, they sometimes proudly refer to themselves as "geeks," "hackers," and "web jockeys." Using such jargon identifies one as a member of the group.

Songs are a form of language that researchers on organizational culture have tended to overlook. Adding music to words can magnify their power and their ability to motivate people (Van Maanen and Kunda, 1989; Trice and Beyer, 1993). National anthems, military music (e.g. the Marine Corps Hymn), and the famous "fight songs" of well-known universities are examples of emotionally charged music

The Elements of Union Culture

Ally walked into the office lunchroom for her break and sat in the corner by herself. On the opposite side of the room several co-workers were earnestly involved in conversation. She could not help but overhear them as their voices grew louder and louder. John said he wasn't surprised the union had decided not to take Angie's grievance to arbitration. "Our union's a joke," he said. Ling chimed in, "The only thing they do right is collect the dues every month." Jose added, "They have to get that right or they couldn't go on all those vacations they call union business." Ally thought to herself, "It seems around our office 'knocking the union' is everyone's favorite sport." She didn't think the union was so bad and thought about telling them so, but she knew that would just single her out as an oddball. So she kept quiet.

Like any other organization, unions have cultures. Some unions may have strong cultures in which the values of the organization are widely known and accepted. Such organizations are likely to have high levels of member commitment and supportive behavior. Other organizations, like Ally's local union, have weak cultures. In such a situation the union is not valued highly. Behavior supportive of the union (like speaking up on its behalf) is not rewarded, and low levels of commitment are the rule. Unions might also have an "organizing" culture, a "servicing" culture, or a culture encompassing elements of both.

Union culture, like that in any organization, is made up of the several elements of culture described earlier.

Rituals, Taboos, Ceremonies, and Rites

Few people in the labor movement probably give much thought to the rituals of their union, but they exist and have a useful role to play. In the distant past, union members would greet each other with a secret handshake or a password. These rituals were designed to identify fellow members and keep spies out.

One contemporary example of a union ritual is the use of uniformity of dress to give people a sense of group identity and to communicate support for shared values. Unions often issue shirts to members participating in rallies, parades, or demonstrations. This helps to build a sense of solidarity and togetherness among members. In certain bargaining units in the Communications Workers of America (CWA), every member is encouraged to wear the same color shirt on the same day every week during the period the union is bargaining a new contract with the employer. The purpose of this ritual is to build unity among the group and to communicate that unity to management.

The labor movement also has a few well-accepted taboos. Crossing a picket line to serve as a strike replacement is seen as one of the worst behaviors in which a union member can engage. Many unions have clauses in their constitutions forbidding this act. Often, members of a union shun members who violate this taboo.

Ceremonies and rites are also a part of modern American labor organizations. National, state, and regional labor groups periodically hold conventions that are ceremonies of a sort. In these conventions union members gather to review the union's priorities, set its policies, and, in some cases, elect its leaders. But these occasions have a larger purpose. Conventions provide an opportunity for the union to reinforce and communicate its values and goals and to build commitment to, and enthusiasm for, the union. These dynamics occur in many ways.

First, the size of union conventions (often more than a thousand members attend, in some cases several thousand) is impressive, particularly to the less experienced union activist. Union members rarely see as many members gathered in one place as they see at a national convention. Simply being a part of such a large group of committed activists tends to reinforce one's own commitment to the union.

Second, conventions are usually held in relatively impressive settings, usually large convention halls in attractive locations like Las Vegas, New Orleans, and cities in Florida and California. The halls are commonly decorated with large banners and other artwork displaying, among other things, the union's logo and current themes, and there is often a band playing union songs. Throughout the convention, delegates hear speeches by union leaders, politicians, and others praising the work of the union and its members. Conventions are, in short, an occasion when union members are bombarded with positive stimuli about the union. The goal is to generate a personal and collective "feeling" or sense of pride in the organization so that participants leave the convention inspired and energized.

Often conventions include union-related rites. Rites are specific activities that are incorporated into ceremonies. Among the rites that are often part of union conventions are the swearing in of officers, moments of silence to honor recently deceased members, and the presentation of awards to members who have made special contributions to the union.

Conventions are not the only union functions that fall under the heading of ceremonies and at which rites occur. Local union meetings also contain elements of ceremonies and rites, although on a far less elaborate scale. New members are commonly sworn in at these meetings, as are new officers. Recognition is bestowed on deserving members, and collections are often taken up for those in need. Union picnics, dinners, and other social events also have ceremonial dimensions.

Some unions also have additional rites involving members' funerals. The International Association of Fire Fighters (IAFF) and the Fraternal Order of Police (FOP) often provide uniformed honor guards for the funerals of deceased members. Some unions provide a brief union-oriented funeral service for members on request, and others make their logo available for inclusion in the member's death notice. Often these gestures are accompanied by union-provided death benefits that help the bereaved family with funeral and burial expenses. These gestures communicate the message that the union was a part of the deceased's life. They can, in turn, have a positive impact on the attitudes toward the union of surviving family, friends, and members.

Heroes, Stories, and Myths

Union culture is also transmitted by the creation of heroes and the telling of stories and myths (Martin, 1982). Like rituals, taboos, ceremonies, and rites, they serve as mechanisms for communicating and reinforcing the values and priorities of the labor movement.

Unions, like other organizations, have their pantheon of heroes. The Railway Workers' Eugene Debs, the UMW's John L. Lewis and Mother Jones, and the UAW's Walter Reuther would probably be on most lists of labor's heroes.

Courtesy of IBEW.

Stories and myths are also part of the union culture and are often the means by which heroes are brought to life. The story of Lewis punching Big Bill Hutcheson, a rival union president, and then walking out of the 1935 AFL Convention to found the CIO is one example. Crystal Rae Sutton, a North Carolina textile worker who tried to organize her mill in the 1970s, became a widely recognized union hero when her story was recounted in the award-winning film *Norma Rae*.

Unions are egalitarian by nature. It is, therefore, not surprising that they often celebrate their members and their struggles as heroic in nature. Union publications often print stories about the tribulations of their members. Often these stories involve individuals banding together to stand up to unfair and unscrupulous employers.

Characterizing these members and their stories as heroic calls attention to the values of the union. While most people may not readily identify with such larger than life heroes as John L. Lewis, many will feel some kinship to people whose circumstances and abilities seem more similar to their own. Publicizing their success inspires others to do the same.

Symbols and Language

In any organization, symbols and language are also an important part of culture. Most unions and union leaders would probably reject the notion that they should market and advertise the labor movement in the same way that marketing executives promote their products.

Many people are cynical about marketers because they believe they are trying to sell substandard products or they are trying to sell products people do not need. Neither of these concerns applies to the labor movement. People who believe that unions play an important, valuable, and necessary role in society should have no compunction about using various means to accurately convey labor's message to the broadest possible audience. This audience might be the current membership of the union, prospective members, or the public at large (which would include current and prospective members).

Part of gaining recognition for an organization is having one or more unique and attractive symbols that people readily associate with the group. In most organizations this will take the form of a logo or emblem. Virtually all unions have such a symbol. In some unions, the emblem represents the occupation or industry in which the members are involved (see the UMW and IBEW logos illustrated below). Other union emblems convey one or more of the basic values of the organization. The AFL-CIO's logo communicates several values. The image of the shaking hands suggests the solidarity and brotherhood central to collective action. In some versions of this emblem one hand is white and the other black, which communicates the principle of racial equality. The hands could also represent the merger of the two groups that joined to form the federation, the AFL and the CIO.

Some unions have adopted colors. AFSCME's colors are green and white, CWA's are purple and gold, and UFCW's are blue and white. When one of these unions holds a rally, participates in a demonstration, or marches in a parade, the members often dress in the union's colors. This clearly identifies one with the group and heightens the sense of solidarity and togetherness felt by the union's members.

An imaginative and creative example of the use of color schemes to build solidarity was the UMW's use of camouflage clothing ("camo" for short) during the Pittston strike of 1989 and 1990. The Pittston strike took place in rural southwest Virginia. As in many rural areas where hunting is a way of life, camouflage clothing (clothing in varying patterns of greens and browns, usually associated with the military) is popular. The UMW adopted camouflage clothing as the symbol of its struggle with the company. UMW members, their families, and the many people who came to support the strikers all donned camo. This served as a means of identifying supporters and helped to build camaraderie among the strikers. Following the successful conclusion of the strike, camo was adopted by the UMW and other unions as a symbol of solidarity and militance.

The use of symbols to strengthen the culture of a union is not limited to logos,

Courtesy of IBEW, AFL-CIO, UAW, and UMW.

emblems, and colors. One of the most common symbols associated with the labor movement is the picket sign. Picket signs communicate one of the fundamental values shared throughout the labor movement—"thou shalt not cross a picket line, anytime, anywhere." This symbol is so strong in some unions that all it takes to shut down a workplace is for someone to prop a picket sign at the entrance; the sign need not be accompanied by an actual person.

The more visible such symbols are, the more impact they can have. There are good reasons behind the efforts of some unions to affix their name and logo to everything from coffee mugs, ball caps, and T-shirts to letter openers, watches, and golf balls. Raising the union's visibility in this way is one means of strengthening and extending its culture (and its values, priorities, and objectives).

Unions can also enhance their visibility by using language. A union's emblem can cause people to think, if only for a second, about the organization. Adding language can add a message to that brief moment of recognition.

Most unions have developed mottoes or slogans that communicate the values of the organization. "Union YES!", for example, is the primary motto or slogan of the AFL-CIO. It communicates the fundamental importance the labor movement places on organizing.

Often unions will employ several mottoes, some for general use and some for use with specific events or programs. For instance, the Service Employees International Union (SEIU) uses the slogan "Leading the Way" for general purposes but has developed specific slogans for different organizing campaigns. "Justice for Janitors" is a widely recognized slogan that was used in SEIU's efforts to organize janitors in major cities in the early 1990s. "Dignity, Rights, and Respect" is a slogan SEIU has developed for its campaign to organize nursing home workers. The latter slogan is a very clear and powerful representation of the values of the union. The more SEIU is able to get that brief message in front of nursing home workers and the more the union becomes associated with those words, the greater its chances of bringing those workers into the union.

Other unions have developed mottoes or slogans that associate the union with an industry or a type of work. For example, CWA uses the slogan "The Union for the Information Age"; the NALC uses "Delivering for America"; and AFSCME uses "In the Public Service."

The use of acronyms is a variation on the theme of mottoes and slogans. The American Federation of Government Employees (AFGE) has built its campaign against the privatization of government services around the acronym SWAMP (*Stop Wasting America's Money on Privatization*). It has developed a colorful logo that can be used on everything from bumper stickers to T-shirts. The SWAMP campaign has garnered significant publicity for AFGE's battle against privatization and has helped generate enthusiasm and support for the campaign among members (AFGE, 1999).

The Association of Flight Attendants (AFA) has also adopted an acronym to describe its strategy of calling surprise job actions at airlines with which it is bargaining. CHAOS stands for *Create Havoc Around Our System*. The strategy has proven to be an effective weapon against recalcitrant employers, and the acronym quickly became a part of the AFA's organizational culture (AFA 1999).

Songs can be an important part of a group's culture because they are able to magnify the power of the written or spoken word. Songs have long been a part of the culture of the labor movement. Most people are familiar with labor's anthem,

Art by Mike Konopacki. Used with the permission of AFGE.

"Solidarity Forever," but there are many other labor songs that often are heard on picket lines and at rallies and benefits in support of workers on strike. Among these songs are "We Shall Not Be Moved," "Which Side Are You On," and "Roll the Union On."

There is one additional way in which language is tied to the concept of organizational culture. Groups sometimes develop their own unique vocabularies that are used to identify individuals as members of that group, to build camaraderie within the group, and to allow members to communicate more effectively and efficiently. In the American labor movement, fellow members are often referred to as brothers or sisters, strikebreakers are often labeled "scabs," and non-dues-payers are called "free riders." Such language can be a general indicator of the strength and pervasiveness of a union's culture, because it tends to be more prevalent in a setting where a union is a strong, accepted, and integral part of the lives of its members.

Emblems, slogans, songs, and other efforts to raise the visibility of a labor organization and to get members to identify with the group can play a positive role in shaping people's attitudes toward unions. And it has been argued throughout this book that attitudes lead to behavior and that fostering the right behavior can increase a union's effectiveness. By themselves, however, these elements of organizational culture can have only a limited impact. Once a union gets its name in front of people, it has an opportunity to begin a relationship. To generate the commitment that will lead to significant involvement and participation in the work of the union, the union will need to show much more than an eye-catching emblem or a clever slogan. Still, these symbols make a contribution.

Assessing Union Culture

This chapter argues that for a union to be as effective as possible it must have a culture that is consistent with, and helps promote, the values and goals of the organization. It is useful for union leaders to be familiar with the role that culture plays in their group, whether it be at the local, regional, or national level.

In addition, union leaders need to be able to evaluate their union's culture and decide whether that culture is consistent with the union's mission. If the present culture is consistent with the objectives of the union, the union needs to work to keep that culture alive and vital. If the goals and values of the union have changed over time, the union needs to change the prevailing culture within the group. Doing nothing is not an alternative for unions that want to maximize their effectiveness.

The initial step in making the decision whether to maintain or change the union's culture is to assess the present culture of the organization as accurately as possible. This assessment is sometimes referred to as an "audit" (different from the financial kind). Although such audits are usually initiated, formally or informally, by the union's leadership, leaders should consider that they themselves may not be in the best position to conduct such an assessment. This may be the case for two reasons.

First, leaders may not be sufficiently detached to be able to analyze the prevailing culture in their organization objectively. Second, while union leaders are, in many ways, organizational experts regarding their own group, they may not have a broad understanding of the role of culture and its various elements in organizations (Trice and Beyer, 1993). For this reason, union leaders should consider employing outside help, when feasible, to assist them with auditing the culture of their organization.

People within an organization can gather much of the information necessary for such an assessment. One place to start is with the elements of culture discussed earlier in this chapter. Identifying these elements—rituals, rites, ceremonies, heroes, myths, stories, symbols, and language—can tell much about the intensity and the nature of the culture. In addition, leaders might consider holding meetings to hear what members have on their minds. Some unions call these exchanges "rap sessions" and hold them on a regular basis. These sessions can either be focused on a single workplace or union-related issue or they can be open forums.

The series of town meetings the AFL-CIO leadership has held around the country in the years since the election of the Sweeney administration is just such an initiative. These meetings are, in essence, efforts by the federation's leadership both to assess the present culture of the labor movement and to try to reshape that culture (Kusnet, 1998).

Unions might also consider employing more systematic means of gaining insight into their organization's culture. Surveys are a useful means of gathering information about members' attitudes. Questions can be posed to members either through written questionnaires or oral interviews. This is one area in which the employment of outside consultants or university-based researchers familiar with the labor movement might be helpful. Not only would these individuals have expertise in the construction and implementation of surveys and the analysis of their results, but members might be more willing to discuss their opinions frankly with such neutral outsiders.

Having gathered relevant information about the culture in the organization, as well as about the attitudes and behaviors of members, unions should compare the values and beliefs expressed by the membership with the stated values, goals, and objectives of the union. If the two are generally the same, the union probably has an appropriate culture already in place. In this situation, the union might consider devoting resources to strengthening this culture.

However, if the union senses that the values and beliefs of the membership differ from the values, goals, and objectives of the organization, perhaps the culture in the group needs to be changed. Also, if the union's leadership believes that the organization needs to go in new directions, it will need to consider changing the culture to make it consistent with that new direction.

Changing Organizational Culture

One of the most consistent findings of research on organizational change is that such change will meet with resistance. This resistance is motivated by different factors. One of the most significant is fear of the unknown. People are both afraid to try something new and to give up that with which they are comfortable. People also are afraid that changes to cultures may threaten their self-interest. People receive a wide variety of economic benefits (wages, pensions, bonuses, vacations), as well as psychological benefits (prestige, recognition, respect, power) that they tie to a given organization's culture. Those receiving the most benefits will likely be most resistant to change.

Change also produces anxiety. By its very nature, change destabilizes an organization and creates uncertainty about the future. If nothing else, change forces people to abandon old habits that help people feel secure.

Finally, change threatens the interpersonal relationships that have developed within an organization. Friendship, loyalty, or even familiarity could lead people to resist any changes that threaten these established relationships (Trice and Beyer, 1993).

Unions, like any other organization, need to be aware of, and prepared for, this resistance. At a national level, the rejection of the proposed NEA-AFT merger by NEA convention delegates in 1998 and the inability of the UAW and USW to consummate a proposed merger with the IAM in the late 1990s are two situations in which members' concerns about changes to their union's cultures appeared to be partly responsible for blocking change (Clark and Gray, 2000).

Another lesson researchers studying change have learned is that any effort to introduce a new culture should include efforts to maintain valued parts of the old culture. This provides some continuity between the old and the new and reduces resistance to the change (Wilkins, 1989; Trice and Beyer, 1993). For example, a new local president elected on a reform platform might decide that sweeping change is the way to move the union in a new direction. The new president might replace all appointed union officers and stewards, move the site of the union office, change the night on which the local meeting is held, revamp the local newsletter, and institute a new procedure for handling grievances. Such change, however, is likely to be disorienting to even the new president's supporters and counterproductive to efforts to bring about positive change.

This does not mean that leaders desiring to change their organizations should approach the process passively. Research has found that strong leadership is a necessary ingredient for successful organizational change. Leaders who desire to change their group's culture need to sell their vision to the membership confidently and aggressively (Trice and Beyer, 1991). In essence, leaders need to adopt a "transformational" approach to leadership. This type of leadership will be addressed in the next chapter.

The implementation of cultural change has been characterized as having three steps. The first step involves providing members with information about the changes. The second step is gaining members' acceptance for the changes. And the third step is actually implementing the change. Moving to the implementation step without informing and gaining the acceptance of group members is a common error that often leads to the failure of the change effort (Beyer and Trice, 1978). This suggests that unions should approach any significant change effort in a systematic and measured way. Leaders must first lay the groundwork by providing members with information about why the change is necessary and how it will occur. If effectively done, this should move members toward acceptance of the planned change.

Very few successful efforts to change an organization's culture occur quickly (Deal and Kennedy, 1982). Over time, one of the areas that should be included in any change process is the socialization of new members. Many of the resistance issues that must be overcome in order to implement change (vested self-interest, habits, interpersonal relationships) are not concerns of new members coming into the organization. New members are likely to be more open to new values and ideas than are established members.

One final point that researchers who study culture change in organizations emphasize is the need to change the elements of culture in the targeted organization. The previous discussion of rituals, ceremonies, rites, heroes, myths, stories, symbols, and language suggests how important these things are in building or changing a culture. Leaders should consciously consider which of these elements might most effectively communicate the values of the new culture the union wants to encourage.

All of this suggests that changing an organization's culture in a significant way is not an easy undertaking. It can be a painful, disruptive, and costly process. And there are no guarantees of success. But ultimately, when confronted with a changing environment, organizations must change. Clearly, an informed and systematic approach to change offers the best chance of success.

A promising strategy for shaping union culture is being explored in the San Francisco Bay area by the Project for Labor Renewal. This project is discussed in the case study at the end of this chapter.

Three Potential Areas for Change

Some unions in the American labor movement have been attempting to move in new directions in recent years. In moving in these new directions these unions have undoubtedly had to address the problems that arise when a group engages in new programs or strategies that are not consistent with a well-entrenched organizational culture.

Three examples of fundamental changes that many unions have pursued or experienced in recent years are the increased emphasis unions have been placing on organizing, the cooperative and participative programs that more and more unions have engaged in with management, and the increasing diversity many unions have seen within their membership.

New Emphasis on Organizing

As discussed in Chapter 3, much of the American labor movement has committed itself in recent years to making the organizing of new members a top priority. This is a significant change for many unions as, in the past, taking care of the present union's membership (servicing, in the language of the labor movement) greatly overshadowed many unions' commitment to bringing in new members. Given the numerous obstacles unions face in the organizing arena, many in the labor movement argue that unions must be prepared to commit themselves 100 percent to the task of organizing new members. This suggests that for labor to succeed, organizing must be an integral part of its culture.

In many unions, this is currently not the case. While most union members probably see organizing as a positive thing, to many it is not a priority or an issue of direct, personal interest. Richard Trumka, currently secretary-treasurer of the AFL-CIO, pointed to the need to change this situation when, in 1995, as president of the UMW, he appointed a special commission to examine the future of his union:

> In the 1930s and '40s, every UMW member really was an organizer. Then, organizing wasn't a job reserved for union officers and staff. It was a mission that every member took seriously, and the entire organization was focused on the task of bringing new members into the UMW. To successfully organize the next generation of workers, our union has to regain that focus and find new ways to involve rank-and-file members in the process (UMW Journal, 1995, p. 7).

In moving toward an organizing culture, members need to be convinced that bringing in new members affects them in significant and positive ways. Because many unions have seen their memberships diminish over the last twenty years, it is clear that without a growing, or at least stable, membership, unions cannot maintain their bargaining or political power. With the percentage of the workforce organized falling from 25 percent in 1956 to 21 percent in 1980 to 14 percent in 1999, the lower wages in the increasingly larger non-union sector have exerted downward pressure on union wages (Gifford, 1999; Bureau of Labor Statistics, 2000). This is a message all union members need to hear.

Some unions have made conscious efforts to develop an organizing culture. These unions make organizing a part of every union activity. At ceremonial occasions such as meetings and conventions, successful organizing campaigns and successful organizers are recognized. These occasions assume the status of rites. Organizing stories and myths start to develop as successful organizers are raised to the status of heroes. These things help make organizing an integral part of a union's culture.

Cooperative versus Adversarial Relationships

The changing nature of unions' relationships with employers is another area of significant change in the labor movement. For most of their history, American unions and employers have seen each other as enemies. The relationships that have developed have been based on the belief that employers and managers have significantly different values and priorities than unions and employees. In their day-to-day dealings in the workplace and in their periodic meetings at the collective bargaining table, each side has often viewed the other with distrust and suspicion. This attitude is reflected in the culture of most unions, as when managers are referred to pejoratively as "bosses" or "suits." This adversarialism creates bonds among members by identifying a common enemy and fortifies the membership for when the union and the employer enter into open conflict during a strike.

This culture, however, created problems as unions began to enter into cooperative programs in the 1980s and 1990s. Increasingly, some union leaders and management officials began talking about common interests and shared values. Instead of the enemy, the employer increasingly became a partner. Unions began signaling to their members that the employer could be trusted. All of this, of course, was in conflict with the prevailing union culture, which often said exactly the opposite (Parker and Slaughter, 1994).

In unions where this culture was strong, members openly resisted this change in the relationship. Some union leaders, while endorsing the exploration of a cooperative relationship with the employer, simultaneously argued that the strong, adversarial culture had to stay in place to keep the employer honest. Not surprisingly, members were confused by these conflicting signals. This suggests the need for a union's culture and its actions to be consistent. It also suggests that if a union desires to make significant changes in policy and strategy, it must make sure that the organization's culture changes as well.

Increasing the Diversity of Union Membership

Another area in which unions have experienced fundamental changes that need to be reflected in the culture of the organization is in the composition of their membership. Women and people of color are becoming a more and more significant part of the American labor movement. In 1986, 34 percent of American union members were women and 21 percent were African American or Hispanic American (Gifford, 1988). In 1998 women made up 39 percent and African Americans and Hispanic Americans made up 24 percent of union members (see Figure 9.2)

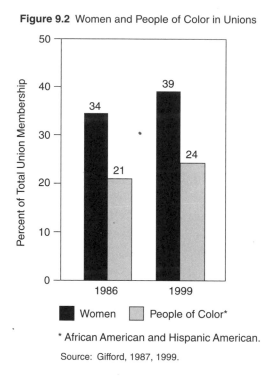

Figure 9.2 Women and People of Color in Unions

* African American and Hispanic American.

Source: Gifford, 1987, 1999.

(Gifford, 1999). These numbers are expected to increase in the years ahead as the labor movement has specifically targeted its organizing efforts toward sectors of the workforce in which these groups have a significant presence.

As women and people of color become a larger part of the American labor movement, union culture is changing. The culture of unions in the past has been shaped largely by white males for white males. The rituals and rites, the heroes and stories, and the symbols and language have reflected this situation.[1] Increasingly, however, women and people of color are assuming the role of heroes and becoming the focus of stories and myths.

We have also seen changes in language. The term "sister" is becoming almost as commonplace as "brother." Some unions have had discussions concerning the appropriateness of the term "brotherhood" in their name (although none have as yet made a change). Increasingly, unions are communicating in Spanish as well as English. Phrases such as "sí, se puede" (translation: yes, we can) are becoming part of the mainstream labor vocabulary. Several unions now include a Spanish-language section in their national magazine or newsletter, and some unions incorporate diversity into their mottoes, as in the case of the UFCW, which uses the slogan "Many Faces, One Union."

1. Most of the heroes in labor's history are white males (e.g., John L. Lewis, Philip Murray, Walter Reuther, Eugene Debs, Big Bill Haywood, Joe Hill). Two exceptions are Mother Jones and Cesar Chavez. Union songs (with some exceptions) also tend to be oriented toward the masculine.

Although the labor movement is changing in the face of growing diversity, for some the change is not happening quickly enough. At least one observer has commented that these changes are occurring at a "snail's pace" (Baden, 1986). During the 1950s and the 1960s, the proportion of women holding top leadership positions in the labor movement was less than 5 percent. In the 1970s, the proportion increased to 11 percent, a level that remained unchanged through 1994 (Gray, 1994). While Linda Chavez-Thompson's election as executive vice-president of the AFL-CIO is significant, clearly there is a need for more women at the top at a time when women make up more than 40 percent of the membership of the labor movement (Gifford, 1998).

This situation is unlikely to change until more women become active and gain leadership experience as union staffers and local leaders. Fortunately, change is occuring in the ranks of union staff. Between the 1970s and the 1980s, the number of women on union staffs doubled, with women holding more than 30 percent of such positions (Gray, 1994).

The greatest change, however, appears to be occurring at the local level. In 1994, AFSCME, AFT, and NEA reported that approximately one-half of their current local union officers were female. The percentage for CWA was 35 percent, and for SEIU it was 40 percent (Gray, 1994). Significant numbers of women seem to be gaining experience at the local level that will prepare them for leadership positions at higher levels, at least in some major American unions.

Nevertheless, women who want to climb from local leadership positions to positions at the top of their unions must overcome barriers, including child-rearing and other homemaking responsibilities, occupational stereotyping based on gender, and male bonding activities that exclude women (Cook, 1968; Needleman and Tanner, 1987; Fellner, 1990). These barriers are part of a union's culture that needs to be systematically identified and changed.

The American labor movement also suffers from a dearth of people of color in top leadership positions (Yates, 1998). With some exceptions (e.g. Linda Chavez-Thompson, Arturo Rodriguez of the United Farm Workers, and Gene Upshaw of the National Football League Players Association), few people of color serve in their union's top leadership positions.

Union leaders may not use the term "culture" regularly, but many instinctively recognize the need to create an organizational environment in which the values, goals, and objectives of the group are promoted and supported. Unions and their leaders can more effectively create such environments if they explicitly recognize the roles that rituals, rites, ceremonies, taboos, heroes, stories, myths, symbols, and language play in their organization. By recognizing these elements, union leaders can monitor their organizations and intervene when necessary to strengthen or change the group's culture. In doing so, they are taking an important step toward building more effective unions.

The case study that follows describes an ambitious effort to fundamentally change the culture of the labor movement in the San Francisco Bay area. Although the project is still in its early stages, it represents one of the most systematic and thoughtful plans undertaken at the local level to revitalize the labor movement.

CASE STUDY

Mission Statement of the Project for Labor Renewal: A Strategy for Changing Union Culture

The general mission of the Project for Labor Renewal is the revitalization of the labor movement. The specific task undertaken by the Project is helping union locals in the San Francisco Bay area to renew their internal life, build their power in the economic and political environment in which they operate, organize unorganized workers, and reconnect with their natural and potential allies in the communities in which their members work and live. The Project seeks to bring unions back into the lives of their members and members back into the lives of their unions.

Renewal of the life of locals is especially important for the organization of unorganized workers. The labor movement simply cannot reach significant numbers of unorganized workers without the substantial involvement of present members of unions. Members for whom their union has become a source of power to affect the quality of their lives and in which they willingly invest their time and energy will become the most enthusiastic and convincing missionaries for unionism within their own families, among their friends, and with unorganized workers generally.

Involved workers will see their self-interest in organizing the unorganized. They will share the vision of a more just society unionized workers can have. They will contribute to society as a whole when there is a strong labor movement. The organizing challenge can be taken up by a large number of union members when unionism has become a deeply meaningful element of their lives as workers.

The Problem and the Challenge

The challenges unions confront, the demands placed upon them, and the expectations they must meet are growing daily. The path to change is often blocked by attitudes and practices that are deeply embedded in their organization's culture and traditional ways of working. The majority of union members continue to look upon their unions as a service provider (some combination of lawyer, social worker, and insurance agent) to which they pay dues with the expectation that the union (something they identify as separate from themselves) will take care of their problems for them.

More recently, some union leaders have also donned the mantle of organizer and mobilizer, but almost always with the intent of activating members around already determined programs, priorities, and activities. In one-on-one conversations with project staff, most of these leaders admit that, with the exception of occasional short-term activities (such as rallies, phone banks, voter registration and education drives, or contract ratifications), the majority of their members continue to be consumers of union services rather than co-creators of union power. The union continues to be identified as a workplace-based contract negotiator and administrator rather than a central institution in the lives of its members—an expression of who they are in the world, a vehicle through which they actively participate in their communities, an instrument through which they exercise power in their own interests and those of their co-workers, families, and communities.

The Solution—A Process of Transformation

The Project for Labor Renewal seeks to recruit a diverse group of local unions in the Bay area to engage in a process of internal renewal that draws an ever-wider circle of members into the life of the union. It is not just another program to implement; it is a process of internal change designed to transform the relationship between the members and their union and between the union and its environment. It will affect how the union approaches everything that it does.

The project begins with a conversation with the principal officer of a local, who, if interested, arranges for similar discussions with other important leaders in the local. If they show interest, the principal officer then convenes a meeting of all those who met with project staff. If there is a consensus to take the next step, these core leaders attend a day-long workshop with those from other locals to prepare them to take the conversation to their members in one-on-one discussions.

These conversations explore the challenges members confront, the pressures they are under, the frustrations they experience, and their aspirations and expectations for themselves, their family, their community, for their local union, and the labor movement. It becomes a conversation about what they want their union to be and what they are willing to do to make it be that. It is also a conversation about the union as the most accessible, reliable, and effective source of power for them, their co-workers, and their families in addressing the myriad of problems they confront—in the workplace, in the community, and in society.

This process leads to the convening of a membership meeting or open executive board meeting of all those who have been drawn into the conversation at which members make the formal decision whether the local should participate in the project during the Action Phase. As this process unfolds in each local, the leaders meet together throughout a year of periodic workshops, reflection, strategic analysis, and planning, training and education, and evaluation which constitute the Action Phase, which begins with an intensive three-day workshop/retreat.

Within each local, the Action Phase will feature campaigns around issues identified by the members during the one-on-one visits that are designed to draw members into action by giving them "ownership" of the campaign itself. Further, the one-on-one conversations engage members in a broader discussion of the relationship between their deeply held democratic values and their union as a vehicle through which these values can be realized. Over the course of time, as the locals proceed step by step, as the process reaches deeper into the union and begins to permeate everything that the union does, these unions should experience a qualitative change in how their members relate to and identify with their unions.

Rather than "What are you (meaning union officials) going to do about————?", members will increasingly say, "What are we going do to about————?" The union will become more than "Contracts-R-Us" or a distant dues collector. It will become an integral part of the lives of its members on the job, in the community, and in society generally.

Present Status

The Project for Labor Renewal is presently in the final stage of the Exploratory Phase, during which it seeks to identify those locals that will make the official decision to participate. The project has garnered the support of a number of Bay area central labor council and building trades council leaders, as well as that of Bill Fletcher, education director of the AFL-CIO and a number of regional and national officials of federation affiliates.

As of January 1999, project staff have met with principal officers of more than fifty-five Bay area locals. More than twenty principal officers have indicated a positive interest. Thirteen have moved beyond the initial step to set up visits for project staff with their core leaders. Eleven sent core leaders to a day-long workshop. Ten are ready to begin visiting the natural leaders among their members, whose support for involvement in the project is key. The aggregate membership of these locals represents a cross section of Bay area industry sectors, occupations, ethnic and gender groups, and income levels. It reflects the diversity of the labor movement itself. Among these members are public employees, transit workers, school bus drivers, construction trades, janitors, clerical workers, college professors, professional and technical employees, and home health care workers. Their incomes range from the "working poor" to over $100,000 a year.

Project Sponsor and Funders

The Project for Labor Renewal is affiliated with Organize Training Center. The center has twenty-five years of experience with civic associations, religious, senior, tenant, labor, small business, merchant, and other grassroots organizations in developing ways to remove barriers to participation on the part of their members, deepening member commitment to their organization, and making the organization a powerful voice for democratic values and for the particular interests of its members. The current project staff bring more than one-hundred years of combined organizing experience to their work.

During this exploratory phase, the project is funded by grants from the following foundations: Ford, Rockefeller, Veatch, Vanguard, and Nu Lambda Trust, and by other individual donors. There was no cost to locals now exploring possible participation in the project. During the next phase, participating local unions will be expected to share substantially in the costs of the project. Project staff are engaged in raising additional funding from foundations to meet its budget for the Action Phase.

Update

Since the above was written, the Project for Labor Renewal has moved forward into the Action Phase with two local unions in an effort to help them shift the way they do their work so that a larger number of members become engaged in the life of the union. With a local of school bus drivers in San Francisco, the project introduced a new way of negotiating contracts which involved a large majority of its members by focusing on the problems they identified and their impact on the lives of the members and their families. Bargaining sessions throughout the summer drew as many as 110 members. Members drew upon their relationships in the community to build support for their demand that management address the problems they identified. The campaign resulted in breakthroughs on guaranteed minimum hours, pay parity for office and support personnel, retention of full cost-of-living protection, and other improvements.

The project also assisted a clerical and professional workers' local to rebuild internal organization and leadership in several large bargaining units that will be in negotiations next year [2000]. Where previously only one or two members were active, the project has helped get many more members involved. In one open shop unit, a dozen new members were signed up within the first few months after the project was introduced. Union staff and leadership who had been consumed with grievances and negotiations (there are 170 contracts) have begun to shift how they do their own work to focus more on strategic goals and new organizing. Members now assume more responsibility for how the union operates where they work and feel ownership of the local.

In each of these cases, and in numerous other locals that are at various stages of involvement, the Project for Labor Renewal has seen positive changes in both members and leaders. The project is now identifying additional locals that might be interested in working with the project in the future.[2]

2. The above overview was written by the Project for Labor Renewal, Michael Eisenscher, project coordinator. It has been slightly edited for inclusion in this book.

10

Union Leadership

Practical Recommendations

- Union leaders should become familiar with the various models of leadership.
- Leaders should consider the potential benefits transformational leadership has for the labor movement.
- Unions should encourage their leaders to engage in self-assessment, mentoring, and training in an effort to promote transformational leadership.

It is well accepted that leadership is critical to the success of any organization. Certainly this is true for unions. Unions are voluntary organizations in the sense that participation in the work of the union (as opposed to the payment of membership dues or agency fees) cannot be compelled. Thus the first great challenge facing union leaders is convincing members to participate in the organization's work, whether that be organizing new members, handling members' grievances, or working on behalf of the union's political action program. The second great challenge union leaders face is using the limited resources of the organization (including active members) in the most effective way possible.

The previous chapters have examined how behavioral science can assist union leaders in meeting these two challenges. This chapter addresses what behavioral science has to say about leadership itself. Unfortunately, research in this area has not found any magic formulas for conjuring up good leaders. It does, however, provide insight into leadership that can help leaders evaluate themselves. It also suggests strategies for the development of future leaders.

Behavioral Models of Leadership

Not surprisingly, the subject of leadership has received a great deal of attention from behavioral researchers. Their work has produced many theories, models, and definitions. Drawing on this work, leadership is defined, for the purposes of this chapter, as the process of influencing the activities of the members of an organized group toward the determination and accomplishment of shared goals.

Earlier in this book a model was described as something that uses words and symbols to help us understand how things work. Three models are often used by behavioral scientists to explain leadership in organizations. They are the laissez-faire, transactional, and transformational models (see Figure 10.1).

> **LEADERSHIP**—the process of influencing the activities of the members of an organized group toward the determination and accomplishment of shared goals.

Laissez-Faire Leadership

Laissez-faire, loosely translated, means "hands-off" in French. When applied to leadership, it suggests a leader who is passive, delays decisions, gives little or no feedback to subordinates, and makes little effort to help members with their problems; in short, someone who takes a hands-off approach (Northouse, 1997). Clearly, this is not an effective style of leadership, and, in the context of a democratic organization like a union, a leader who consistently employed this approach would probably not remain in office very long. Still, some labor leaders probably do exhibit at least some of the characteristics of a laissez-faire leader.

Transactional Leadership

A second model, transactional leadership, is a more traditional approach and is more readily found in the labor movement. This type of leadership motivates people by using rewards and punishments. A transactional leader identifies the roles organizational members must play for the organization to achieve its objectives. The leader then discerns what the members need from the organization and

Figure 10.1 Approaches to Leadership

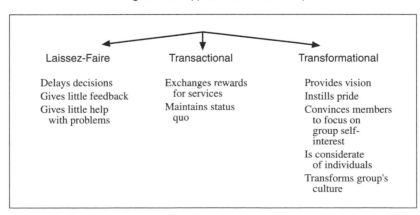

communicates to them how the organization will fulfill those needs in exchange for the members performing the necessary roles (Bass, 1990; Northouse, 1997). Alternatively, the leader determines what punishment the members fear and uses the threat of that punishment to get the members to assume the desired roles.

The terms "exchange" or "transaction," used in this context, do not suggest anything unethical or illegal. Rather, they describe a situation in which, for example, a union leader suggests that members can receive higher wages or better benefits in exchange for supporting a strike. On a more personal level, a leader might ask for members' votes in a union election in exchange for better union services the leader promises to provide. Or a candidate for union office might promise to appoint a particularly influential member to a union position in exchange for his or her active help in the candidate's campaign. Alternatively, the candidate might threaten to withhold services or appointments if support is not forthcoming. Such transactions are a part of the politics of most democratic organizations. The success of a transactional leader is tied to that leader's ability to appeal to the self-interest of the individual member. Specifically, this type of leader must be skilled in identifying and fulfilling the members' priorities.

Research on transactional leadership suggests that it is an approach that is particularly well suited to stable organizations. If the overarching goal of an organization is to maintain the status quo, transactional leadership can be an effective leadership style. In a union context, a leader engaging in transactional leadership would focus largely on traditional union functions like bargaining contracts and handling grievances.

Transformational Leadership

A third model of leadership that will be examined in some detail is transformational leadership. Transformational leaders focus their efforts on communicating group goals to the organization's members and convincing members to put those goals above their own (Wagner and Hollenbeck, 1998). In this sense, such a leader causes members to look beyond their own self-interest for the good of the group. This type of leader works to transform the organizational culture, instilling new values and challenging members to do more than has been asked of them previously.

Throughout, this book has stressed that changing members' attitudes and beliefs is a critical step in increasing participation and building more effective unions. It has also emphasized that appealing to members' self-interest is a critical part of changing attitudes. Transformational leadership, with its emphasis on what is good for the group, may not appear at first to be a particularly useful approach, given the important role played by individual self-interest. But, this would be the case only if the interests of the group and the individual were ultimately in conflict.

The case can be made that in a union context an individual's self-interest, in general, can be advanced only as part of the group's interest. In the short run, this may mean that individuals may have to postpone the attainment of their agenda for the good of the group. This might be the case, for example, when a union decides to devote more of its resources to organizing than it has in the past. In the short run, the union may need to reduce services to current members to do this. The long-run benefits of increased organizing may not be readily apparent to those members. Convincing members that this is in their long-run interest may not be easy to do, but it is a fundamental challenge of transformational leadership.

More than thirty-five studies on this topic have found that transformational leadership is associated with higher levels of member satisfaction with, and commitment to, an organization than are other leadership approaches. A transformational leadership style is also associated with higher levels of member participation and performance (Bass and Avolio, 1994; Shamir, House, and Arthur, 1993). Some of these studies have looked at union officer and steward leadership styles and have concluded that transformational leadership has a positive effect on union members' "loyalty, sense of responsibility, and actual participation in union activities" (Kelloway and Barling, 1993, p. 263).

In addition, work on transformational leadership has found that leaders can be taught to practice this style of leadership (Bass, 1998). This suggests that transformational leaders are not simply "born" but rather can be developed.

The research on this approach to leadership has also identified a number of characteristics of transformational leaders. First, transformational leaders act as strong role models whom others wish to emulate. They have high standards and are greatly respected.

Second, these leaders present members with a clear vision of what their organization can or should be. This vision inspires and excites members. Transformational leaders are optimistic, positive, and enthusiastic. They instill pride, confidence, and a sense of mission in members and communicate high expectations. In this way, they cause members to believe they can accomplish great things with extra effort (Bass, 1990).

Although this optimism and sense of mission are not easily instilled, many would argue that they are precisely what is needed in the American labor movement today. Years of emphasizing the servicing function of unions—the negotiation of contracts and the handling of grievances on behalf of the members—has caused the "movement" part of the labor movement to atrophy. Union members of fifty or a hundred years ago recognized that sacrifice on behalf of the common good was necessary if progress was to be made. One could make the case that members of the last twenty years have thought more about getting "their money's worth" for the dues they pay.

Third, transformational leaders touch people on a personal level. They are not aloof or condescending; rather, they are aware of people's emotional needs and communicate their concern for members as individuals. They take time to advise and counsel people and to share their expertise and experience. They are concerned with helping members grow and develop, particularly in terms of the contributions those members can make to the organization.

Last, leaders who employ the transformational style approach difficulties as problems to be solved and are constantly looking for new ways to deal with old problems. They involve members in decision making and constantly challenge them to think creatively (Bass, 1990).

John F. Kennedy is an example of a largely transformational leader who, on a societal level, challenged the American people to examine their values and rise to meet the adversity of a changing world when he said, "Ask not what your country can do for you; ask what you can do for your country" (Northouse, 1997, p. 132).

Martin Luther King and Mahatma Gandhi are other examples of transformational leaders. King led a movement to change American society in very fundamental ways by appealing to people to rise above hatred and vengeance and to engage in nonviolent protest. His "I Have a Dream" speech personified his manner of leadership (Northouse, 1997). Gandhi, in his own right, used nonviolence as a means to transform India from a British colony into a free nation.

The Leadership Continuum

Leaders usually do not employ one style of leadership—laissez-faire, transactional, or transformational—exclusively. Rather, they choose different approaches in different situations. Also, the approach a leader employs in a given situation will often simultaneously draw on more than one of the styles of leadership. Specifically, leadership provided in any given situation can be characterized on a continuum (see Figure 10.2) as being part transactional and part transformational or part laissez-faire and part transactional.

Figure 10.2 suggests that it is probably rare for leaders to combine laissez-faire and transformational styles at the same time because the two approaches tend to be diametrically opposed. It would not be uncommon, however, for a largely transformational leader occasionally to employ a laissez-faire approach to deal with a given issue (Bass, 1990). Leaders do tend to draw more heavily on one approach than another. This is the basis for characterizing leaders as largely laissez-faire, transactional, or transformational.

Researchers who have studied leadership styles make the case that while such

Figure 10.2 Leadership Continuum

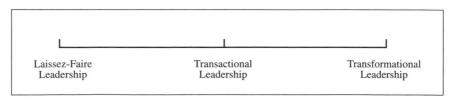

noted leaders as Abraham Lincoln, Franklin D. Roosevelt, and John F. Kennedy employed largely transformational approaches in dealing with the great challenges they faced, they were also skilled in the transactional style of leadership (Bass, 1990). For example, each was probably well-versed in the transactions of political patronage, where campaign workers and supporters sometimes receive government positions in exchange for their efforts. Their approaches to leadership, in those situations, would probably be plotted on the continuum much closer to transactional leadership than to transformational leadership. Another transformational leader, Mahatma Gandhi, engaged in the transactional approach to a far lesser extent. His leadership style, more purely transformational in nature than those of most leaders, would probably be plotted much closer to that end of the continuum.

Transformational Leadership in the Labor Movement

Transformational Leadership at the National Level

The labor movement has had its share of leaders who employed a largely transformational style of leadership to steer the movement through turbulent times. Such leaders recognized that maintaining the status quo was not sufficient for unions to develop to their full potential. Probably the best example of such a transformational leader was John L. Lewis, president of the UMW from 1920 to 1960. Charismatic in every way, Lewis founded the CIO and led the movement for industrial unionism, a radical new type of unionism that reshaped the labor movement by organizing the auto, steel, and rubber industries in the 1930s.

Walter Reuther, president of the UAW and third president of the CIO, is another example. Reuther was one of the earliest labor leaders to advocate a role for labor beyond improving pay and benefits for union members. Reuther led the UAW into the forefront of the movement for social justice in the 1960s. In doing so he suggested that labor had an obligation to be concerned about more than just the welfare of its members.

John Sweeney, current president of the AFL-CIO, is a more contemporary example of a leader whose style incorporates elements of the transformational approach. This is particularly apparent when his approach to leadership is contrasted with that of his predecessor, Lane Kirkland. Kirkland was a highly intelligent yet somewhat hesitant leader, with a low-key personality. He depended largely on the political and public relations strategies of the past in responding to the dramatic changes labor faced in the 1980s and early 1990s. His desire to adhere to the status quo is characteristic of a transactional approach to leadership.

In contrast, Sweeney put together a leadership team that consisted of Rich Trumka, the relatively young and very dynamic president of the UMW, and Linda Chavez-Thompson, a Hispanic American whose gender and ethnic background signaled that the Sweeney administration would not conduct business as usual. The Sweeney slate ran on a ticket that promised change. Most significant was the principal plank of the Sweeney platform that called for a greatly increased role for the AFL-CIO in organizing (Bryne, 1995).

Traditionally, the AFL-CIO had left the organizing of new members to its member unions. The AFL-CIO would talk about the importance of organizing, but rarely did it engage in concrete action. For the most part, the labor federation concentrated on politics, public relations, and international affairs. Upon its election, the Sweeney administration immediately created a new Organizing Department at the AFL-CIO, convinced the Executive Board to approve a special organizing fund that would spend at least $20 million per year, and announced that in the future "organizing [would be] a joint responsibility of the AFL-CIO, the affiliates and every one of the rank-and-file members" (Cooper, 1996).

Many people, both inside and out of the labor movement, have argued that American unions are in the midst of a crisis. Structural changes in the economy of North America, brought about by deindustrialization and the rise of a global economy, have contributed to steadily declining union membership in the United States. Unless the bleeding is stopped, the labor movement will inevitably reach the point at which it is no longer a significant player in American society.

Since the election of the Sweeney administration in 1995, the AFL-CIO and some unions have made significant changes. Some critics of the administration, however, have argued that these reforms have not gone far enough. They contend that the changes the AFL-CIO and many of its member unions have made are superficial in nature and wholly inadequate to meet the rapidly changing circumstances they face. In terms of the leadership models just discussed, this criticism suggests that the American labor movement is not, as a whole, employing a leadership style that is sufficiently transformational in nature.

Transformational Leadership at the Local Level

Up to this point, the examples used to illustrate transformational leadership have been well-known national and world leaders, both in and out of the labor movement. This does not mean that this model has relevance only to leadership at these levels. This approach is very relevant to all levels of leadership (Bass and Avolio, 1990).

In fact, several studies have examined the extent to which union stewards can be taught to use the transformational leadership approach and the impact this approach has on members' attitudes toward the union and on members' participation. In one such study some of the stewards in a local union of Canadian public employees were given a one-day training session on transformational leadership while others were not. Those who received the training were also given periodic follow-up sessions to ensure that they were practicing effective transformational leadership (Kelloway and Barling, 1996; Kelloway, Barling, and Catano, 1996).

After several months, members in the units with stewards who were practicing transformational leadership showed significantly greater satisfaction with their local union. Those in units led by stewards who had not received training showed no increase in membership satisfaction (Kelloway and Barling, 1996; Kelloway, Barling, and Catano, 1996). Additional research at the local union level has also found links between transformational leadership, as practiced by stewards, and increased membership commitment and participation (Kelloway and Barling, 1993).

These findings are significant because they demonstrate the effectiveness of transformational leadership in a union context. The research shows that local union leaders can, with appropriate training, learn to practice the transformational style of leadership. It also shows that transformational leadership is more effective at shaping members' attitudes toward the union and increasing members' participation in the organization than the more common transactional approach.

The research also suggests that transformational leadership not only benefits the organization, it also reflects well on the leaders employing it. Unions are democratic organizations, and many union leaders hold elective office. On a practical level, these leaders are concerned both with the welfare of the union and with how they are perceived by those who elected them—the union members. If practiced effectively, transformational leadership can increase members' commitment and participation, thereby improving the performance of the union. Transformational leadership can also increase members' satisfaction with the union. Both of these phenomena, improved union performance and increased member satisfaction, should reflect positively on elected union leaders.

Developing Transformational Leaders

Transformational leadership appears to be the most effective leadership approach for organizations facing significant changes and challenges. Clearly, this is the situation facing American unions as they enter the twenty-first century. The evidence suggests that union leaders who employ the transformational approach to leadership can positively influence members' satisfaction and commitment, thus better equipping their organizations to meet these challenges than those who do not (Bass and Avolio, 1994; Shamir, House, and Arthur, 1993).

Most researchers who study leadership believe that transformational leadership is something that can be taught and learned. It is possible for individuals and organizations to consciously adopt this approach to leadership. The first step toward this end is for current leaders to critically assess, or take inventory of, their own leadership styles and begin to incorporate the transformational approach where possible.

The second step toward increasing transformational leadership throughout the labor movement is for current leaders to assume responsibility for developing other such leaders through mentoring. The next stage is the development and implementation of training programs. Such programs can build transformational leadership in an organization only if they touch all levels of leadership and occur on an ongoing basis.

Self-Assessment

If a leader is serious about moving toward the more effective leadership that the transformational approach represents, that leader must first understand his or her own leadership style and the aspects of that style that need to be changed. A good way to arrive at an accurate assessment of one's leadership approach is to have it evaluated by a trained leadership consultant. Unions that have the resources to retain such an expert should seriously consider doing so. If that is not feasible, individuals can use a well-accepted instrument to assess their own leadership styles.

The Multifactor Leadership Questionnaire (MLQ) (on the following pages) is a series of items that measure the degree to which a leader practices the three major approaches to leadership described in this chapter—transformational, transactional, and laissez-faire (Bass and Avolio, 1992). Individuals can answer the questions and use the directions to gain a better sense of their own style of leadership.

Those who take the MLQ should pay particular attention to the nine factors listed on page 179. Examining one's scores for each of these factors can give concrete insights into the style of leadership one practices. The first five factors, Idealized Attributes, Idealized Behavior, Inspirational Motivation, Intellectual Stimulation, and Individualized Consideration, are aspects of the transformational approach. The next three factors, Contingent Reward, Management-by-Exception (Active), and Management-by-Exception (Passive), are characteristic of transactional leadership, while the ninth factor represents the laissez-faire approach to leadership. If one's goal is to be more of a transformational leader, one should carefully consider those leadership characteristics and skills listed on page 179 under the first five factors and work to develop those skills.

Because we sometimes do not see ourselves as others do, an additional way to gain insight into the kind of leadership we practice is to have people on the receiving end of one's leadership complete the questionnaire, substituting "the leader" for "I" in the questions. It can be useful to compare the self-assessment of one's leadership style with the way others perceive our approach. In many ways, it is probably more important how other people see us than how we see ourselves.

Mentoring

The transformational leadership approach has relevance for leadership at all levels (Bass and Avolio, 1990). It is unreasonable to expect leaders elected to higher office suddenly to develop transformational leadership skills. These skills need to be cul-

MULTIFACTOR LEADERSHIP QUESTIONNAIRE – SHORT FORM 6S (rev. 12/99)

Bernard M. Bass and Bruce J. Avolio
Center for Leadership Studies
Binghamton University
State University of New York State
Binghamton, NY 13902-6015
cls@binghamton.edu

This questionnaire provides a description of your leadership style. The items used here are <u>sample items</u> from the longer MLQ 5X survey. This survey was designed to familiarize readers with the MLQ survey and should only be used for that purpose. Please leave the answer blank when a statement is irrelevant or does not apply, or when you are uncertain or don't know the answer. Use the following key for the five possible responses:

0	1	2	3	4
Not at all	Once in a while	Sometimes	Fairly often	Frequently, if not always

1.   Circle (O) the number beside the statement that best represents your opinion regarding what you believe you **OUGHT** to do.

2.   Next, cross out (X) the number beside the statement that indicates what you **ACTUALLY** do.

Example: 0 1 X ③ 4 - I listen carefully

0 1 2 3 4	1.	I make personal sacrifices for the benefit of others.
0 1 2 3 4	2.	I champion exciting new possibilities.
0 1 2 3 4	3.	I provide an exciting image of what is essential to consider.
0 1 2 3 4	4.	I encourage non-traditional thinking to deal with traditional problems.
0 1 2 3 4	5.	I listen attentively to others' concerns.
0 1 2 3 4	6.	I clarify what outcomes are expected of others
0 1 2 3 4	7.	I arrange to know if and when things go wrong.
0 1 2 3 4	8.	I take no action until complaints are received.
0 1 2 3 4	9.	I avoid dealing with chronic problems.
0 1 2 3 4	10.	I reassure others that obstacles will be overcome.
0 1 2 3 4	11.	I talk about the importance of trusting each other.
0 1 2 3 4	12.	I take a stand on controversial issues.
0 1 2 3 4	13.	I encourage rethinking those ideas which have never been questioned before.
0 1 2 3 4	14.	I promote self-development with others.
0 1 2 3 4	15.	I deliver what I have promised in exchange for others' support.
0 1 2 3 4	16.	I watch for any infractions of rules and regulations.
0 1 2 3 4	17.	I have to be told what went wrong before taking any action.
0 1 2 3 4	18.	I fail to follow-up requests for assistance.

Phone: (650) 261-3500   **Fax:** (650) 261-3505   **E-mail:** robbmost@mindgarden.com

SELF-SCORING DIRECTIONS
MULTIFACTOR LEADERSHIP QUESTIONNAIRE-Short Form 6S

1. Using a pencil, write the circled (ought to do) numeric answer you gave for each item 1 to 18 in the spaces (not shaded) below.
2. Add each column for a total score.
3. Divide the total score by the number 2, which is the number of items you answered for each scale. By dividing each column, you will be computing your mean or average score (on a scale of 0–4) per scale.
4. After erasing the circled answers, repeat the above steps for the answers you marked with an X (actually do).

Item	Transformational					Transactional			Non
	IIA	IIB	IM	IS	IC	CR	MBE A	MBE P	LF
1									
2									
3									
4									
5									
6									
7									
8									
9									
10									
11									
12									
13									
14									
15									
16									
17									
18									
Total Score	$\overline{IIA}$	$\overline{IIB}$	$\overline{IM}$	$\overline{IS}$	$\overline{IC}$	$\overline{CR}$	$\overline{MBE}$ A	$\overline{MBE}$ P	$\overline{LF}$
Mean	$\overline{IIA}$	$\overline{IIB}$	$\overline{IM}$	$\overline{IS}$	$\overline{IC}$	$\overline{CR}$	$\overline{MBE}$ A	$\overline{MBE}$ P	$\overline{LF}$

Legend:
IIA - Idealized Attributes
IIB - Idealized Behavior
IM - Inspirational Motivation
IS - Intellectual Stimulation
IC - Individualized Consideration

CR - Contingent Reward
MBEA - Management-by-Exception (Active)
MBEP - Management-by-Exception (Passive)
LF - Laissez-faire

tivated and practiced over a period of time. This suggests that national and international union leaders should work to cultivate such skills among officials at the district and regional levels, district and regional leaders should cultivate such skills among local officers, and local officers should cultivate such skills among first-line union representatives, such as stewards, as well as among the general membership. Mentoring is one means of cultivating such skills.

Mentoring involves "modeling" or demonstrating for others the kind of behavior one hopes will be emulated. For instance, one of the most important things a transformational leader does is to present a "vision" of what the organization can and

---

Score Interpretation

TRANSFORMATIONAL

IIA - Idealized Attributes indicates whether you instill trust, faith, and respect among people by showing dedication to them and appealing to their hopes and dreams.

IIB - Idealized Behavior indicates whether you serve as a role model for people by doing what is morally and ethically right, by following through on commitments, and by taking responsibility for actions taken.

IM - Inspirational Motivation measures the degree to which you provide a vision, use appropriate symbols and images to help others focus on their work, and try to make others feel their work is significant.

IS - Intellectual Stimulation shows the degree to which you encourage others to be creative in looking at old problems in new ways, create an environment that is tolerant of seemingly extreme positions, and nurture people to question their own values and beliefs and those of the organization.

IC - Individualized Consideration indicates the degree to which you show interest in others' well-being, assign projects individually, and pay attention to those who seem less involved in the group.

TRANSACTIONAL

CR - Contingent Reward shows the degree to which you tell others what to do in order to be rewarded, emphasize what you expect from them, and recognize their accomplishments.

MBEA - Management-by-Exception (Active) assesses the degree to which you actively monitor whether people deviate from their responsibilities or do not live up to expectations and the degree to which you take corrective action to remedy the situation.

MBEP - Management-by-Exception (Passive) assesses the degree to which you wait for problems to arise as a result of people deviating from their responsibilities or not living up to expectations before taking corrective action to remedy the situation.

NON-TRANSACTIONAL/LAISSEZ-FAIRE

LF - Laissez-Faire measures whether you require little of others, are content to let things ride, and let others do their own thing.

Source: Bass and Avolio, 1992;, Avolio, 1999.

Permission to use the MLQ survey was provided by Drs. Bruce Avolio and Bernard Bass. please contact Mind Garden at www.mindgarden.com for further information on the use of the MLQ.

should be, as well as to convince other leaders and members to embrace that vision as their own. Truly transformational leaders inspire others to put the long-term interests of the organization ahead of their own individual short-term interests, and they accomplish this, in part, by doing it themselves. They demonstrate optimism, enthusiasm, and energy, and, by example, they communicate to subordinate leaders and to members that this is the way a leader should behave (Bass, 1990).

Transformational leaders also touch people on a personal level. They demonstrate a sincere consideration for others and attempt to assist them when possible. They act as coaches and advisers and provide constructive feedback to people.

This can be particularly helpful to less experienced leaders who are trying to develop their own leadership skills.

Good leaders are not only concerned about the state of their union today or tomorrow; they are also concerned about its long-term success. They look beyond their own time in office and work to ensure the viability of the organization after they are gone. One important way to do this is to make sure that the organization has a cadre of people ready and willing to assume future leadership positions. Today's leaders need to see the identification and development of future leaders as part of the responsibilities they take on when they assume office.

Often, individuals with potential can be introduced to leadership roles through appointed positions in the union structure. As suggested in earlier chapters, individuals are most likely to take on such responsibilities when the work meshes with interests they already have. For instance, a member who already holds positive attitudes toward the union's political agenda is more likely to accept an invitation to work on a union's lobbying campaign than someone who opposes, or is uninterested in, the union's political positions. And as the earlier models suggest, if an interest in politics (attitudes) leads to working on a union political campaign (behavior), and that experience is positive, the individual's attitudes about that work will be reinforced and the person will become even more active.

Sometimes leaders holding elected positions are reluctant to mentor potential leaders for fear that those individuals could challenge them in future elections. Or they will choose individuals to mentor whose primary qualification is loyalty rather than ability. This is a shortsighted philosophy that is more consistent with transactional than with transformational leadership because it puts the interests of the leader above the interests of the organization.

It would be naive to suggest that developing potential leaders does not include some risk to the mentor's position, but it also must be recognized that a failure to develop competent leaders also carries significant risk. Except in the smallest of local unions, one person cannot alone provide the leadership necessary to ensure the success of the organization. A key part of leadership is identifying and involving capable people in the work of the group. A failure to do so will ultimately be reflected in the ineffectiveness of the organization. Ineffectiveness is an equally, if not a greater, danger to tenure in office than competent rivals.

Training

A training program for introducing leaders to transformational leadership, suggested by the researchers who have done the most work in this area, involves a three-day basic training session, a three-day advanced follow-up session run three months after the basic program, and a follow-up program one year later (Bass, 1998). In a model training program, each of these sessions would be taught by leadership consultants with significant expertise and experience in transformational leadership.

Some unions may have the resources to train their leaders in this way; others may not. Certainly more modest programs than the one described above can have a positive effect on leaders; however, an organization must expect that a lesser program will have a lesser impact.

Included among the many elements of such a training program would be the MLQ. Participants, and possibly those who work with the participants, would take the MLQ as part of the program. Trainers would discuss the results with the individual participants. This gives participants a chance to reflect on their styles of leadership as they go through the training.

Another critical part of a training program involves getting participants to think consciously and analytically about leadership. Discussing the significant challenges facing the labor movement and the critical role leadership can play in helping unions face those challenges is a useful exercise. A leadership training program should also introduce participants to the various approaches to leadership—transformational, transactional, and laissez-faire—and to the potential impact each approach has on the organization. Ultimately, the trainers need to make a convincing case that moving from laissez-faire and transactional leadership toward the transformational approach has significant benefits for the leader, the members, and the organization.

Introducing Leadership: An Exercise

One way to get participants in a training program to begin to think analytically about leadership is to have them think of a leader, past or present, inside or outside of the organization, who has had a lasting impact on their development. They can be asked to write a summary of their relationship with this leader, the attributes that made this individual an effective leader, and what they learned from him or her.

A group discussion can follow in which participants discuss the leaders they chose as models. This exercise brings to the fore key elements of successful leadership that resonate with participants because of their personal experience with the leaders they have identified. (Bass, 1998)

Relevant cases and role plays can be an important part of any leadership training program. These exercises provide participants with a chance to apply leadership principles to situations they might encounter in their work. Comparing the responses of a transformational versus a transactional leader in various scenarios, as well as the outcomes that might result from each approach, is an excellent way of illustrating the advantages of transformational leadership.

Discussing each of the components of transformational leadership is another important part of an effective training program. First, it must be clearly communicated to aspiring leaders that they must have high standards of behavior and act as strong role models for their memberships.

Second, transformational leaders must present members with a clear vision of what their organization can or should be. They must inspire and excite their members with this vision and have the energy and enthusiasm to pursue it. An exercise that helps leaders to think in this way might involve asking participants to look into the future and envision the shape, form, or direction they would like to see their organization take. This should be followed by a discussion of concrete steps that could move the union in this direction.

Third, transformational leaders touch people on a personal level. They are aware of people's emotional needs and communicate their concern about members as individuals. They take time to advise and counsel people and to help individuals grow and develop. An effective training program might discuss how such concern can play a role in developing future leaders.

Finally, it is important for leaders interested in moving toward the transformational style to develop the tools necessary to be creative and innovative problem solvers. This requires leaders to be thoughtful, open-minded, and, to a degree, bold in addressing problems they encounter. Individual and group problem-solving exercises, along with feedback from trainers, can be helpful in this regard.

The purpose of having a period of time between training sessions is to give participants an opportunity to put into practice the approaches to leadership addressed in the program. To make the most of this trial period, participants should establish some specific objectives during their training program that will move them closer to transformational leadership. Such objectives might include the following:

—I will always be conscious of the need to maintain high standards of behavior and to be a role model to others.
—I will take advantage of opportunities to communicate to members my vision for our local, district, or national union.
—I will encourage members to think in a creative and innovative way about problems that face us.
—I will delegate responsibility in a way that will help others develop their own leadership skills.

Participants should also decide on some concrete steps they can take to move toward those objectives during the trial period.

Research and training experience have found that it is important that participants in the original training program be brought back together following their trial period. This advanced training program should provide a chance for participants to debrief about their experiences with the transformational approach. Discussing with other leaders the progress or the difficulties they experienced can be a very useful exercise.

This advanced training should include a review of the information presented about leadership styles in the first training session. It should also provide an opportunity for participants to review and revise the objectives they set for themselves in the first training program.

This chapter has focused on leadership within organizations. It has presented a continuum of leadership styles—laissez-faire, transactional, and transformational—and has suggested that transformational leadership has the most potential for increasing members' commitment and participation. This book has argued that maximizing members' commitment and participation is necessary for unions to effectively confront the many challenges they face today and in the years ahead. Transformational leadership is one tool, among many, that unions can use to move toward this objective.

Throughout this book ideas, approaches, programs, and strategies that unions, union leaders, and active union members can use to build stronger organizations have been suggested. None are radical; many are not even particularly novel. But all are based on some, and in many cases, substantial, behavioral science research. Using behavioral science as a basis, or at least part of the basis, for adopting such strategies is unusual in labor's ranks. Ironically, anyone who seriously looks to behavioral science for assistance, considers the many suggestions presented here in a systematic way, and moves to implement even a few of them is engaging in transformational leadership. Because the labor movement is unlikely to be transformed without transformational leadership, this is a step in the right direction.

The case study that follows depicts a local union leader whose approach to leadership includes elements of both transformational and transactional leadership. Through her leadership skills this leader has built a strong local union and developed a cadre of committed and experienced activists in the local that will ensure its continued success well after she leaves office.

CASE STUDY
Transformational Leadership at the Local Level

As suggested in this chapter, it is, in some ways, easier to envision transformational leadership operating at the national, international, or federation levels. After all, that is where leaders have the resources to have a meaningful impact, to "transform" an organization. But transformational leadership can be practiced in a local union setting, and it can make a difference at that level.

The case study that follows is the account of a local union leader whose approach to leadership includes aspects of both transformational and transactional styles. While very capable, this leader does not possess unusual skills or abilities, and the membership she leads is made up of good, but not exceptional, people. So as not to bring undue attention to this local and its president, their names have been changed, as has the context in which the case takes place.

Gena is the president of a local union representing a large group of public employees in a major American city. Gena's union career is somewhat typical for local union leaders. She started working for a government agency in an entry-level position and gradually moved up through various job classifications. Along the way, she became active in her local union. She first volunteered to help with a couple of the local's committees and later became an elected steward. She demonstrated a lot of ability and enthusiasm in that position and was asked to run for local vice-president when the position opened up. She lost that election, but when the vice-president stepped down after one term, she ran again and won. After two terms in that position, she ran for president and was elected.

During her first term in office, Gena made her share of mistakes. But she was a quick learner and was reelected to a second term. One of the most important things she had learned was that her local's old way of doing things was not working particularly well. She realized that the organization faced many new challenges. Gena looked down the road and realized that the local could not survive unless it changed in significant ways.

Gena decided that she needed to communicate this message to her membership. She decided that one way to send this message was by changing the most tangible symbol of the local—its office. For some years the local had rented space in an office complex. During that time its treasury, as well as its level of activity, had grown. Finding space for committee and membership meetings was always a problem. On a trip across the city, Gena passed an old movie theater in a declining neighborhood. It had been closed for a few years but at one time was a vibrant, attractive place with an art deco facade. A few months later she drove by it again and saw the "for sale" sign still out in front.

It occurred to Gena that it might make a good headquarters for the local. It was not in the best part of town, but that made the property more affordable. It also was very close to the complex where many of the local's members worked. Gena knew it would not be easy to convince the local's executive board to buy and renovate the building, but she decided to present her request as part of a strategic planning report on which she and a committee had been working for some time. Gena painted a picture of the local's future and what it would need to do to continue to serve its members. The building was an important part of that plan. After a series of meetings, the executive board agreed to make a down payment and secure a mortgage. Gena presented her proposal at a general membership meeting which ratified the board's decision.

After considerable renovations, the local moved in. The local occupied a suite of offices that included a conference room for committee meetings. It also had a large hall for membership meetings that could be rented out for parties, weddings, and other gatherings. It leased excess space to some other local unions, which helped to pay the mortgage, and donated space to a local community development group that was working to restore the neighborhood. The local's occupation of this landmark building was seen by many in the community as an opportunity to turn the area around.

The local's purchase of the building was a bold step, and it had some interesting ramifications. The building stood out in the neighborhood, and many of the local's members drove by it as they went to and from work each day. Because the building was restored to its former glory, the members began to feel a sense of pride in their building. These positive feelings seemed to energize the local. As the building was conveniently located, more members began attending the local's meetings. Initially, some were just curious to see what the building looked like inside, but many returned meeting after meeting. Gena seized the opportunity and personally invited each of these members to get involved in the union's committees. The additional manpower enabled the local to expand its community service, political action, and social activities. The social activities, in particular, attracted even more members, some of whom were then recruited to participate in the local's work.

Gena realized that to keep many of the newly active members involved, the local needed to make them feel more and more connected to the organization. Toward this end, Gena initiated an education program for the local. With the help of a local university's labor education program, the union offered a series of evening classes to be held in the new union building. Initially, the local offered four eight-week courses over a two-year period. The courses focused both on skills, such as effective grievance handling and leadership techniques, and on broader issues like labor history and politics.

The local hosted a dinner at the end of each course and presented the participants with a certificate. When they completed the four classes, they were presented with a framed diploma indicating their successful completion of the program. The participants enjoyed the classes so much that Gena was persuaded to add a series of advanced courses to the curriculum.

Gena personally attended many of the classes. From observing the classes and from her involvement with the local's committees, Gena was able to identify members with significant leadership potential, and she began to mentor these activists, even though she probably did not consciously use that term to describe what she was doing. Gena took every opportunity to involve these individuals in other local activities. She also rewarded them in small ways, such as sending them to the union's regional education conference in Atlantic City, helping them to get elected as delegates so they could attend the national union's biennial convention, or having them represent the local at union-related dinners and ceremonies. While they did serve as rewards, Gena realized that these experiences also would most likely serve to strengthen the members' commitment to the organization.

The end result was a group of knowledgeable, deeply committed local union activists who were ready and willing to take on any task necessary to move the union forward. When Gena was appointed to the union's national staff, she left behind a significant number of capable people to carry on the work she had begun.

If we analyze Gena's leadership in light of our discussion of the different leadership approaches, we find elements of both transformational and transactional approaches. Characteristic of a transformational leader, Gena had a vision of where the local union needed to go to meet the challenges it faced. She shared this vision with her executive board and the union's membership. The new building that she proposed served to build pride in the local. It also served as a catalyst for energizing the local.

Gena acted to take advantage of the increased interest in the union spurred by the new building. She got to know the newly interested members and personally invited them to participate in the union's activities. She instigated an education program that simultaneously informed these budding activists about the union and the union movement and built commitment to the local, and she actively mentored members she saw as having significant leadership potential.

Gena's approach to leadership also included some transactional aspects. Specifically, she offered rewards to members who performed particular services. These rewards were authorized by the executive board and consisted of travel to regional and national union functions and other perks. These rewards sent the message that individuals who gave of themselves on the local's behalf would be recognized and rewarded for their contributions.

Not surprisingly, Gena's local stood out as an exceptionally active and effective organization, both in the local labor community and in the national union. Her leadership capabilities were acknowledged by her appointment to the union's staff. Certainly, Gena had some advantages that many local unions do not have. She had a healthy treasury that resulted from a stable membership who were relatively well paid and whose jobs were not threatened by the vagaries of the economy. These conditions are not necessary for leaders to practice transformational leadership, however. It can, and should, be practiced regardless of the circumstances.

11

Conclusion

Recognizing the many challenges unions and their members face, this book proposes that the American labor movement add behavioral science to its arsenal of resources. Based on the premise that maximizing the involvement and participation of members is central to building more effective unions, the book has examined some findings of behavioral science research that can be helpful toward this end.

It should be reiterated that unions have clearly developed, over time, many tried and tested tools, techniques, and strategies to build and rebuild their organizations. The premise of this book is that the insights of behavioral science can add to, and increase, the effectiveness of these proven approaches.

At the very least, behavioral science and its findings may help union activists and leaders better understand the human behavior they observe. An understanding of the principles of behavioral science can also help to place the lessons of experience in a broader perspective. This broader perspective can be helpful to union leaders interested in initiating changes or in analyzing the success or failure of particular initiatives.

Understandably, unions and union leaders have been suspicious or skeptical of behavioral scientists because in the past they have worked mostly with employers and, in some instances, against unions (Gordon and Burt, 1981; Gordon and Nurick, 1981). It should be clear by this point, however, that behavioral science is only a tool, available for use by any type of organization. Behavioral science provides great insight into people and their behavior. To use those insights ethically, honestly, and toward a socially acceptable end is the responsibility of those who adopt them.

It should also be clear that, over the last twenty-five years, numerous behavioral scientists have chosen to work with unions and union leaders in an effort to generate information about members' attitudes and behavior. Underlying much of this

Figure 11.1 What Makes an Effective Union?

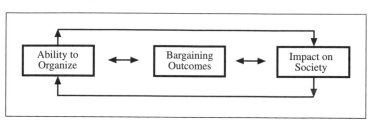

work has been the goal of building more effective unions. This collaboration has produced a growing body of research about unions, union members, and union leaders. This book has been an effort to bring as much of that work as possible together in an organized and coherent way and to suggest tangible strategies based on the insights generated.

In Chapter 1, the groundwork for the rest of the book was laid by attempting to define what is meant by an "effective" union. Figure 11.1 reiterates the three elements or measures of an effective union. It was suggested that if behavioral science is to be of genuine help to the labor movement, its insights would have to help unions improve their performance in each of these areas. It was also suggested that one of the most important areas in which behavioral science could make a contribution is member participation. Member participation is critical to all three elements of effective unionism. If behavioral science can help unions generate more positive and constructive membership participation, it will indeed be helping to build more effective labor organizations.

Toward this end, Chapter 2 presented a model of union participation that suggested numerous factors that influence a member's decision to participate in the union. This book has focused, to a large degree, on two of these factors over which unions have some influence—members' attitudes and beliefs, particularly toward the union, and that part of the environment over which the union has some control, namely the union's culture and its leadership.

The Importance of Attitudes

One of the basic findings of behavioral science, and a key premise of this book, is that people's behaviors are shaped by their attitudes. Behavioral science also has concluded that individuals are not born with their attitudes in place; rather, attitudes are developed by the influences, information, and experiences to which people are exposed. It also proposes that new experiences or new information can change a person's attitude (Fishbein and Ajzen, 1975).

When applied to a union context, these findings suggest that if participation and involvement in the union are behaviors that unions want to encourage, they need

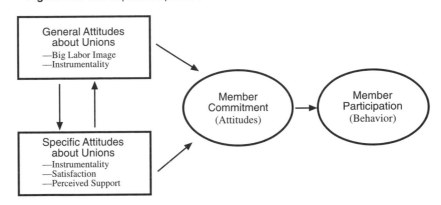

Figure 11.2 The Impact of Specific and General Attitudes on Union Commitment

to focus their efforts on fostering those attitudes that will lead to the desired behavior of participation.

One of the more useful contributions of behavioral science research on unions has been the identification of the construct of union commitment and the development of a scale to measure it. Union commitment brings together a wide variety of relevant and significant attitudes and opinions about unions and the union experience. It also has been found to be closely related to participation in union activities. Strategically, this suggests that if a union wishes to become more effective through increased member participation, it can do so by raising the level of members' commitment to the union.

Factors that have been found to be closely related to union commitment and that can be influenced by a union and its representatives include a person's overall attitudes about unions in general and a person's beliefs about a specific union that might be attempting to, or currently does, represent that person (Figure 11.2).

Much of this book has focused on ways unions and union leaders can positively influence a member or nonmember's general and specific attitudes toward unions. By doing so, that individual's level of commitment to the union would also be positively influenced and his or her likelihood of participating in the work of the union would increase.

This can occur in a wide variety of union settings, including organizing drives, socialization and orientation programs, political action programs, and grievance procedures. Also discussed were the importance and value of communication skills, information, and image-building activities in influencing people's attitudes.

The Role of the Environment

Individual characteristics such as attitudes are only one of the two major influences the model suggests are central to shaping an individual's behavior. The environment in which the behavior takes place will also influence the way a person behaves. There are many dimensions to the environment in which a person lives. Among them are the social, political, economic, organizational, and physical environment.

The organizational environment may be the environment that has the most immediate influence over a person's behavior. Of all the many different aspects of the environment, unions have the most control over their own organizational environment. If union leaders can create an environment in their union that encourages and rewards participation in, and support for, the organization, they can encourage behavior that will most benefit the group.

Unions and union leaders can do this by building a strong union culture. Members' attitudes in general, and their commitment, involvement, and participation in particular, can be strongly influenced by an organization's culture. Though union leaders may not use the term "culture," many do instinctively recognize the need to create an organizational environment in which the values, goals, and objectives of the group are promoted and supported. Unions and their leaders can more effectively create such environments if they explicitly recognize the roles that rituals, rites, ceremonies, taboos, heroes, stories, myths, symbols, and language play in their organization. By recognizing these elements, leaders can monitor their organizations and intervene when necessary to strengthen or change the group's culture. In doing so, they are taking an important step toward building more effective unions.

Another important environmental factor that has significant potential for influencing people's attitudes toward the union and, ultimately, for encouraging participation is leadership. This book presented a continuum of leadership styles—laissez-faire, transactional, and transformational—and suggested that transformational leadership has the most potential for increasing members' commitment and participation.

Throughout the book, ideas, approaches, programs, and strategies that unions, union leaders, and active union members can use to build stronger organizations have been suggested. None are radical; many are not even particularly novel. But all are based on some, and in many cases substantial, behavioral science research. Anyone who seriously looks to behavioral science for assistance, considers the many suggestions presented here in a systematic way, and moves to implement even a few of them is engaging in transformational leadership. Because the labor movement is unlikely to be transformed without transformational leadership, this is a step in the right direction. Thus the labor movement needs to encourage transformational leadership as an important tool in bringing about necessary change.

Building More Effective Unions Systematically

As the number of different areas discussed in this book suggest, virtually every aspect of union activity presents an opportunity to build a more effective union. An optimal union-building strategy would require a union and its leaders to look at every decision, action, and activity of the organization as a chance to influence members' attitudes and build commitment.

This is, of course, very difficult to do when a union is constantly dealing with crises, when it does not possess adequate human or financial resources to deal with the problems at hand, and when it is continually fighting for its very existence. It is just such circumstances that gave rise in the 1980s to an increased interest on the part of the labor movement in a tool successfully used for many years by other organizations. That tool is strategic planning (Clark and Gray, 1991).

The concept of strategic, or long-range, planning once was regarded with skepticism by many in the labor movement because of its close association with management (Fitzpatrick and Waldstein, 1994). A study in the 1980s found that only 25 percent of North American unions surveyed engaged in such planning at the national level (Reshaf and Stratton-Devine, 1990). Surveys conducted in the United States in 1990 and in Canada in 1993 found an increased use of strategic planning, with 40 percent (U.S.) and 58 percent (Canada) of national unions in the two countries using this tool (Clark et al., 1998). Anecdotal evidence suggests that the number of national unions engaging in strategic planning has continued to rise.

While there is little hard evidence on the use of strategic planning at the district/regional and local levels of the labor movement, it is probably safe to assume that strategic planning is less common (probably far less common) than at the national union level.

Labor organizations, at all levels, tend by their nature to be reactive. Unions mount organizing drives in reaction to employee dissatisfaction. They file grievances in reaction to management's violation of a contract. And, as was the case in the 1980s, the labor movement has tended to wait until it comes under attack before it reacts and begins to formulate a defensive strategy.

Strategic planning, in contrast, is a proactive process that looks to the future and attempts to anticipate the challenges an organization will face. This process also systematically identifies ways in which an organization can pursue its mission and achieve its goals in the face of such challenges.

As was suggested earlier, examples of such forward looking planning are numerous in the labor movement. One of the most widely publicized was the AFL-CIO's Committee on the Evolution of Work, which was formed in the mid-1980s to help the labor movement respond to the many challenges it faced at that time. Numerous national unions have since formed committees on the future to help them develop strategic plans for the years ahead (Clark and Gray, 1991).

It is critical that local and district unions and local and state labor federations also engage in such strategic and systematic planning. Such an undertaking should include consideration of the importance of members' participation, the manner in which members' attitudes shape such behavior, and the individual and environmental (structure, culture, and leadership) considerations that influence members' attitudes.

Many of the insights discussed in this book can be translated into action as opportunities present themselves (e.g., a member files a grievance that presents a steward with a chance to educate the member about the important role the union plays in bringing due process to the workplace or a new employee is hired, giving the union a chance to make a positive first impression on a potential new member). To have the most impact, however, these insights and the strategies they suggest need to be implemented on a systematic basis. Ideally, unions and their leaders, at all levels, should consciously strive to consider the implications every decision, action, and activity has for shaping members' attitudes and behaviors. Such important considerations should not be left to chance.

This book does not suggest that behavioral science is a panacea or a cure-all for the tremendous challenges facing the American labor movement as it enters the twenty-first century. Rather, as has been stated numerous times, behavioral science is a tool that unions and union leaders can use, along with many others, to build more effective organizations. To deal effectively with the challenges it faces, the labor movement must marshal every resource available to it. Behavioral science is one such resource it should use to its advantage.

References

Abramowitch, Rona, and Laura Johnson. 1992. "Children's Perceptions of Parental Work." *Canadian Journal of Behavioral Science* 24:319–33.

AFA. 1999. "What Is Chaos." AFA Website. http://www.flightattendant-afa.org/ chaos_what_is_it.htm.

AFGE. 1999. "Join the Fight to Clean Up the SWAMP." *Government Standard*, September-October, 1.

AFL-CIO. 1984. "How AFL-CIO Members Voted in the 1984 Election." *AFL-CIO News*, December 1, 5–8.

——. 1985a. "Public Support for Unions Gaining." *AFL-CIO News*, June 15, 1.

——. 1985b. *The Changing Situation of Workers and Their Unions*. Washington, D.C.: AFL-CIO.

——. 1996a. "America Needs a Raise." AFL-CIO Executive Council Statement, February 19, AFL-CIO Website, http://www.aflcio.org/publ/estatements/feb1996/ecraise.htm

——. 1996b. "Delegates to Raise Workers' Political Voice." *AFL-CIO News*, March 22, 1.

——. 1997–98. *America@Work*, December-January, 20.

——. 1998. *Economic Development*. Washington, D.C.: AFL-CIO.

——. 1999a. "Americans' Attitudes toward Unions." AFL-CIO Website, http://www.aflcio.org/labor99/am_attitude.htm.

——. 1999b. "The Union Advantage." AFL-CIO Website, http://www.aflcio.org/ uniondifference/uniondiff4.htm.

——. 1999c. "Talking Union to Your Kids." *America@Work*, August, 18–19.

——. 1999d. "Talking Union to Your Kids." AFL-CIO Website, http://www.aflcio.org/ articles/talk_union_to_kids/talk_union.htm.

AFSCME. 1987. "Active Stewards: The Union's Energy Source." *AFSCME Steward*, Spring, 8–12.

Aldrich, John. 1993. "Rational Choice and Turnout." *American Journal of Political Science* 37:246–78.

Allen, Steven G. 1988. "Declining Unionization in Construction: The Facts and the Reasons." *Industrial and Labor Relations Review* 41:343–59.

Ambrose, M. L., L. K. Harland, and C. T. Kulik. 1991. "Influence of Social Comparisons on Perceptions of Organizational Fairness." *Journal of Applied Psychology* 76:239–46.

Anderson, John C. 1979. "Local Union Participation: A Reexamination." *Industrial Relations* 29:18–31.

Anderson, John C., Charles O'Reilly, and Gloria Busman. 1980. "Union Decertification in the U.S.: 1947–1977." *Industrial Relations* 19:100–107.

Anderson, Kenneth. 1978. *Persuasion: Theory and Practice*. Boston: Allyn and Bacon.

Angle, H. L., and J. L. Perry. 1984. "Union Member Attitudes and Bargaining Unit Stability in Urban Transit." In *Proceedings of the Thirty-Sixth Annual Meeting of the Industrial Relations Research Association*, edited by B. D. Dennis, 284–90. Madison, Wisc.: Industrial Relations Research Association.

Avolio, Bruce. 1999. *Full Leadership Development: Building the Vital Forces in Organizations*. Thousand Oaks, Calif.: Sage.

Axelrod, Robert. 1972. "Where the Votes Come From: An Analysis of Electoral Coalitions, 1952–1968." *American Political Science Review* 66 (March): 11–20.

———. 1982. "Communication." *American Political Science Review* 76:393–96.

Baden, Naomi. 1986. "Developing an Agenda: Expanding the Role of Women in Unions." *Labor Studies Journal*, 11 (Winter): 229–49.

Bandura, Albert. 1977. *Social Learning Theory*. Englewood Cliffs, N.J.: Prentice-Hall.

———. 1986. *Social Foundations of Thought and Action: A Social Cognitive Theory*. Englewood Cliffs, N.J.: Prentice-Hall.

Banks, Andy, and Jack Metzgar. 1989. "Participating in Management: Union Organizing on a New Terrain." *Labor Research Review* 14 (Fall): 1–55.

Barbash, Jack. 1969. "Rationalization in the American Union." In *Essays in Industrial Relations Theory*, edited by Gerald G. Somers, 147–62. Ames: Iowa State University Press.

Barling, Julian. 1990. *Employment, Stress, and Family Functioning*. New York: Wiley.

Barling, Julian, Clive Fullagar, and Kevin Kelloway. 1992. *The Union and Its Members: A Psychological Approach*. New York: Oxford University Press.

Barling, Julian, Clive Fullagar, Kevin Kelloway, and Leanne McElvie. 1992. "Union Loyalty and Strike Propensity." *Journal of Social Psychology* 132:581–90.

Barling, Julian, Kevin Kelloway, and Eric Bremermann. 1991. "Pre-Employment Predictors of Union Attitudes: The Role of Family Socialization and Work Beliefs." *Journal of Applied Psychology* 76:725–31.

Bass, B. M. 1990. *Bass & Stodgill's Handbook of Leadership: Theory, Research, and Applications*. New York: Free Press.

———. 1998. *Transformational Leadership: Industrial, Military, and Educational Impact*. Mahwah, N.J.: Lawrence Erlbaum Associates.

Bass, B. M., and Avolio, B. J. 1990. "The Implications of Transactional and Transformational Leadership for Individual, Team, and Organizational Development." *Research in Organizational Change and Development* 4:231–72.

———. 1992. *Multifactor Leadership Questionnaire—Short Form 6S*. Binghamton, N.Y.: Center for Leadership Studies.

———. 1994. *Improving Organizational Effectiveness through Transformational Leadership*. Thousand Oaks, Calif.: Sage.

Becker, B. E., and R. U. Miller. 1981. "Patterns and Determinants of Union Growth in the Hospital Industry." *Journal of Labor Research* 2:309–28.

Becker, T. E., R. S. Billings, D. M. Eveleth, and N. L. Gilbert. 1996. "Foci and Bases of Employee Commitment: Implications for Job Performance." *Academy of Management Journal* 39:264–82.

Bettinghaus, E. P., and M. J. Cody. 1994. *Persuasive Communications*. 5th ed. Fort Worth, Tex.: Harcourt Brace.

Beyer, Janice, and Harrison Trice. 1978. *Implementing Change: Alcoholism Programs in Work Organizations*. New York: Free Press.

Bigoness, W. J., and H. L. Tosi. 1984. "Correlates of Voting Behavior in a Union Decertification Election." *Academy of Management Journal* 27:654–59.

Bourne, P. G. 1967. "Some Observations on the Psychosocial Phenomena Seen in Basic Training." *Psychiatry* 30:187–97.

Bray, D. W. 1978. "The AT&T Assessment Center Program." Paper presented at the Annual Meeting of the Academy of Management, San Francisco, August.

Brett, J. M. 1980. "Why Employees Want Unions." *Organizational Dynamics* 8:47–59.

Briggs, Stephen. 1984. *The Municipal Grievance Procedure*. Los Angeles: Institute of Industrial Relations, UCLA.

Bronfenbrenner, Kate. 1993. "Seeds of Resurgence: Successful Union Strategies for Winning Certification Elections and First Contracts in the 1980s and Beyond." Ph.D. diss., Cornell University.

———. 1994. "The Impact of Employer Opposition on Union Certification Win Rates: A Private/Public Sector Comparison." Working Paper 113, Economic Policy Institute, October.

———. 1997. "The Role of Union Strategies in NLRB Certification Elections." *Industrial and Labor Relations Review* 50:195–212.

Bronfenbrenner, Kate, and Tom Juravich. 1998. "It Takes More Than House Calls: Organizing to Win with a Comprehensive Union-Building Strategy." In *Organizing to Win*, edited by Kate Bronfenbrenner, S. Friedman, R. Hurd, R. Oswald, and R. Seeber, 19–36. Ithaca, N.Y.: Cornell ILR Press.

Brummer, Alex. 1990. "The $1,000 Billion S&L Debacle Could Never Happen Here." *Guardian*, June 7, 12.

Bruno, Robert. 1999. "Democratic Goods: Teamster Reform and Collective Bargaining Outcomes." Paper presented at the Conference on Union Governance and Democracy, Atlanta, Ga., May.

Bulger, Carrie A., and Steven Mellor. 1997. "Self-Efficacy as a Mediator of the Relationship between Perceived Union Barriers and Women's Participation in Union Activities." *Journal of Applied Psychology* 82:935–44.

Buono, A. F., J. L. Bowditch, and J. W. Lewis. 1985. "When Cultures Collide: The Anatomy of a Merger." *Human Relations* 38:477–500.

Bureau of Labor Statistics. 2000. Website, http://stats.bls.gov:80/datahome.htm.

Byrne, Michael. 1995. "Sweeney Heralds 'a Moment of Hope.' " *AFL-CIO News* November 6, AFL-CIO Website, http://www.aflcio.org/publ/newsonline/95nov6/conwrap.html.

Byrne, Michael, and James Parks. 1996. "Delegates to Raise Workers' Political Voice." *AFL-CIO News* AFL-CIO Website, http://www.aflcio.org/publ/newsonline/96mar22/politic.html.

Callaghan, Polly, and Heidi Hartmann. 1991. *Contingent Work*. Washington, D.C.: Economic Policy Institute.

Canadian Labour Confederation. 1979. *Canadian Labour*, October 12.

Carre, Françoise, Virginia duRivage, and Chris Tilly. 1998. "Making Labor Law Work for Part-Time and Contingent Workers." In *Contingent Work: American Employment Relations in Transition*, edited by Kathleen Barker and Kathleen Christensen. Ithaca, N.Y.: Cornell ILR Press.

Cascio, Wayne. 1991. *Applied Psychology in Personnel Management*. 4th ed. Englewood Cliffs, N.J.: Prentice-Hall.

Chafetz, I., and C. Fraser. 1979. "Union Decertification: An Exploratory Analysis." *Industrial Relations* 18:59–69.

Chaison, Gary. 1996. *Union Mergers in Hard Times: The View from Five Countries*. Ithaca, N.Y.: Cornell ILR Press.

Chamberlain, Neil, and James Kuhn. 1965. *Collective Bargaining*. New York: McGraw-Hill.

Chermish, Ron. 1982. "Press Criteria for Strike Reporting: Counting or Selective Presentation," *Social Science Research* 11 (March): 88–101.

Clark, Paul F. 1986. "Union Member Attitudes toward the Grievance Procedure: Measurement, Correlates, and Relationship to Union Commitment." Ph.D. diss., University of Pittsburgh.

———. 1989. "Union Image-Building at the Local Level: Labor Education Techniques and Resources." *Labor Studies Journal* 14 (3): 48–68.

———. 1998. "Conservative Interest Group Impact on Union Voters: The Link between Social and Economic Issues." *Labor Studies Journal* 22 (4): 47–61.

———. 1999. "Using Members' Dues for Political Purposes: The Paycheck Protection Act." *Journal of Labor Research* 20:329–42.

Clark, Paul F., Darlene A. Clark, David Day, and Dennis Shea. 1999. In "Health Care Reform's Impact on Hospitals: Implications for Union Organizing." In *Proceedings of the Fifty-First Annual Meeting of the Industrial Relations Research Association*, 61–67. Madison, Wisc: Industrial Relations Research Association.

Clark, Paul F., Clive Fullagar, Michael Gordon, and Daniel G. Gallagher. 1993. "Building Commitment among New Union Members: The Role of Formal and Informal Socialization." *Labor Studies Journal* 18 (3): 3–16.

Clark, Paul F., and Daniel G. Gallagher. 1992. "Report on the NALC Socialization Survey." Department of Labor Studies and Industrial Relations, Penn State University.

Clark, Paul F., Daniel G. Gallagher, and Thomas Pavlak. 1990. "Member Commitment in an American Union: The Role of the Grievance Procedure." *Industrial Relations Journal* 21:147–57.

———. 1991. "Due Process in the Workplace: Member Attitudes toward the Grievance Procedure." In *Resolving Disputes in the Public Sector*, edited by Miriam Mills, 58–80. Chicago: Nelson Hall Press.

Clark, Paul F., Kay Gilbert, Lois S. Gray, and Norman Solomon. 1998. "Union Adminstrative Practices: A Comparative Analysis." *Journal of Labor Research* 19:149–61.

Clark, Paul F., and Lois S. Gray. 1991. "Union Administration." In *The State of the Union*, edited by George Strauss, Daniel G. Gallagher, and Jack Fiorito, 175–200. Madison, Wisc.: Industrial Relations Research Association.

———. 2000. "Assessing the Proposed U.A.W., U.S.W., and I.A.M. Merger: Structural Alternatives and Potential Outcomes." *Journal of Labor Research* 21:65–82.

Clark, Paul F., and Marick Masters. 1996. "Pennsylvania AFL-CIO COPE Union Member Survey: A Final Report." Department of Labor Studies and Industrial Relations, Penn State University.

Clark, R. A. 1984. *Persuasive Messages*. New York: Harper & Row.

Cobble, Dorothy Sue. 1993. "Remaking Unions for the New Majority." In *Women and Unions: Forging a Partnership*, edited by Dorothy Sue Cobble, 3–18. Ithaca, N.Y.: Cornell ILR Press.

Cohen, Larry, and Richard Hurd. 1998. "Fear, Conflict, and Union Organizing." In *Organizing to Win*, edited by Kate Bronfenbrenner, S. Friedman, R. Hurd, R. Oswald, and R. Seeber, 181–97. Ithaca, N.Y.: Cornell ILR Press.

Cohen, Noam. 1999. "Corporations Battling to Bar Use of E-Mail for Unions." *New York Times* August 23, C-1.

Cohen, Peter. 1973. *The Gospel According to the Harvard Business School*. Garden City, N.J.: Doubleday.

Conrow, Theresa. 1991. "Contract Servicing from an Organizing Model." *Labor Research Review* 17:45–59.

Cook, Alice. 1968. "Women and American Trade Unions." *Annals of the American Academy of Political and Social Science* 375 (January): 124–32.

Cooper, Muriel. 1996. "Organizing Program Seeks Innovation." *AFL-CIO News*, March 8, AFL-CIO Website, http://www.aflcio.org/publ/newsonline/96mar8/ecorgan.html.

Cornfield, Daniel. 1987. "Decline and Diversification: Causes and Consequences for Organizational Governance." *Research in the Sociology of Organization* 5:187–216.

Davies, Julia, and Mark Easterby-Smith. 1984. "Learning and Developing from Managerial Work Experiences." *Journal of Management Studies* 21:169–83.

Deal, Terrence, and Alan Kennedy. 1982. *Corporate Cultures: The Rites and Rituals of Corporate Life*. Reading, Mass.: Addison-Wesley.

Delaney, John, Jack Fiorito, and Marick Masters. 1988. "The Effects of Union, Organizational, and Environmental Characteristics on Union Political Action." *American Journal of Political Science* 32:616–42.

Delaney, John, and Marick Masters. 1991. "Unions and Political Action." In *The State of the Union*, edited by George Strauss, Daniel G. Gallagher, and Jack Fiorito, 313–46. Madison, Wisc.: Industrial Relations Research Association.

Delaney, John, Marick Masters, and Susan Schwochau. 1990. "Union Membership and Voting for COPE-Endorsed Candidates." *Industrial and Labor Relations Review* 43:621–35.

Derry, Stephen J., and Roderick D. Iverson. 1997. "Antecedents and Consequences of Dual and Unilaterial Commitment: A Longitudinal Study." Paper presented at the Third International Conference on Emerging Union Structures: Reshaping Labour Market Institutions, Canberra, Australia.

Deshpande, Satish, and Jack Fiorito. 1989. "Specific and General Beliefs in Union Voting Models." *Academy of Management* 32(4): 883–97.

Diamond, Virginia. 1988. *Numbers That Count: A Manual on Internal Organizing*. Washington, D.C.: AFL-CIO.

Dickens, W. T., J. R. Wholey, and J. C. Robinson. 1987. "Correlates of Union Support in NLRB Elections." *Industrial Relations* 26:240–52.

duRivage, V. L. 1992. "New Policies for the Contingent Workforce." In *New Policies for the Part-Time and Contingent Workforce*, edited by V. L. duRivage, 12–18. Armonk, N.Y.: Sharpe.

Eaton, Adrienne, Michael Gordon, and Jeffrey Keefe. 1992. "The Impact of Quality of Work Life Programs and Grievance System Effectiveness on Union Commitment." *Industrial and Labor Relations Review* 45:591–604.

Edelstein, J. David, and Malcolm Warner. 1975. *Comparative Union Democracy: Organization and Opposition in British and American Unions*. New York: Halsted Press.

Faunce, William. 1962. "Size of Locals and Union Democracy." *American Journal of Sociology* 48:291–98.

Fellner, Kim. 1990. "Women Still Have No Standing in Unions." *New York Times*, September 3, 21.

Fields, Mitchell W., Marick F. Masters, and James W. Thacker. 1987. "Union Commitment and Membership Support for Union Political Action: An Exploratory Analysis." *Journal of Labor Research* 8:143–57.

Fierman, Jaclyn. 1994. "The Contingency Workforce." *Fortune*, January 24, 30–36.

Filippelli, Ronald. 1984. *Labor in the USA: A History*. New York: Knopf.

Fiorito, Jack. 1987. "Political Instrumentality Perceptions and Desires for Union Representation." *Journal of Labor Research* 8:271–89.

——. 1992. "Unionism and Altruism." *Labor Studies Journal* 17 (3): 19–34.

Fiorito, Jack, Daniel G. Gallagher, and Charles Greer. 1986. "Determinants of Unionism: A Review of the Literature." In *Research in Personnel and Human Resources Management*, edited by Kenneth Rowland and Gerald Ferris, 269–306. Greenwich, Conn.: JAI Press.

Fiorito, Jack, Daniel G. Gallagher, and C. V. Fukami. 1988. "Satisfaction with Union Representation." *Industrial and Labor Relations Review* 41 (2): 294–307.

Fiorito, Jack, Cynthia Gramm, and Wallace Hendricks. 1991. "Union Structure." In *The State of the Union*, edited by George Strauss, Daniel G. Gallagher, and Jack Fiorito, 103–38. Madison, Wisc.: Industrial Relations Research Association.

Fiorito, Jack, and Wallace Hendricks. 1987. "The Characteristics of National Unions." *Advances in Industrial and Labor Relations* 4:1–42.

Fiorito, Jack, Paul Jarley, and John Delaney. 1995. "National Union Effectiveness in Organizing: Measurement and Influences." *Industrial and Labor Relations Review* 48:613–35.

Fiorito, Jack, Paul Jarley, John Delaney, and Robert Kolodinsky. 2000. "Unions and Information Technology: From Luddites to Cyber unions?" *Labor Studies Journal* 24 (4): 3–34.

Fiorito, Jack, Christopher Lowman, and Forrest Nelson. 1987. "The Impact of Human Resource Policies on Union Organizing." *Industrial Relations* 26:113–26.

Fiorito, Jack, and Angela Young. 1998. "Union Voting Intentions: Human Resource Policies, Organizational Characteristics, and Attitudes." In *Organizing to Win*, edited by Kate Bronfenbrenner, S. Friedman, R. Hurd, R. Oswald, and R. Seeber, 232–46. Ithaca, N.Y.: Cornell ILR Press.

Fishbein, Martin, and Icek Ajzen. 1975. *Belief, Attitude, Intention, and Behavior: An Introduction to Theory and Research*. Reading, Mass.: Addison-Wesley.

——. 1981. "Attitudes and Voting Behavior: An Application of the Theory of Reasoned Action." In *Progress in Applied Social Psychology*, Vol. 1, edited by G. M. Stephenson and J. M. Davis, 253–314. London: Wiley.

Fitzpatrick, Tracy, and Weezy Waldstein. 1994. "Challenges to Strategic Planning in International Unions." In *Proceedings of the Forty-Second Annual Meeting of the Industrial Relations Research Association*, 73–84. Madison, Wisc.: Industrial Relations Research Association.

Fletcher, Bill, and Richard Hurd. 1998. "Beyond the Organizing Model: The Transformation Process in Local Unions." In *Organizing to Win*, edited by Kate Bronfenbrenner, S. Friedman, R. Hurd, R. Oswald, and R. Seeber, 37–53. Ithaca, N.Y.: Cornell ILR Press.

Fones-Wolf, Kenneth. 1989. *Trade Union Gospel: Christianity and Labor in Industrial Philadelphia, 1865–1915*. Philadelphia: Temple University Press.

Freeman, Richard B. 1985. "Why are Unions Faring So Poorly in NLRB Representation Elections?" In *Challenges and Choices Facing American Labor*, edited by Thomas Kochan, 45–64. Cambridge: MIT Press.

Freeman, Richard, and James Medoff. 1979. "The Two Faces of Unionism." *Public Interest* 57 (Fall): 69–93.

———. 1984. *What Do Unions Do?* New York: Basic Books.

Freeman, Richard, and Joel Rogers. 1999. *What Workers Want*. Ithaca, N.Y.: Cornell University Press.

Fukami, Cynthia, and Erik Larson. 1984. "Commitment to Company and Union: Parallel Models." *Journal of Applied Psychology* 69:367–71.

Fullagar, Clive, and Julian Barling. 1987. "Toward a Model of Union Commitment." *Advances in Industrial and Labor Relations* 4:43–78.

———. 1989. "A Longitudinal Test of a Model of the Antecedents and Consequences of Union Loyalty." *Journal of Applied Psychology* 44:213–27.

Fullagar, Clive, Daniel G. Gallagher, Michael Gordon, and Paul F. Clark. 1995. "A Longitudinal Study of Union Member Commitment and Participation." *Journal of Applied Psychology* 80:147–57.

Fullagar, Clive, Judi McLean Parks, Paul F. Clark, and Daniel G. Gallagher. 1995. "Organizational Citizenship and Union Participation: Measuring Discretionary Membership Behaviors." In *The Psychology of Industrial Relations under Changing Employment Relationships: An International Perspective*, edited by Julian Barling and Lois Tetrick, 311–332. Washington, D.C.: American Psychological Association.

Fuller, J. B., and K. Hester. 1998. "Extending the Social Exchange Model of Union Commitment: An Examination of Steward Leadership and Union Justice." Paper presented at the Fifty-Eighth Annual Meeting of the Academy of Management, San Diego, August 9–12.

Gallagher, Daniel G. 1999. "Youth and Labor Representation." In *Young Workers: Varieties of Experience*, edited by Julian Barling and Kevin Kelloway, 235–55. Washington, D.C.: American Psychological Association.

Gallagher, Daniel G., and Paul F. Clark. 1989. "Research on Union Commitment: Implications for Labor." *Labor Studies Journal* 14 (1): 52–71.

Gallagher, Daniel G., Judi McLean Parks, and Kurt Wetzel. 1987. "Methodological Considerations in the Measurement of Union Participation: The Issue of a Multidimensional Construct." In *Proceedings of the Nineteenth Annual Meeting of the Decision Sciences Institute*, 530–33. Boston: Design Sciences Institute.

Gallagher, Daniel G., and George Strauss. 1991. "Union Membership Attitudes and Participation." In *The State of the Union*, edited by George Strauss, Daniel G. Gallagher, and Jack Fiorito, 139–74. Madison, Wisc.: Industrial Relations Research Association.

Gallagher, Daniel G. and Kurt Wetzel. 1988. "Employer and Union Commitment: A Comparative Analysis of Full-Time and Part-Time Workers." In *Proceedings of the Forty-First Annual Meeting of the Industrial Relations Research Association*, edited by B. D. Dennis, 192–200. Madison, Wisc.: Industrial Relations Research Association.

Gallup Poll, 1994. *The Gallup Poll: Public Opinion 1993*. Wilmington, Del.: Scholarly Resources.

Garin, Geoffrey, and Guy Molyneux. 1998. "Informing and Empowering American Workers: Ten Rules for Union Political Action." In *Not Your Father's Union Movement*, edited by Jo-Ann Mort, 113–26. New York: Verso.

Getman, J. G., S. B. Goldberg, and J. B. Herman. 1976. *Union Representation Elections*. New York: Russell Sage Foundation.

Gifford, Courtney. 1987. *Directory of U.S. Labor Organizations, 1986–87 Edition*. Washington, D.C.: Bureau of National Affairs.

———. 1988. *Directory of U.S. Labor Organizations, 1988–89 Edition*. Washington, D.C.: Bureau of National Affairs.

——. 1998. *Directory of U.S. Labor Organizations, 1998 Edition.* Washington, D.C.: Bureau of National Affairs.

——. 1999. *Directory of U.S. Labor Organizations, 1999 Edition.* Washington, D.C.: Bureau of National Affairs.

Gordon, M. E., and R. L. Bowlby. 1988. "Propositions about Grievance Settlements: Finally, Consultation with Grievants," *Personnel Psychology* 41:107–23.

Gordon, M. E., and R. E. Burt. 1981. "A History of Industrial Psychology's Relationship with American Unions: Lessons from the Past and Directions for the Future." *International Review of Applied Psychology* 30:137–56.

Gordon, M. E., and G. E. Fryxell. 1993. "The Role of Interpersonal Justice in Organizational Grievance Systems." In *Justice in the Workplace: Approaching Fairness in Human Resource Management*, edited by Russell Cropanzano, 231–55. Hillsdale, N.J.: Lawrence Erlbaum Associates.

Gordon, M. E., and R. T. Ladd. 1990. "Dual Allegiance: Renewal, Reconsideration, and Recantation." *Personnel Psychology* 43:37–69.

Gordon, M. E., and A. J. Nurick. 1981. "Psychological Approaches to the Study of Unions and Union Management Relations." *Psychological Bulletin* 90:293–306.

Gordon, M. E., J. W. Philpot, R. E. Burt, C. A. Thompson, and W. E. Spiller. 1980. "Commitment to the Union: Development of a Measure and an Examination of Its Correlates." *Journal of Applied Psychology* 65 (1): 479–99.

Grabelsky, Jeff. 1995. "Lighting the Spark: COMET Program Mobilizes the Ranks for Construction Organizing." *Labor Studies Journal* 20 (2): 4–21.

Grabelsky, Jeff, Adam Pagnucco, and Steve Rockafellow. 1999. "Fanning the Flames (After Lighting the Spark): Multi-Trade COMET Programs," *Labor Studies Journal* 23 (4): 34–50.

Gramm, C. L., and J. F. Schnell. 1997. "Following the Leader: Race and Player Behavior in the 1987 NFL Strike." In *Advances in the Economics of Sport*, Vol. 2, edited by Wallace Hendricks, 115–43. Greenwich, Conn.: JAI Press.

Gray, Lois. 1993. "The Route to the Top: Female Union Leaders and Union Policy." In *Women and Unions: Forging a Partnership*, edited by Dorothy Sue Cobble, 363–77. Ithaca, N.Y.: Cornell ILR Press.

Greenberg, Jerald. 1990. "Organizational Justice: Yesterday, Today, and Tomorrow." *Journal of Management* 16:399–432.

Greenhouse, Steven. 1998. "Union Organization Drive Exposes Flaws in Nation's Labor Laws." *New York Times*, July 10, 1.

Grenier, Guillermo. 1987. *Inhuman Relations: Quality Circles and Anti-Unionism in American Industry*. Philadelphia: Temple University Press.

Grossinger, Ken. 1998. "How Labor Defeated California Proposition 226." *Working USA* September-October, 84–90.

Hammer, Tove, and David Wazeter. 1993. "Dimensions of Local Union Effectiveness." *Industrial and Labor Relations Review* 46:302–19.

Hart Research Associates. 1996. *Results of Post-Election Membership Survey*. Report submitted to AFL-CIO, November 8.

——. 1999. *AFL-CIO Membership Survey*. Washington, D.C.: AFL-CIO.

Hepburn, C. Gail, and Julian Barling. 1997. "Predicting the Decision to Abstain in Union Elections." Unpublished manuscript. Department of Psychology, Queen's University, Kingston, Ontario.

Hepburn, C. Gail, Catherine Loughlin, and Julian Barling. 1997. "Abstaining from Voting in Union Certification Elections." In *The Future of Trade Unionism*, edited by Magnus Sverke, 249–62. Aldershot, England: Ashgate.

Heshizer, Brian. 1985. "Unions and Public Opinion: Why the Declining Relationship." *Labor Studies Journal* 9 (4): 254–70.

Heshizer, Brian, and Mary C. Wilson. 1995. "The Role of Referent Beliefs in the Socialization of Union Attitudes." *Journal of Social Behavior and Personality* 10:771–90.

Hindman, H. D. 1988. "Determinants of Union Representation Election Outcomes: Evidence from the Public Sector." Paper presented at the Forty-First Annual Meeting of the Industrial Relations Research Association, New York, December 28–30.

Hirschman, A. O. 1970. *Exit, Voice, and Loyalty: Responses to Decline in Firms, Organizations, and States.* Cambridge, Mass.: Harvard University Press.

Hochner, Arthur, Karen Koziara, and Stuart Schmidt. 1980. "Thinking about Democracy and Participation in Unions." *Proceedings of the Thirty-Second Annual Meeting of the Industrial Relations Research Association,* 12–19. Madison, Wisc.: Industrial Relations Research Association.

Hovland, Carl, Irving Janis, and Harold Kelley. 1964. *Communications and Persuasion.* New Haven: Yale University Press.

Hurd, Richard. 1989. "Learning from Clerical Unions: Two Cases of Organizing Success." *Labor Studies Journal* 14 (1): 30–51.

Huszczo, G. E. 1983. "Attitudinal and Behavioral Variables Related to Participation in Union Activities." *Journal of Labor Research* 4:289–97.

IBEW. 1996. *IBEW Journal,* July, 11.

IBT. 1984. *Membership Manual.* Washington, D.C.: IBT Education Department.

ICEM-USW. 1999. ICEM-USW Website on Continental Tire, http://www.icem.org/campaigns/conticamp/.

Janis, Irving. 1959. *Personality and Persuasibility.* New Haven: Yale University Press.

Jarley, Paul, Jack Fiorito, and John Delaney. 1998. "What's Inside the Black Box? Union Differences, Innovations, and Outcomes." In *Advances in Industrial and Labor Relations,* Vol. 8, 139–81. Greenwich, Conn.: JAI Press.

Jarley, Paul, Sarosh Kuruvilla, and Douglas Casteel. 1990. "Member-Union Relations and Union Satisfaction." *Industrial Relations* 29:129–34.

Joel, Billy. 1982. *Nylon Curtain Album.* New York: Columbia Records.

Johnson, Nancy Brown, Philip Bobko, and Linda S. Hartenian. 1992. "Union Influence on Local Union Leaders' Perceptions of Job Insecurity: An Empirical Test." *British Journal of Industrial Relations* 30:45–60.

Kelloway, Kevin, and Julian Barling. 1993. "Members' Participation in Local Union Activities: Measurement, Prediction, and Replication." *Journal of Applied Psychology* 78:262–79.

———. 1996. "Predictors of Satisfaction with Local and National Unions." Unpublished manuscript. Department of Psychology, University of Guelph, Ontario.

Kelloway, Kevin, Julian Barling, and Victor Catano. 1996. "Training Shop Stewards in Transformational Leadership." Unpublished manuscript. Department of Psychology, University of Guelph, Ontario.

Kelloway, Kevin, and Laura Watts. 1994. "Preemployment Predictors of Union Attitudes: Replication and Extension." *Journal of Applied Psychology* 79:631–34.

Kelman, H. C. 1961. "Processes of Opinion Change," *Public Opinion Quarterly.* 25:57–78.

Kerlinger, F. N. 1973. *Foundations of Behavioral Research,* 2d ed. New York: Holt, Rinehart, and Winston.

Kilgour, J. C. 1987. "Decertifying a Union: A Matter of Choice." *Personnel Administrator* 32 (7): 42–51.

Klandermans, Bert. 1984a. "Mobilization and Participation in Trade Union Action: Acting and Quitting." *Journal of Occupational Psychology* 59:189–204.

———. 1984b. "Mobilization and Participation: Social Psychological Expansions of Resource Mobilization Theory." *American Sociological Review* 40:583–600.

———. 1986. "Union Commitment: Replications and Tests in the Dutch Context." *Journal of Applied Psychology* 74:869–75.

Kochan, Thomas. 1979. "How Americans View Labor Unions." *Monthly Labor Review* 102:23–31.

———. 1980. *Collective Bargaining and Industrial Relations: From Theory to Policy and Practice.* Homewood, Ill.: Richard D. Irwin.

Kochan, Thomas, Harry Katz, and Robert McKersie. 1986. *The Transformation of American Industrial Relations.* New York: Basic Books.

Kochan, Thomas, Robert McKersie, and J. Chalykoff. 1986. "The Effects of Corporate Strategy and Workplace Innovations on Union Representation." *Industrial and Labor Relations Review* 39 (4): 487–501.

Konovsky, M. A., R. Foger, and D. S. Fogel. 1990. "A Panel Analysis of Distributive and Procedural Justice on Employee Commitment and Pay Satisfaction." Working Paper 90-HRMG-05, Tulane University.

Kram, K. E. 1985. *Mentoring at Work: Developmental Readings in Organizational Life.* Glenview, Ill.: Scott, Foresman.

Krosnick, J. A., and D. F. Alwin. 1989. "Aging and Susceptibility to Attitude Change." *Journal of Personality and Social Psychology* 57:416–25.

Kusnet, David. 1998. "The 'America Needs a Raise' Campaign." In *Not Your Father's Union Movement,* edited by Jo-Ann Mort, 167–78. New York: Verso.

Lawler, J. J. 1986. "Union Growth and Decline: The Impact of Employer and Union Tactics." *Journal of Occupational Psychology* 59:217–30.

Lazarovici, Laureen. 1999. "Virtual Organizing." *America@Work,* September, 8–11.

Lee, Eric. 1996. *The Labour Movement and the Internet: The New Internationalism.* Chicago: Pluto Press.

———, ed. 1999. *Global Labournet* (an online newsletter), http://www.labournet.org/

Leroy, Michael. 1990. "The 1988 Elections: Re-Emergence of the Labor Bloc Vote?" *Labor Studies Journal* 15 (1): 5–32.

Lewin, Kurt. 1943. "Defining the 'Field at a Given Time.'" *Psychological Review* 50:292–310.

Likert, Rensis. 1961. *New Perspectives on Management.* New York: McGraw-Hill.

Lipset, S. M., M. A. Trow, and J. B. Coleman. 1956. *Union Democracy: The Internal Politics of the International Typographical Union.* Glencoe, Ill.: Free Press.

Lynch, Lisa, and Sandra Black. 1998. *How to Compete: The Impact of Workplace Practices and Information.* Cambridge, Mass.: National Bureau of Economic Research.

MacEwen, Karyl, and Julian Barling. 1991. "Effects of Maternal Employment Experiences on Children's Behavior via Mood, Cognitive Difficulties, and Parenting Behavior." *Journal of Marriage and the Family* 53:635–44.

Maranto, Cheryl. 1988. "Corporate Characteristics and Union Organizing," *Industrial Relations* 27:352–70

Maranto, Cheryl, and Jack Fiorito. 1987. "The Effect of Union Characteristics on the Outcome of NLRB Certification Elections." *Industrial and Labor Relations Review* 40:225–40.

Martin, James. 1986. "Predictors of Individual Propensity to Strike." *Industrial and Labor Relations Review* 38:365–76.

Martin, Joanne. 1982. "Stories and Scripts in Organizational Settings." In *Cognitive Social Psychology,* edited by Albert Hastorf and Alice Isen, 225–305. New York: Elsevier–North Holland.

Masters, Marick. 1997. *Unions at the Crossroads: Strategic Membership, Financial, and Political Perspectives.* Westport, Conn.: Quorum.

McGuire, W. J. 1957. "Order of Presentation as a Factor in 'Conditioning' Persuasiveness." In *Order of Presentation in Persuasion,* edited by Carl Hovland, 98–114. New Haven: Yale University Press.

———. 1964. "Inducing Resistance to Persuasion: Some Contemporary Approaches." In *Advances in Experimental Social Psychology,* Vol. 1, edited by Leonard Berkowitz, 192–231. New York: Academic Press.

———. 1985. "The Nature of Attitudes and Attitude Change." In *The Handbook of Social Psychology,* 3d ed., edited by Gardner Lindzey and Elliot Aronson, 233–46. New York: Random House.

———. 1989. "Theoretical Foundations of Campaigns." In *Public Communications Campaigns,* 2d ed., edited by Ronald Rice and Charles Atkin, 43–65. Newbury Park, Calif.: Sage.

McKay, Jim. 1999. "AFL-CIO Sees Solidarity via Online Network." *Pittsburgh Post-Gazette,* October 12, F-1.

McLean Parks, Judi, Daniel G. Gallagher, and Clive Fullagar. 1995. "Operationalizing the Outcomes of Union Commitment: The Dimensionality of Participation." *Journal of Organizational Behavior* 16:533–55.

McShane, S. L. 1986. "The Multidimensionality of Union Participation." *Journal of Occupational Psychology* 59:177–87.

Mellor, Steve. 1990. "The Relationship between Membership Decline and Union Commitment: A Field Study of Local Unions in Crisis." *Journal of Applied Psychology* 75:258–67.

Mendels, Pamela. 1999. "Unions Organizing Workers Via E-mail." *New York Times*, June 30, Website.

Meyer, J. P. and N. J. Allen. 1997. *Commitment in the Workplace: Theory, Research, and Application.* Thousand Oaks, Calif.: Sage.

Michels, Robert. 1962. *Political Parties.* New York: Free Press.

Mobley, W. H. 1977. "Intermediate Linkages in the Relationship between Job Satisfaction and Employee Turnover." *Journal of Applied Psychology* 62:237–40.

——. 1982. *Employee Turnover: Causes, Consequences, and Control.* Reading, Mass.: Addison-Wesley.

Moorhead, Gregory, and Ricky W. Griffin. 1998. *Organizational Behavior: Managing People and Organizations.* Boston: Houghton Mifflin.

Morrison, E. W. 1993. "Longitudinal Study of the Effects of Information Seeking on Newcomer Socialization." *Journal of Applied Psychology* 73:173–83.

Mowday, R. T., R. M. Steers, and L. W. Porter. 1979. "The Measurement of Organizational Commitment." *Journal of Vocational Behavior* 14:224–47.

Muste, A. J. 1928. "Factional Fights in Trade Unions." In *American Labor Dynamics,* edited by J. B. S. Hardman, 332–48. New York: Harcourt Brace Jovanovich.

NALC. 1983. *Letter Carrier's Guide.* Washington, D.C.: NALC.

Nash, Al. 1984. "British and American Stewards: A Comparative Analysis." *Labor Studies Journal* 9 (1): 46–65.

National Labor Relations Board. 1997. *NLRB Annual Report for 1997.* Washington, D.C.: U.S. Government Printing Office.

Needleman, Ruth, and Lucretia Dewey Tanner. 1987. "Women in Unions: Current Issues." In *Working Women: Past, Present, and Future,* edited by K. Koziara, M. H. Moscow, and L. D. Tanner, 205–18. Washington, D.C.: Bureau of National Affairs.

Neuman, W. Russell. 1986. *The Paradox of Mass Politics: Knowledge and Opinion in the American Electorate.* Cambridge, Mass.: Harvard University Press.

Nicholson, Nigel, Gill Ursell, and Paul Blyton. 1981. *The Dynamics of White Collar Unionism: A Study of Local Union Participation.* San Diego: Academic Press.

Northouse, Peter. 1997. *Leadership: Theory and Practice.* Thousand Oaks, Calif.: Sage.

OCAW. 1998. "How to Work with the Media and Love It." *OCAW Reporter* 54 (May–June): 12–13.

Organ, Dennis. 1988. *Organizational Citizenship Behavior: The Good Soldier Syndrome.* Lexington, Mass.: Lexington Books.

Organ, Dennis, and Mary Konovsky. 1989. "Cognitive versus Affective Determinants of Organizational Citizenship Behavior." *Journal of Applied Psychology* 12:157–64.

Parker, Mike, and Jane Slaughter. 1994. *Working Smart: A Union Guide to Participation and Reengineering.* Detroit: Labor Notes.

Patton, David B., and John J. Marrone. 1984. "The Impact of Labor Endorsements: Union Members and the 1980 Presidential Vote." *Labor Studies Journal* 9 (1): 3–18.

Patton, David B., John J. Marrone, and Hugh Hindman. 1986. "Unions and Politics: 1984 and Beyond." In *Proceedings of the Thirty-Eighth Annual Meeting of the Industrial Relations Research Association,* edited by B. D. Dennis, 490–94. Madison, Wisc.: Industrial Relations Research Association.

Petty, Richard and John Cacioppo. 1984. "The Effects of Involvement on Responses to Argument Quantity and Quality." *Journal of Personality and Social Psychology* 46:69–81.

Porter, L. W., and F. J. Smith. 1970. "The Etiology of Organizational Commitment." Unpublished paper. Graduate School of Administration, University of California, Irvine.

Premack, Steven and John Hunter. 1988. "Workplace Hazards and Workers' Desires for Union Representation." *Journal of Labor Research* 9:237–49.

Puette, William. 1992. *Through Jaundiced Eyes: How the Media View Organized Labor.* Ithaca, N.Y.: Cornell ILR Press.

Purcell, T. V. 1953. *The Worker Speaks His Mind on Company and Union.* Cambridge, Mass.: Harvard University Press.

Quaglieri, Philip. 1989. *America's Labor Leaders.* Lexington, Mass.: Lexington Books.

Reardon, K. K. 1991. *Persuasion in Practice.* Newbury Park, Calif.: Sage.

Reitz, Joseph. 1987. *Behavior in Organizations.* Homewood, Ill.: Irwin.

Reshaf, Yonatan, and Kay Stratton-Devine. 1990. "Long-Range Planning in North American Unions: Preliminary Findings." *Relations Industrielles* 48:250–66.

Robbins, Stephen P., and Mary Coulter. 1996. *Management,* 5th ed. Upper Saddle River, N.J.: Prentice-Hall.

Rogers, Jackie Krasas. 2000. *Temps: The Many Faces of the Changing Workplace.* Ithaca, N.Y.: Cornell ILR Press.

Roomkin, Myron, and Richard Block. 1981. "Case Processing Time and the Outcomes of Representation Elections: Some Empirical Evidence." *University of Illinois Law Review* 1:75–97.

Rundle, James. 1998. "Winning Hearts and Minds in an Era of Employee Involvement Programs." In *Organizing to Win,* edited by Kate Bronfenbrenner, S. Friedman, R. Hurd, R. Oswald, and R. Seeber, 213–31. Ithaca, N.Y.: Cornell ILR Press.

Sandver, M. H. 1980. "Predictors of Outcomes in NLRB Certification Elections." *Proceedings of the Twenty-Third Annual Meeting of the Midwest Academy of Management,* 174–81. Cincinnati: Midwest Academy of Management.

Schein, E. H. 1968. "Organizational Socialization and the Profession of Management." *Industrial Management Review* 9:1–16.

Schlossberg, S. I. 1994. "Turning Point for America: Resolving the Crisis at the Workplace." *Labor Law Journal* 45 (October): 603–17.

SEIU, 1988. *Proceedings of the Nineteenth Convention of the Service Employees International Union.* Washington, D.C.: SEIU.

Shamir, Boas, Robert House, and Michael Arthur. 1993. "The Motivational Effects of Charismatic Leadership: A Self-Concept Based Theory." *Organizational Science* 4 (4): 577–94.

Shore, L. M., L. E. Tetrick, R. R. Sinclair, and L. A. Newton. 1994. "A Validation of a Measure of Perceived Union Support." *Journal of Applied Psychology* 79:971–77.

Shostak, Arthur. 1991. *Robust Unionism: Innovations in the Labor Movement.* Ithaca, N.Y.: Cornell ILR Press.

———. 1999. *Cyberunion: Empowering Labor Through Computer Technology.* Armonk, N.Y.: M. E. Sharpe.

———, ed. 1995. *For Labor's Sake: Gains and Pains as Told by 28 Creative Union Insiders.* Lanham, Md.: University Press of America.

Skratek, Sylvia. 1997. "Conflictive Partnerships under Collective Bargaining." In *Workplace Dispute Resolution,* edited by Sandra Gleason, 57–58. East Lansing: Michigan State University Press.

Sousa, David J. 1993. "Organized Labor in the Electorate, 1960–1988." *Political Research Quarterly* 46:741–58.

Staats, Arthur. 1968. *Learning, Language, and Cognition.* New York: Holt, Rinehart, and Winston.

Stewart, Wendy, and Julian Barling. 1996. "Fathers' Work Experiences Affect Children's Behaviors via Job-Related Affect and Parenting Behaviors." *Journal of Organizational Behavior* 16:221–32.

Strauss, George. 1977. "Bridging the Gap between Law and Psychology: A First but Difficult Step." *Contemporary Psychology* 22:833–34.

———. 1991. "Union Democracy." In *The State of the Union,* edited by George Strauss, Daniel G. Gallagher, and Jack Fiorito, 201–36. Madison, Wisc.: Industrial Relations Research Association.

———. 1993. "Issues in Union Structure." *Research in the Sociology of Organization* 12:1–49.

———. 1999. "What's Happening Inside U.S. Unions: Hunches and a Few Hard Facts." Paper presented at the Conference on Union Governance and Democracy, Atlanta, Ga., May.

Summers, Clyde. 1999. "From Industrial Democracy to Union Democracy." Paper presented at the Conference on Union Governance and Democracy, Atlanta, Ga., May.

Summers, T. P., J. H. Betton, and T. A. DeCotiis. 1986. "Voting for and against Unions: A Decision Model." *Academy of Management Review* 11:643–55.

Sverke, Magnus, ed. 1997. *The Future of Trade Unionism*. Aldershot, England: Ashgate.

Sverke, Magnus, and Sarosh Kuruvilla. 1995. "A New Conceptualization of Union Commitment: Development and Test of an Integrated Theory." *Journal of Organizational Behavior* 16:505–32.

Sweeney, John J. 1996. *America Needs a Raise*. Boston: Houghton Mifflin.

Thacker, J. W., M. W. Fields, and L. A. Barclay. 1990. "Union Commitment: An Examination of Antecedent and Outcome Factors." *Journal of Occupational Psychology* 63:33–48.

Thomson, A. W. J. 1974. *The Grievance Procedure in the Private Sector*. Ithaca, N.Y.: Cornell ILR Press.

Trice, Harrison, and Janice Beyer. 1991. "Cultural Leadership in Organizations." *Organization Science* 2 (2): 149–69.

———. 1993. *The Cultures of Work Organizations*. Englewood Cliffs, N.J.: Prentice-Hall.

Tsui, A. S., and C. A. O'Reilly. 1989. "Beyond Simple Demographic Effects: The Importance of Relational Demography in Supervisor-Subordinate Dyads," *Academy of Management Journal* 32:402–23.

Tyler, T. R. 1986. "When Does Procedural Justice Matter in Organizational Settings?" In *Research on Negotiation in Organizations*, edited by R. J. Lewicki, B. H. Sheppard, and M. H. Bazerman, 7–24. Greenwich, Conn.: JAI Press.

UAW. 1986. "The Naked Truth about Unions." *UAW AMMO* 24(1).

———. 1999. "Black Lake." UAW Website, http://www.uaw.org/.

UFCW. 1997. "Crossing Borders." *UFCW Action*, May-June: 4–5.

UMW. 1995. "Commission on Future Named." *UMW Journal*, July-August: 7.

USW. n.d. *The Union Is You: The Grievance Committee Handbook*. Pittsburgh: USW.

———. 1996. "Union Effort in Election Nets Gains for Workers." *Steelabor*, November/December, 17.

Van Maanen, John. 1976. "Rookie Cops and Rookie Managers." *Wharton Magazine* 1:49–55.

Van Maanen, John, and Gideon Kunda. 1989. " 'False Real Feelings': Emotional Expression and Organizational Culture." *Research in Organizational Behavior* 11:43–103.

Van Maanen, John, and Edgar Schein. 1979. "Toward a Theory of Organizational Socialization." In *Research in Organizational Behavior*, Vol. 1, edited by B. M. Staw, 209–64. Greenwich, Conn.: JAI Press.

Velasquez, Joe. 1999. "Political Update." Speech presented to the 1999 Pennsylvania AFL-CIO COPE Conference, Hershey, Pa.

Wagner, John, and John Hollenbeck. 1998. *Organizational Behavior*. Upper Saddle River, N.J.: Simon and Schuster.

Wallihan, James. 1985. *Union Government and Administration*. Washington, D.C.: Bureau of National Affairs.

Wanous, John. 1980. *Organizational Entry: Recruitment, Selection, and Socialization of Newcomers*. Reading, Mass.: Addison-Wesley.

Weiler, Paul. 1983. "Promises to Keep: Securing Workers' Rights to Self-Organization under the NLRA." *Harvard Law Review* 96:1769–1827.

Wilayto, Phil, and Dave Cormier. 1990. *We Won't Go Back: The Story of the UMWA against Pittston Coal Company*. New York: United Labor Action.

Wilkins, Alan. 1989. *Developing Corporate Character: How to Successfully Change an Organization without Destroying It*. San Francisco: Jossey-Bass.

"Workers Assess Conditions, Unions, Pay." 1997. *USA Today*, August 28.

Yates, Michael. 1998. *Why Unions Matter*. New York: Monthly Review Press.

Youngblood, S. A., A. Denisi, J. L Molleston, and W. Mobley. 1984. "The Impact of Work Environment, Instrumentality Beliefs, Perceived Labor Union Image, and Subjective Norms on Union Voting Intentions," *Academy of Management Journal* 27:576–90.

Zimbardo, Philip, and Ebbe Ebbesen. 1970. *Influencing Attitudes and Changing Behavior*. Reading, Mass.: Addison-Wesley.

Index